To Dr. Getty

GIVE ME THAT BOOK!
by T.S. Rendall

Ted S. Rendall

"Oh, give me that Book—the Book of God!"
—John Wesley

Give Me That Book!
By T.S. Rendall

ISBN 978-1-940791-09-8

First printing, 1982

Current edition published in 2015 by
Victory Baptist Press
Milton, Florida – USA

Cover design by Trinity Lorimer
Layout by Sarah Berg and Trinity Lorimer

Dedication

I dedicate this study of the Book of God, the Holy Scriptures, to all who have participated in classes on "anointed, expository preaching," on the campus of Olford Ministries Intl., Memphis, TN. In the symbols used to describe the Bible itself, we have twenty-four powerful reasons why we should "preach the Word" in the power of the Spirit!

CONTENTS

Acknowledgments

I want to thank the following publishers for permission to use quotations from books copyrighted by them: Abingdon, Eerdmans, Hodder & Stoughton, A.J. Holman, Kregel, Loizeaux, Moody Press, MOVE Press, National Geographic Society, *Newsweek*, Inc., Oliphants, Paternoster, Pickering & Inglis, Presbyterian and Reformed, Regal, Revell and Zondervan.

I have not been able to give sources for a number of quotations; however, rather than eliminating the quotations, I have used them, indicating the fact that I have not been able to trace author or title. If, inadvertently, I have used copyrighted materials, I would appreciate hearing from the authors.

Preface

Another book on the Bible?

We offer no apology for this study of the symbols used in the Bible to set forth the excellence and the effectiveness of the Word of God when appropriated by us. To the best of our knowledge, no one has attempted a systematic and thorough examination of this aspect of Bible study.[1] Amid the plethora of books on the inspiration and the inerrancy of Scripture, surely there is room for one that deals not with the problems of the Bible but with the profit of the Scriptures in the life of the Christian.

In terms of classification, this series of studies deals with what we may term Bible appreciation. Our aim is not to offer methods of Bible study as such, but to create a desire in the reader's heart to appreciate the Bible's freshness and to appropriate the Bible's fullness. This book, then, is really preparatory to Bible study, each chapter providing a biblical reason why we should live by the Book.

There are, of course, many symbols in the Bible. I am in complete agreement with A.C. Thiselton, who wrote: "All God's pictures, all God's symbols, are worthy of the most careful and reverent study."[2] This book, however, deals only with those symbols which are employed by the biblical writers to express their evaluation of the Word of God. Other writers have dealt in detail with other symbols.[3]

This series of studies first appeared in *The Prairie Overcomer*, the monthly magazine of the Prairie Bible Institute, with which I had the privilege of being identified for many years. The original title of the series was, "In Praise of God's Word."

The reader will notice that we have included a large number of quotations relative to the symbols of the Bible. In making this selection, we have had in mind the counsel of S.T. Coleridge:

> Why are not more gems from our great authors scattered over the country? Great books are not in everybody's reach; and though it is better to know them thoroughly than to know them only here and there, yet it is a good work to give a little to

those who have neither time nor means to get more. Let every bookworm, when in any fragrant scarce old tome he discovers a sentence, a story, an illustration, that does his heart good, hasten to give it to others.

It is because many of these quotations have done my own heart good that I share them with my readers. As I do so, I take the words of Thomas Fuller as my own: "If the reader may reap in a few hours what cost me more months, just cause have I to rejoice, and he (I hope) none to complain. Thus may the faults of this book redound to myself, the profit to others, and the glory to God."

Ted S. Rendall

The Book of Books

There never was a book like the Bible, and there never will be another.

— **Thomas Carlyle**

The Bible is truly a Wonder Book. It contains, and is, the wonderful record of a wonderful revelation given to a wonderful people by a wonderful God through men who were prepared for their tasks in a wonderful way. It is a matter of wonder that God should bridge the distance which separates Him from men, that He should break the silence which enfolds all life by speaking through men to all mankind. It is an even greater wonder that He should—on the lips of His divine-human Son—speak to men in the final phases of that amazing revelation which He has given.

— **Allon Poole**

Were I but a great poet I would write a magnificent poem on the utility and efficacy of the divine Word. Without that Word where should we be? For several years I read the whole Bible twice in every twelve months. It is a great and powerful tree, each word of which is a mighty branch: each of these branches I have shaken.

— **Martin Luther**

The Bible is the Book of books, because it is the Word of God. It is my Guide and Light, and Food for my soul. Experience has shown and proved the fact that there is no other book in the world beside this which can meet the spiritual needs of men. In reading it I have found untold and eternal wealth of riches, of which I never thought or dreamed before; and now in passing on its message to others and sharing it with them, its blessing to me and to them continually increases.

— **Sadhu Sundar Singh**

The Scriptures are of preeminent value in their clear solution of the problems of the spiritual life.

— **D.J. Burrell**

STUDY 1
God's Word Is Superlative

Our Key Scripture—"My heart standeth in awe of thy word" (Psalm 119:161).

Supplementary Scriptures—Job 23:12; Psalm 19:7–11; Psalm 119; 138:2; Jeremiah 15:16; Luke 4:36; 24:32; Acts 12:24; Romans 15:4; 2 Timothy 3:15–17.

A minister was about to leave his home on a long journey. As he packed his suitcase, he found that he had a little room left in it. Speaking to a friend, the minister said, "There is still enough room in my suitcase for me to pack a guidebook, a lamp, a mirror, a telescope, a book of poems, a number of biographies, a bundle of old letters, a hymn book, a sharp sword, and a small library of thirty volumes."

The minister's friend looked at the small space and gasped: "How can you manage to fit all that in the space left?"

"Oh, that's easy," said the minister, "for my Bible contains all of these things!"[1]

And indeed it does! The Bible is superlative in its ability to meet all our spiritual needs. Concerning the Bible, we may exclaim in the words of those who listened to the authoritative teaching of the Lord Jesus, "What a word *is* this!" (Luke 4:36). As we contemplate the resources of the divine Word, we confess with the psalmist, "My heart standeth in awe of thy word" (Psalm 119:161).

In this series of studies we shall be examining the symbols that are used in the Bible to set forth the power and purpose of God's Word in the

Christian's life. Our findings lead us to agree with F.E. Marsh, "Many are the similes which are used in the Scriptures about the Word of God, and various are their uses to elucidate its intrinsic value, its inherent virtue, and its inspiring vitality."[2] "The best way to evaluate God's Word," according to Dr. Norman B. Harrison, "is through the statements it makes regarding itself."[3]

L.M. Perry and R.D. Culver comment:

> The Christian who feels no urgency to study his Bible needs his appetite whetted. He could do nothing better than to thumb through the Bible, pausing along the way to meditate on the many statements it makes concerning itself. He should thereby come to a new appreciation of the Word of God and a new hunger to know its contents.[4]

BASIC OUTLINE

In addition to other aspects the symbols speak of the *variety* of God's Word, the *value* of God's Word, and the *vitality* of God's Word. Let's examine these three aspects in some depth.

Variety

A systematic study of the symbols reveals the great *variety* of God's spiritual truth to be found in the Bible. In his book, *The Key Words of the Bible*, Dr. A.T. Pierson refers to symbols as "twelve conspicuous symbols chosen in the Word of God to represent its uses and the range and scope of its application to our needs."

We classify these under seven divisions:

1. The mirror to show us ourselves as we are and may be (James 1:23–25).
2. The laver to wash away our sin and defilement (Ephesians 5:26).
3. The lamp and light to guide us in the right way (Psalm 119:105).
4. The milk, bread, strong meat, and honey, affording sustenance and satisfaction to the believer at all stages of spiritual development (Hebrews 5:12–14; Psalm 19:10).
5. The fine gold to enrich us with heavenly treasure (Psalm 19:10).

6. The fire, hammer, and sword to be used in the work and warfare of life (Jeremiah 23:29; Hebrews 4:12; Ephesians 6:17).
7. The seed to beget souls in God's image and to plant harvest fields for God (James 1:18; 1 Peter 1:23; Matthew 13).[5]

Dr. Pierson returns to the same topic in his magnum opus, *Knowing the Scriptures*:

> There are about twelve or thirteen conspicuous symbols used to express the range and scope of the application of Holy Scripture to daily needs. They abundantly repay study from their great suggestiveness and comprehensiveness. Taken alphabetically, they are the following: bread, fire, gold, hammer, honey, lamp, laver, light, meat, milk, mirror, seed, sword. Here four symbols refer to food, and food in its nutritious and delicious qualities; four more to the uses of the Word in self-revealing, self-cleansing, and self-guiding; four others to its power as a force or weapon, etc.[6]

In their book, *How to Search the Scriptures*, Drs. Perry and Culver invite us to consider "eleven illustrations by which the Bible is pictured." Here is their list:

1. The Bible is a priceless possession (Psalm 19:7–10, 119:72).
2. The Bible is a light (Psalm 119:105, 130; Proverbs 6:23).
3. The Bible is rain which produces life and fruit (Isaiah 55:10, 11).
4. The Bible is food (Jeremiah 15:16; 1 Corinthians 3:1, 2; Hebrews 5:12–14; 1 Peter 2:1, 2).
5. The Bible is a fire which burns away the chaff and which ignites us to action (Jeremiah 23:29, 20:9).
6. The Bible is a hammer which disintegrates our pretenses and reveals our true nature (Jeremiah 23:29).
7. The Bible is a seed which when it falls on good soil grows and bears fruit in a new divine life (Matthew 13:1–23; Mark 4:1–20; Luke 8:4–15; 1 Peter 1:23).
8. The Bible is a mirror in which we find ourselves revealed (James 1:22–25) and in which the Lord Jesus Christ can be seen (2 Corinthians 3:18).

9. The Bible is water whereby we are washed and cleansed (Ephesians 5:26).
10. The Bible is a sword to be wielded in our defence against the enemy (Ephesians 6:17).
11. The Bible is a critic which pierces our innermost being, discerning our thoughts and motives (Hebrews 4:12).[7]

In the light of this great variety Dr. W.H. Griffith Thomas affirms—

> The Word becomes all-sufficient and all-powerful in our life—the mirror to reveal (James 1); the water to cleanse (Ephesians 5); the milk to nourish (1 Peter 2); the strong meat to invigorate (Hebrews 5); the honey to delight (Psalm 119); the fire to warm (Jeremiah 23); the hammer to break and fasten (Jeremiah 23); the sword to fight (Ephesians 6); the seed to grow (Matthew 13); the lamp to guide (Psalm 119); the statute book to legislate (Psalm 119); and the gold to treasure in time and for eternity (Psalm 19).[8]

Allon Poole claims that:

> The Bible is the traveller's guide through this life to the life to come. It is to the believer what chart, compass, and Pole star are to the navigator. It is the truth of the ages God-given to the sons of time. It is to man's spiritual life what bread is to his body. It is his armoury where he is thoroughly furnished unto all good works. Mortal and weak, he needs no less; possessing it, he can have no more.[9]

In our series of studies, we have included a number of symbols not dealt with by the preceding authors. We are convinced that there are still other symbols to be found through a careful search of the Scriptures. We challenge our readers to keep searching for more of these fruitful and fascinating symbols.

Value

A study of the symbols used in the Bible to illustrate its power and pre-eminence has led to a large number of eulogies in which the *value* of the Bible has been extolled. W.A. Rice wrote the following:

From whatever angle the Book is regarded, on whatever aspect of it attention is fixed—its excellence as literature, the range and variety of its contents, its freshness and permanence, its enormous circulation increasing year-by-year, its availability in-whole or in-part for the vast majority of mankind, or its spiritual fervor and challenge—it is impossible to be guilty of exaggeration when speaking the praises of this unrivalled Book.[10]

Asked what his favourite text was, Robert Burdette answered:

When I think of a favourite text, half a dozen dear ones leap to my lips. Stormy days, I want a cloak; cold days I want the sunny side of the wall; hot days I want a shady path; now I want a shower of manna; now I want a drink of cool living water; now I want an arbour to rest in; now I want a pilgrim staff; now I want a sword, a right Jerusalem blade.[11]

In his *Introduction to the King James Version of the Bible*, Miles Smith, one of the principal translators of that version, wrote beautifully:

When the Scriptures are acknowledged to be so full and perfect, how can we excuse our negligence if we do not study them? And how can we excuse our curiosity if we are not content with them? Men talk much about the many good and sweet things the harvest wreath had hanging on it. They say that the philosopher's stone turns copper to gold, that the cornucopia contains all things necessary for food, that the herb Panaces was good for all diseases, that the drug Catholicon replaces all purges, that Vulcan's armour was invulnerable to all thrusts and blows.

What men so falsely and vainly attribute to these for physical good, we may justly and with full measure ascribe to the Scriptures for spiritual good. It is not only armour, it is also a whole supply depot full of offensive and defensive weapons. By it we save ourselves and put the enemy to flight.

It is not merely a herb, but a tree; rather, a whole orchard full of trees of life which bear fruit every month. Their fruit is for food and their leaves for medicine.

It is not merely a memorial pot of manna or cruse of oil sufficient for a host of people, be that host ever so great. It is, as it were, a whole cellar full of oil containers adequate to provide for all our necessities and pay up all our debts.

In a word, it is a storeroom full of fresh food, not like mouldy tradition. St. Basil calls it a drug store full of antidotes against the poison of heresies. It is an encyclopedia of profitable laws for the control of rebellious spirits. It is a treasure chest full of the most costly jewels in contrast to the barest essentials of life. It is a fountain of the most pure water which is springing up to everlasting life.[12]

Here is the well-known tribute of praise for God's Word written by Bishop Anderson.

The Bible is—
The charter of all true liberty.
The forerunner of civilization.
The moulder of institutions and governments.
The fashioner of law.
The secret of national progress.
The guide of history.
The ornament and mainspring of literature.
The friend of science.
The inspiration of philosophies.
The textbook of ethics.
The light of intellect.
The answer to the deepest human heart hungerings.
The soul of all strong heart life.
The illuminator of darkness.
The foe of superstition.
The enemy of oppression.
The uprooter of sin.

The regulator of all high and worthy standards.
The comfort in sorrow.
The strength in weakness.
The pathway in perplexity.
The escape from temptation.
The steadier in the day of power.
The embodiment of all lofty ideals.
The begetter of life.
The promise of the future.
The star of death's night.
The revealer of God.
The guide and hope and inspiration of man.[13]

In addition to these eulogies, there are a number of "orphan" quotations which have become part of the heritage of Christian writing. Here are the best known of these quotations:

The Bible contains the mind of God, the state of man, the way of salvation, the doom of sinners, the happiness of believers, light to direct you, food to support you, comfort to cheer you.

It is the traveller's map, the pilgrim's staff, the pilot's compass, the soldier's sword, the Christian's charter, a mine of wealth, a paradise of glory, a river of pleasure. Its doctrines are holy, its precepts are binding, its decisions are immutable. Christ is its grand subject, our good is its design, the glory of God its end.

Read it to be wise; believe it to be safe; practise it to be holy.

Read it slowly, frequently, prayerfully.

It should fill the memory, rule the heart, and guide the feet.

It is given you in life; it will be opened at the Judgment, and be remembered forever.

It involves the highest responsibility, will reward the greatest labour, and condemns all who trifle with its sacred contents. It is the Word of God, which shall stand forever."[14]

An unknown writer gives the Bible a voice and imagines it to say:

I am the Bible.
I am God's wonderful Library.
I am always—and above all—the Truth.
To the weary pilgrim, I am a good strong Staff.
To the one who sits in black gloom, I am the glorious Light.
To those who stoop beneath heavy burdens, I am sweet Rest.
To him who has lost his way, I am a safe Guide.
To those who have been hurt by sin, I am healing Balm.
To the discouraged, I whisper a glad message of Hope.
To those who are distressed by the storms of life, I am an Anchor, sure and steadfast.
To those who suffer in lonely solitude, I am as a cool, soft Hand resting upon a fevered brow.
O child of man, to best defend me, just use me![15]

Catching the wonder of the Bible's survival, the following entitled "Yet It Lives" is a tribute to it:

Generation follows generation—yet it lives.
Nations rise and fall—yet it lives.
Kings, dictators, presidents come and go—yet it lives.
Hated, despised, cursed—yet it lives.
Doubted, suspected, criticized—yet it lives.
Condemned by atheists—yet it lives.
Scoffed at by scorners—yet it lives.
Exaggerated by fanatics—yet it lives.
Misconstrued and misstated—yet it lives.
Ranted and raved about—yet it lives.
Yet it lives—as a lamp to our feet.
Yet it lives—as a light to our path.
Yet it lives—as the gate to Heaven.
Yet it lives—as a standard for childhood.

Yet it lives—as a guide for youth.
Yet it lives—as an inspiration for the mature.
Yet it lives—as a comfort for the aged.
Yet it lives—as food for the hungry.
Yet it lives—as water for the thirsty.
Yet it lives—as rest for the weary.
Yet it lives—as light for the heathen.
Yet it lives—as salvation for the sinner.
Yet it lives—as grace for the Christian.
To know it is to love it.
To love it is to accept it.
To accept it means life eternal.[16]

Our final testimony as to the value of the Bible comes from the pen of Dr. Will H. Houghton:

How well I remember the day when, sitting in my office with my Bible open before me, I looked up at the books surrounding me on the wall. Some of them have lived long and intimately with me, and I value their friendship greatly. Sitting there alone, I talked out loud, and said something like this:

"Books, some of you have been my companions for many years. When lame, I have leaned upon you as a crutch. When tired, I have found rest in you, even as upon a couch. Hungry and thirsty, I have come to you to find food and the water of refreshing. Books, I value you for what you are and for what you have meant to me. As I look at you, ranged on the shelves, I think of each one of you as a bottle of pure spring water. Thirsty, I reach up to drink from your pages that which will bring the slaking of thirst and deep satisfaction."

And then, taking in my hand my open Bible, I continued, "But, books, this is more than a bottle of spring water, this is the spring itself, and if you have anything of truth in your pages, that truth was first in embryo here."[17]

Vitality

As we study the symbols used in the Bible to express the power of God's Word, we are impressed by a sense of the *vitality* of the Scriptures. The symbols themselves are vital words: seed, fire, sword, rain—to name but a few—are words that bring before us thoughts of life and power and energy.

There is a verse in Acts 12 that may be taken as descriptive of the written Word of God. Primarily the verse refers to the spread of the word or teaching of God and its reproduction in the lives of Christian disciples. We do it no injustice, however, to take it as a description of the history of the Bible. Here is the verse: "The word of God grew and multiplied" (Acts 12:24).

The Bible is like a growth. We must not look upon its various parts as so many bricks in a building, but as so many branches of a tree. It is correct to speak of this book as "the living Bible," because it has within it a wonderful vitality. The Word of God grew through the centuries because it has this amazing life.

The Word of God not only grew; it multiplied—that is, it was fruitful and reproduced itself in the hearts of those who read it with trust and obedience.

At the end of his ministry Dr. D.J. Burrell wrote:

> It is not enough to say, in looking back over these five and forty years, that the Bible has forced itself on my confidence by its intrinsic reasonableness. I have seen it making men; and I have cherished the hope that it might ultimately build me up into "the fullness of the measure of the stature of a man." My own and most lamentable failures and shortcomings have served the more to emphasize its reliability as an "infallible rule of faith and practice."[18]

"The Bible," writes Allon Poole, "is as supreme among books as God is above men. It abides because God lives. It lives because God's vitality throbs in it. It is invulnerable and invincible."[19]

This book, then, is to be trusted, and our study of the symbol used to set forth its vitality will have been in vain if there is not a greater appreciation of its power and a greater appropriation of its promises.

Our study of the Bible leads us to agree with Dr. Sewell in his last words concerning the New Testament: "Twelve years of uninterrupted leisure have enabled me to examine a portion of it with a most minute and impartial criticism as a Greek scholar. I cannot describe the awe, the wonder, the loving thankfulness, the entire unshaken trust which the examination has impressed upon my mind."[20]

This book is also to be obeyed. In *Crown of Wild Olive*, John Ruskin wrote:

> The English people are in possession of a book which tells them, straight from the lips of God, all they ought to do, and need to know. I have read that book, with as much care as most of them, for forty years; and am thankful that, on these who trust it, I can press its pleadings. My endeavour has been to make them trust it more deeply than they do; trust it, not in their own favourite verses only, but in the sum of it all; trust it, not as a fetish or talisman, which they are to save by daily repetitions of; but as a captain's order to be heard and obeyed at their peril.[21]

Finally, the book is to be reverenced. Let that great preacher, Dr. D.J. Burrell, bring this introductory study to a close with the magnificent apostrophe to the Bible:

> Dear Bible! Book of the Church militant and triumphant; Book that our fathers touched with reverent hands and our mothers stained with grateful tears; Book that no bonfires have been able to consume nor fuming acids to impair; Book of comfort for the sorrowing, of strength for the weary, of courage for the living, and hope for the dying; my Saviour's book and mine. If I forget thee may my right hand forget its cunning! If I preach thee not, may the living coal no longer kindle on my lips! May my tongue cleave to the roof of my mouth if I find not in thy saving truths my chiefest joy![22]

FOR YOUR FURTHER STUDY

1. Write down all the symbols used in the Scriptures for the Word of God that you can recall.
2. Now attempt your own classification of these symbols.
3. How do the symbols illustrate 2 Timothy 3:16, 17?
4. Here is a quotation from Dr. W.H. Houghton.[23] What practical point does he make?

> The Bible calls itself food. The value of food is not in the discussion it arouses, but in the nourishment it imparts. The Bible calls itself water. The unclean are not cleansed by a dissertation on water, but by the application of water. The Bible calls itself a sword. Battles are not won by successfully debating the value of swords, but by using them.

A Lamp to My Feet

When I read the Bible, I find it is as useful as a light in the darkness.

—**a Chinese Christian**

The Bible? That's the Book — the Book indeed,
The Book of books,
Of which who looks,
As he should do, aright, shall never need
Wish for a better light
To guide him in the night.

—**Christopher Harvey**

The entrance of God's Word gives light under all the changing circumstances of life. It gives light in adversity—in trouble—in temptation—in affliction—under bereavements. It illumines the dark valley and shadow of death. The divine Word is the light of God's sanctuary—of the Christian family—of the believer's closet.

—**Dr. Jabez Burns**

Most wondrous Book! Bright candle of the Lord!
This Book—this holy Book, on every line
Mark'd with the seal of high divinity,
On every leaf bedew'd with drops of love
Divine; and with the eternal heraldry
And signature of God Almighty stamp'd
From first to last; this ray of sacred light,
This lamp, from off the everlasting Throne,
Mercy took down, and in the night of time
Stood, casting on the dark her gracious bow;
And evermore beseeching men, with tears
And earnest signs, to read, believe, and live.

—**Robert Pollock**

"I am convinced," said John Robinson in his farewell address to the Pilgrim fathers before they sailed in the Mayflower from Delft harbor, "I am convinced that the Lord hath yet more light and truth to break forth from His Holy Word."

There spring...those rays
Of light, that turn our darkest nights to days.

—**John Bunyan**

STUDY 2
God's Word Is Illuminative

Our Key Scripture—"Thy word *is* a lamp unto my feet, and a light unto my path" (Psalm 119:105).

Supplementary Scriptures—Psalm 43:3; Psalm 119:130; Proverbs 6:23; 2 Peter 1:19.

P ROBABLY the most familiar of all the symbols used to set forth the power and purpose of God's Word is that of a shining lamp. In joyful appreciation of God's Word, the psalmist once exclaimed: "Thy word *is* a lamp unto my feet, and a light unto my path." And while initially his reference here is to God's law given to Israel, it constitutes the entire written Word of God.

The symbol suggests to us a traveller making his way home in the darkness of the night, guided by the light of a lamp clutched tightly in his hand.

BASIC OUTLINE

In seeking to determine the points of comparison between a shining lamp and the Word of God, let us consider five aspects: the *source*, the *sufficiency*, the *supremacy*, the *securing*, and the *sharing* of the Bible's Light.

The Source of the Bible's Light

Let us first look at the *source* of the Bible's light. Why is it possible to describe God's Word as a lamp and as a light?

Surely the answer to that question is that the Bible is light because it is the Word of God, and God is light. "God is light," affirms the Apostle John, "and in him is no darkness at all" (1 John 1:5). The Bible shines clearly and continually because it is fed by the oil of the Holy Spirit. "All scripture," explains Paul, "*is* given by inspiration of God" (2 Timothy 3:16).

Because God is light, the Bible transmits light. The Book partakes of the character and nature of the Author. We say, for example, that God is holy (Revelation 4:8); His Word, too, is holy (2 Timothy 3:15). We say that God is faithful (1 Peter 4:19); His Word, too, is faithful (Revelation 21:5, 6). We say that God is living (John 6:57); His Word also is living (John 6:63). In the same way, we say that God is light, and His Word shares that quality.

We are told that on one occasion an agnostic asked a Christian woman how she could prove the Bible is the Word of God.

The Christian woman immediately asked, "How can you prove there is a sun in the sky?"

"That's easy," was the reply; "because it warms me and gives me light."

"And so it is with me," replied the Christian. "The proof that this Book is the Word of God lies in the fact that it warms my soul and gives me light."[1]

While we consider the Bible as the Word of God, shedding its light on our pathway, we join William W. How in praising God:

> We praise Thee for the radiance
> That from the hallowed page,
> A lantern to our footsteps,
> Shines on from age to age.[2]

It is because the Bible is the Word of God that its enemies have not been able to extinguish its light. Many attempts have been made either to supplant or to stifle the light of God's Word. But in spite of the winds of adversity the lamp of God's Word has continued to shine.

Dr. A.T. Pierson concluded his book, *The Bible and Spiritual Criticism*, with this paragraph:

> The Statue of Liberty in the harbor of New York lifts its great light for the guidance of mariners, and, though the birds of the night fling themselves madly against its crystal, as if to put out its flame, they only beat themselves into insensibility,

and fall dead at its base; so, whatever antagonism there may be to this, God's Beacon Light, those who assault it will only damage themselves, while the light shines on, safe and serene![3]

The Sufficiency of the Bible's Light

We have seen the source of the Bible's light. The Bible's light is derived from the God of light. This fact suggests to us the *sufficiency* of the Bible's light. Concerning itself the Bible could well say: "Our sufficiency is of God" (2 Corinthians 3:5). Unlike the lamps in the Tabernacle, which needed daily to be replenished with oil, the lamp of the Bible burns on strongly and steadily, fed from an inexhaustible Source.

The light of the Bible lamp is sufficient to dispel our darkness. "The entrance of thy words giveth light," testified the psalmist (Psalm 119:130).

In her book, *Windows*, Miss Sarah Stock states there is the darkness of ignorance (Psalm 82:5); the darkness of sin (Proverbs 2:13); and the darkness of this world (Ephesians 6:12).[4] The glorious fact with regard to the Bible is that it is powerful enough to dispel all the darkness that envelops us.

Concerning this power of the Bible, Robert E. Lee wrote: "The Bible is a book in comparison with which all others in my eyes are of minor importance, and which in all my perplexities and distresses has never failed to give me light and strength."[5]

The light of the Bible is sufficient to disclose all the dangers in our pathway. After having referred to the statutes of the Lord, the psalmist testified: "Moreover by them is thy servant warned" (Psalm 19:11). No danger lies concealed from our eyes if we walk with the Lamp of God's truth in our hearts. No error or evil can trick us or trap us if our trust is in God's Word.

David Hume was a Scottish agnostic who believed in the sufficiency of the light of nature. One evening Hume visited in the home of Principal Robertson, a godly evangelical minister who firmly believed in the necessity of revelation and in the insufficiency of the light of nature. The two men discussed the subject. Friends of both were present, and it was reported that Robertson reasoned with unusual clarity and power. Whether Hume was convinced by Robertson's reasoning, we do not know; at any rate he did not acknowledge his conviction. Hume was very much of a gentleman in his manners, and, as he rose to depart, bowed politely to those in the room, while, as he retired through the door, Robertson took the lamp to show him the way. Hume was still facing the door.

"Oh, sir," said he, "I find the light of nature always sufficient," and continuing with, "pray, don't trouble yourself, sir," he walked on.

The door was opened, and presently, as he went along the hall, he stumbled over something concealed, and pitched down the steps into the street.

Robertson ran after him with the light, and as he held it over him, whispered softly.

"You had better have a light from above, Mr. Hume," and, raising him up, bade him good night, and returned to his friends.[6]

Finally, the light of the Bible is sufficient to deliver us from disaster. Hence Peter exhorts us to take heed to the "more sure word of prophecy ... as unto a light that shineth in a dark place" (2 Peter 1:19). If we wish to avoid making shipwreck (see 1 Timothy 1:19), we must pay full attention to the instruction of God's Word. "Made up of many parts," Matthew Henry wrote about the Bible, "proceeding from the pen of many writers, it is yet so beautifully blended in its rays of various hues as to make one brilliant light to shine upon man's pathway from time to eternity."[7]

To reject the light of God's lamp, then, is to court disaster and ruin. Bishop Villiers of the 19th century illustrated the danger of rejecting God's light by an incident which he had witnessed:

> I once happened to be on a visit to a great castle situated on the top of a hill. There was a steep cliff, at the bottom of which was a rapid river. Late one night there was a woman anxious to get home from that castle in the midst of a thunderstorm. The night was blackness itself; the woman was asked to stop till the storm was over, but she declined; next they begged her to take a lantern, that she might be able to keep upon the road from the castle to her home. She replied that she did not require a lantern, but could do very well without one.

The woman left. Perhaps she was frightened by the storm—I know not the cause—but in the midst of the darkness she wandered from the path and fell over the cliff. The next day that swollen river washed to the shore the poor lifeless body of this foolish woman!

How many foolish ones there are who, when the light is offered to them, say, "I am not afraid; I fear not my end!" And how many have perished because they have refused the light of God's truth, which would have guided them on the road to Heaven![8]

The Superiority of the Bible's Light

But consider now the *superiority* of the Bible's light. There are other books that claim to be luminous and enlightening, but the light of the Bible outshines them all.

From those who walk in the light of God's Word, there is a unanimous agreement that its light is superior to the light of its competitors.

Sir Monier Williams, who was an outstanding authority on the sacred books of the East—the Koran, the Hindu Vedas, the Buddhist Tripitaka, and the Zend Avesta—said: "They all begin with some flashes of true light, and end in utter darkness. There is a gulf between the Bible and the so-called sacred books of the East which severs the one from the other utterly, hopelessly, and forever, a veritable gulf which cannot be bridged over by a science of religious thought."[9]

In this day of religious syncretism we need to hold high the torch of God's Word; it will dispel the darkness of man-made religion.

But not only is the light of the Bible superior to the light of its competitors, it is superior to the light of its critics. The *Sunday School Times* once quoted a newspaper editor who had been enlightened regarding the critics of the Bible. He said:

I would rather trust a bunch of blind men to take a few old lanterns and a string of lightning bugs someday at high noon and go out to examine the noonday sun and analyze it by the power of the lanterns and the lightning bugs, than to trust the advocates of modernism to take their own light and examine and analyze the Sun of righteousness and the Word that reveals Him.[10]

Archibald Naismith tells us that during the 1938 Empire Exhibition, held in Glasgow, Scotland, a number of zealous Christians sought to maintain an effective Gospel witness to visitors at the Exhibition. A booth was set up for the distribution of Scriptures and tracts. In the large window of the booth was a Bible, opened at John 8, with the words of the Lord Jesus, "I am the light of the world," underlined in red ink, and a hand pointing to the verse. Beneath the Bible were printed the words, "The only Way out of the Dark."[11]

The Securing of the Bible's Light

We have traced the source of the Bible's light to God Himself. We have assured ourselves of the sufficiency and the superiority of the Bible's light. We must now ask ourselves how the light of the Bible is *secured* and enjoyed by us.

There are people who read the Bible, and it does not seem to give them any light. Are there conditions to be fulfilled, then, with regard to the securing of the Bible's light? Indeed there are.

First, you must come to the Bible without prejudice against it. Let John Newton tell us how he dealt with Dr. Taylor of Norwich:

> Dr. Taylor said to me: "Sir, I have collated every word in the Hebrew Scriptures seventeen times; and it is very strange if the doctrine of the Atonement you hold be there, that it should not have been found by me."

> I replied: "I am not surprised at that. I once went to light my candle with the extinguisher on it. Now prejudices from education, learning, etc., often form an extinguisher. It is not enough that you bring the candle; you must remove the extinguisher."[12]

Come to the Bible, then, without prejudice. But come to it with prayer. Let your prayer be that of the psalmist: "O send out thy light and thy truth: let them lead me" (Psalm 43:3).

And come to the Bible, finally, with a promise to do God's Will. Light is not given for analysis, but for action. God's Word is a lamp unto our feet. Let us be like the psalmist who could say: "I . . . turned my feet unto thy testimonies" (Psalm 119:59), and "I have refrained my feet from every evil way, that I might keep thy word" (Psalm 119:101). "God's Word," according to Mildred Cable and Francesca French, "is a light, but not of such a kind that a man may use it to explore hidden mysteries for his own gratification; it is given so that there may be illumination on the path of duty."[13]

The point is well made by Samuel Hayes:

> The sacred page
> With calm attention scan. If on thy soul,
> As thou dost read, a ray of purer light
> Break in, oh, check it not; give it full scope!
> Admitted, it will break the clouds which long
> Have dimmed thy sight, and lead thee, till at last,
> Convictions, like the sun's meridian beams,
> Illuminate thy mind.[14]

The Sharing of God's Light

But God has given us His luminous Word, not that we may selfishly enjoy it, but that we may gratefully share it with others. Our final consideration, then, relates to our sharing of the Bible's light, "To give light to them that sit in darkness and *in* the shadow of death" (Luke 1:79). Wherever the Bible has gone, the primeval announcement has been repeated: "Let there be light," and the darkness of ignorance, superstition, and sin has been vanquished.

Various hymn writers present the missionary appeal of this symbol in their compositions. Reginald Heber puts the issue to us clearly in his well-known missionary hymn:

> Shall we, whose souls are lighted
> With wisdom from on high,
> Shall we to men benighted
> The lamp of life deny?[15]

Give Me That Book!

Horatius Bonar, the preacher-poet of Scotland, indicates to us the only response that is right for us to make:

> Men die in darkness at your side,
> Without a hope to cheer the tomb;
> Take up the torch, and wave it wide,
> The torch that lights time's thickest gloom.[16]

Henry M. King assures us what will happen if we share the light of God's Word:

> Where'er it goes its golden light
> Streaming as from an unveil'd sun,
> Shall dissipate the clouds of night,
> Undo the work that sin has done.[17]

An unknown hymn writer summarizes the missionary aspect of our study:

> God's Word is our great heritage,
> And shall be ours forever;
> To spread its light from age to age
> Shall be our chief endeavour.[18]

In the pioneer days of the American west a minister once went far into a backwoods settlement to hold an evangelistic meeting. After holding the meeting, he found it necessary to return to his home late in the very dark night.

A woodsman kindly provided him with a torch of pitch-pine wood.

The minister, who had never seen anything of the kind before, said, "It will soon burn out."

"It will light you home," was the assurance.

"But the wind may blow it out," said the evangelist.

"It will light you home," the assurance continued.

"But what if it should rain?" was the minister's next question.

"It will light you!"

Armed with the assurance the minister set out for home, and to his surprise the torch lit his way right to the door of his house.[19]

The Word of God is a lamp placed in our hands. What if it rains? What if the winds blow? What if our adversaries attempt to blow it out? If we will trust in the Lord and hold high our torch, it will light us all the way Home. Praise God, His Word is illuminative!

FOR YOUR FURTHER STUDY

1. On what do you base your confidence that the enemies of God's Word will never be able to blow out the divine lamp of Scripture?
2. List some of life's dark experiences for which the Bible's light is sufficient.
3. In what ways is the light of the Bible superior to the light of every other book?
4. What may be wrong with us when we come to the Bible only to discover that it sheds no light on our path?
5. What is the missionary challenge of the symbol we have been studying—namely, the lamp of God's Word?

The Seed Is the Word of God

When the Word of God is truly heard and thereby received into a prepared heart, the word becomes truly a seed, spiritual and incorruptible in nature, which, when quickened by the Spirit of God, becomes the life-germ of a new creature—a son of God.

—**Philip Mauro**

The sower went forth sowing;
The seed in secret slept
Through weeks of faith and patience,
Till out the green blade crept;
And warmed by golden sunshine,
And fed by silver rain,
At last the fields were whitened
To harvest once again.
Oh, praise the heavenly Sower,
Who gave the fruitful seed,
And watched and watered duly,
And ripened for our need.

Behold, the heavenly Sower
Goes forth with better seed,
The word of sure salvation,
With feet and hands that bleed;
Here in His church 'tis scattered,
Our spirits are the soil;
Then let an ample fruitage
Repay his pain and toil;
Oh, beauteous is the harvest
Wherein all goodness thrives,
And this the true thanksgiving,
The first fruits of our lives.

— **Author Unknown**

Sometimes the harvest is slow, sometimes swift.

—**R.E.O. White**

The weakest and unworthiest of human instrumentalities can sow the seed, God's Word. The life is not in the sower, but in the seed.

—**Walter B. Knight**

If there were no sowing in tears, there would be no reaping in joy.

—**C.H. Spurgeon**

STUDY 3
God's Word Is Regenerative

Our Key Scripture—"Being born again, not of corruptible seed, but of incorruptible, by the Word of God, which liveth and abideth forever" (1 Peter 1:23).

Supplementary Scriptures—Jeremiah 23:28; Luke 8:11; Philippians 2:16; Colossians 1:5, 6; Hebrews 4:12; James 1:18.

A wise old professor of biology stood before his class of eager students. The professor held a little brown seed in his hand. Quietly he spoke to his class.

"I know just exactly the composition of this seed," he said. "It has in it nitrogen, hydrogen, oxygen, and carbon. I know the exact proportions. I can make a seed that will look exactly like it. But if I plant my seed it will come to nought; its elements will be simply absorbed into the soil. If I plant the seed God made, it will become a plant, because it contains the mysterious principle which we call the 'life principle.' "[1]

The Bible, according to the Apostle Peter, is like the seed God made. It alone of all books contains the mysterious life principle. Plant it in good ground, and it will demonstrate its life principle by germinating, growing, and bearing fruit. In Peter's words the Word of God is an incorruptible seed, and when planted in human hearts it is used by the Holy Spirit to bring new life.

BASIC OUTLINE

In order to explore the wealth of teaching that is implicit in our key Scripture, let us enlarge upon three aspects of the regenerating seed of

God's Word. Peter's words suggest to us lessons about the *properties*, the *power*, and the *propagation* of God's Word.

That there is much more that could be studied with regard to the life-giving Word of God is obvious, but these three aspects will perhaps promote a deeper and fuller study.

The Properties of God's Word

First, let us examine together the *properties* of God's Word. In order that we may see Peter's words in their full context we now look at 1 Peter 1:22–25.

> Seeing ye have purified your souls in obeying the truth through the Spirit unto unfeigned love of the brethren, *see that ye* love one another with a pure heart fervently: Being born again, not of corruptible seed, but of incorruptible, by the word of God, which liveth and abideth for ever. For all flesh *is* as grass, and all the glory of man as the flower of grass. The grass withereth, and the flower thereof falleth away: But the word of the Lord endureth for ever. And this is the word which by the gospel is preached unto you.

Here, indeed, is a rich portion of Scripture for our study. We are looking for the properties of God's Word as compared with the properties of seed. According to Peter, the Word by which we are born again is divine, dynamic, durable, and distinctive.

First, the Bible is a divine Word. Here we learn by contrast. Because we are the descendants of Adam and Eve, Peter tells us that we are born of corruptible seed. When Adam fell, he was cut off from the life-giving Spirit of God. Consequently, when we read that Adam "begat *a son* in his own likeness, after his image" (Genesis 5:3), we may conclude that the son was born devoid of the Spirit of God, a "natural" descendant of Adam. All those born of blood, or of the will of the flesh, or of the will of man (see John 1:13) are born of corruptible seed. "That which is born of the flesh is flesh" (John 3:6).

But, Peter teaches that believers are born again of incorruptible seed, by the Word of God. That the Bible in its entirety is not only truly human but fully divine is taught in many passages of Scripture (e.g., 2 Timothy 3:16; 2 Peter 1:20, 21; etc.). All other books are the products of men and women who wrote without the direct inspiration of the Holy Spirit. It is because the Bible is the product of the Holy Spirit's work of inspiration that we can speak of it as incorruptible seed.

In a remarkable passage in Jeremiah 23:28 the Lord challenges the false prophets of Jeremiah's day in the words: "The prophet that hath a dream, let him tell a dream; and he that hath my word, let him speak my word faithfully. What *is* the chaff to the wheat? saith the LORD."

Here the messages of the false prophets are described as chaff, and the messages of the true prophet are described as wheat. Why? Surely because the message of the true prophet was the product of the Spirit's inspiration, and contained the life principle. Nothing could depict more clearly the deadness and dryness of the false prophet's message than the symbol of chaff. What a rebuke is therefore contained in this passage for all those who speak or preach "another gospel!"

But Peter has more to say. He instructs us that not only is the Bible a divine word, it is also a dynamic Word. By it we are "born again."

In John 3 the Lord Jesus seeks to impress upon the heart of Nicodemus both the miracle and the mystery of the new birth. The Lord Jesus speaks to the ruler of the Jews: "Marvel not that I said unto thee, Ye must be born again. The wind bloweth where it listeth, and thou hearest the sound thereof, but canst not tell whence it cometh, and whither it goeth: so is every one that is born of the Spirit" (John 3:7, 8).

But while fully acknowledging the fact that ultimately the miracle of the new birth defies explanation, we learn from other Scriptures, such as Peter's definitive statement, that the Spirit of God employs the Word of God in His work of regeneration. With regard to the believers whom Peter addressed in his first letter, G.J. Polkinghorne wrote: "The Word of God is described as the formal cause of their new life."[2]

Daniel W. Whittle, then, was right when he combined both the mystery and the means of the new birth in the words of his song:

Give Me That Book!

> I know not how the Spirit moves,
> Convincing men of sin,
> Revealing Jesus through the Word,
> Creating faith in Him.[3]

The words and writings of such men as Erasmus led to the Renaissance. The words and writings of Marx and Lenin have led to revolution. But it is the words and writings of the Holy Spirit that alone lead to regeneration. "For the word of God *is* quick [living]" (Hebrews 4:12). Commenting on 1 Peter 1:23–25, Dr. Wilbur M. Smith states:

> The virtue, the mystery, the significance of any seed is that it consists of living substance. It is able to reproduce the plant or animal from which it came: the word here, *sperma*, has entered vitally into our modern scientific nomenclature. As we have our first life from the sperm of our human parents, so we are born the second time by a power containing and communicating divine life, namely, the seed of the Word which proceeds from the living God.[4]

The Bible is divine and dynamic. But according to Peter it is also durable. It lives and abides forever. The characteristic of humanity—those born of corruptible seed—is *temporality*; the characteristic of Holy Writ is *permanency*.

From the Book of Jeremiah (Chapter 36) comes a graphic illustration of the abiding character of God's Word. Jehoiakim had listened to the message of the scroll, dictated by Jeremiah, and recorded by Baruch. In anger at God's message of judgment the king cut up the scroll as column after column was read to him. He then burned the leaves in the fire which was placed before him.

He destroyed the manuscript, but he could not destroy the message. He got rid of the parchment but not the pronouncement. That Word of the Lord came to pass, and Jehoiakim was destroyed. In token of the certainty of that fulfillment, Jeremiah was commanded by the Lord to produce a second scroll containing the same message of judgment. Jehoiakim imagined that he would abide, and that the Word of the Lord would be forgotten. In the end it was the king who faded away, while the Word of God remained sure and steadfast.

We learn of one more property of the Bible from Peter's inspired words; and that is the Bible has a distinctive message. "The Word of the Lord endureth forever. And this is the word which by the Gospel is preached unto you." In the case of the early Christians the Word of God was preached verbally to them by the Apostles. Eventually that Word was given literary form, and now the Word of the Lord is to be equated with the Scriptures.

The supreme subject of the written Word of God, as it was the supreme subject of the Apostles' preaching, is the Gospel—the good news of God's saving acts in Christ. While it is undoubtedly true that the entire Word of God—that is, the whole canon of Scripture—shares in the "seed" nature, and is thereby a living word, Peter indicates that it is the Gospel that the Holy Spirit primarily uses in His regenerating work.

This means that normally we would not expect the Holy Spirit to use portions or passages where there is no direct mention of the plan of salvation. (We say "normally" because there are illustrations and incidents where individuals were led to Christ by very unusual texts!) But it is the testimony of history that the Spirit generally employs the great facts of the Gospel to arouse conviction, to promote concern, and to lead to conversion. It is in this fact that there lies the necessity of true Gospel preaching, namely, the announcement and affirmation of what God has done in Christ.

Paul's words in 1 Thessalonians 2:13 are most relevant at this point. Paul wrote to the Thessalonian converts. We thank "God without ceasing, because, when ye received the word of God which ye heard of us, ye received *it* not *as* the word of men, but as it is in truth, the word of God, which effectually worketh also in you that believe."

The Power of God's Word

We have reviewed briefly what Peter says about the properties of God's Word. It is time now to look in more detail at the *power* of God's Word. Peter describes God's Word as a seed. According to our dictionary, from a botanical standpoint, a seed is "the small body produced by flowering plants which contains an embryo capable of developing by germination."

Give Me That Book!

God's Word has this unique power.

As seed God's Word has power to germinate when it is placed in suitable and prepared soil. Indeed, it is one of the remarkable features of God's Word as seed that, regardless of country, class, culture, or colour, provided it falls into an honest heart, that seed has power to germinate.

We have already indicated the importance of a prepared heart to receive the seed which is God's Word. This evidently is the meaning of Christ's parable of the sower, the seed, and the soils (see Matthew 13:3–9, 18–23; Mark 4:2–9, 13–29; and Luke 8:4–15). We quote Christ's interpretation of that parable as given by Luke:

Now the parable is this:

The seed is the Word of God. Those by the way side are they that hear, then cometh the devil, and taketh away the word out of their hearts, lest they should believe and be saved.

They on the rock *are they*, which, when they hear, receive the word with joy; and these have no root, which for a while believe, and in time of temptation fall away.

And that which fell among thorns are they, which, when they have heard, go forth, and are choked with cares and riches and pleasures of *this* life, and bring no fruit to perfection.

But that on the good ground are they, which in an honest and good heart, having heard the word, keep *it*, and bring forth fruit with patience.

Note well Christ's statement. The divine seed has to have an honest and good heart as its depository before it can fully accomplish its purpose.

But not only does the Word of God as seed have power to germinate; it has power to grow amid all kinds of unfavourable circumstances. Provided it has been rooted in an honest and good heart, no outward condition can prevent that seed from developing to maturity. Just as the edelweiss can grow amid the Alpine snows, so the Word of God can flourish amid the most chilling conditions. Just as the desert flower survives in the heat and drought of the desert, so the Bible, because it is the Word of God, can survive amid the most barren circumstances.

English writer E.L. Langston in one of his books tells of a strange plant in Jamaica. It is known as the "life plant." It is called this because it is almost impossible to kill or destroy any portion of it. When a leaf is cut off and hung by a string, instead of shrivelling up and dying like any other leaf, it sends out white threadlike roots and thus gathers moisture from the air, and begins to grow new leaves.

The Bible is the life plant of the moral and spiritual world. Circulate the Bible or portions of it anywhere, and it will soon take root in the affections and heart of mankind and send out tendrils of life. In the heart of Africa, or among the aborigines of South America, or among the Eskimos of the Arctic Circle, it has the same quickening power which no climate or heathenism has the power to kill.[5]

As seed, God's Word has power to germinate, to grow, and to give an abundant harvest of spiritual fruit. This is Paul's declaration in Colossians 1:6. Speaking of the Word of the truth of the Gospel, Paul says it has "come unto you, as *it is* in all the world; and bringeth forth fruit, as *it doth* also in you, since the day ye heard *of it,* and knew the grace of God in truth." George F. Pentecost wrote that: "The Word of God is a living seed, containing within itself God's own life, which, when it is received into our hearts, springs up within us and 'brings forth fruit after its kind;' for Jesus Christ, the eternal Word of God, is the living germ hidden in His written Word."[6]

This is the history of Christian missions. Wherever the good seed of God's Word has been carried, it has germinated, grown, and given an abundant harvest. In Europe, Africa, India, South America, and the islands of the sea, wherever this dynamic seed of God's Word has been deposited, there has been a harvest.

The Propagation of God's Word

We have completed our lesson on the properties and the power of God's Word.

We now look at the *propagation* of God's Word. God's Word as seed must be sown, and that responsibility has been given to the Christian Church.

Give Me That Book!

As sowers of God's Word we must sow carefully.

The people of Israel were given clear commandments concerning the sowing of seed in their fields. "Thou shalt not sow thy vineyard with divers seeds: lest the fruit of thy seed which thou hast sown, and the fruit of thy vineyard, be defiled" (Deuteronomy 22:9). It is easy to pass from the world of nature to the realm of spiritual things, and to apply this prohibition to those who sow the Gospel seed. God's command may be applied in a three-fold way to us today.

First, we must not sow the seed of God's truth with the seed of human error. How easy—and how fatal—to sow a thought of error, or to suggest some question as to the inspiration of Scripture, and for that seed to produce a harvest that is described as defiled.

We must not sow the seed of God's wisdom with the seed of human folly. We must shun all that savors of man's proud intellect.

We must not sow the seed of God's Gospel with the seed of man's glib optimism.

Our seed must not be mixed, but rather it must be pure in God's sight—"the unadulterated" Word of God.

As sowers of God's seed we must sow faithfully. "In the morning sow thy seed, and in the evening withhold not thine hand: for thou knowest not whether shall prosper, either this or that, or whether they both *shall be* alike good" (Ecclesiastes 11:6). "Blessed *are* ye that sow beside all waters" (Isaiah 32:20).

As sowers of God's seed, we must sow liberally. "He which soweth sparingly shall reap also sparingly; and he which soweth bountifully shall reap also bountifully" (2 Corinthians 9:6). Here is how Allon Poole concludes:

> No force is so potent for good as the hand which circulates the Word of God. No Christian enterprise holds within it such vast possibilities of blessing as the scattering of the Scriptures. God would have His people ever broadcasting the truth which He has so wondrously given and preserved, with His divine

guarantee as the inspiration of their service: "My word...shall not return unto me void."[7]

Again, as sowers of God's Word we must sow confidently. "Let us not be weary in well doing: for in due season we shall reap, if we faint not" (Galatians 6:9). Here is how Mary Warburton Booth, herself a missionary in India, expressed her confidence in God's Word as she visited villages and sowed God's Word:

> The only comfort we have as we leave them is that the seed has been sown, and the Seed is the Word of God. It does not matter if they do forget what we say. It does not matter if they do not remember how we were sent to them in their sickness and need. It does matter whether we were careful to give to them the Words of Life, for they can never die. They will live forever in the hearts of those who receive them, and some will bring forth a hundredfold and some sixtyfold and some thirtyfold when the harvest is gathered in.

> And I sow and keep on sowing
> The Book that is God's Word;
> The Word that tells of Jesus,
> The Lord Who is the Word.

> I'm sowing and believing
> There must a harvest be;
> The seed that is life giving,
> God trusted this to me.[8]

Again, we must prayerfully sow the seed which is God's Word. Fay Inchfawn wrote a beautiful poem entitled, "A Preacher's Thoughts." Here is the section marked, "After the Sermon:"

> Lord, with an eager hand indeed
> I scattered wide the germ-filled seed.
> Oh, may Thy four winds bear it far,
> Where little-watered cornfields are,
> And to the wilderness which knows
> Not fruit, nor yet rejoicing rose.

> And where my fingers could not reach,
> And all my effort failed to teach,
> Where my poor tongue could not express
> Thy beauty and Thy holiness—
> Yes, where my memory gave way,
> And where my best points went astray—
> Do Thou come in, O Quickening Breath,
> And bring triumphant life from death![9]

Finally, we must sow compassionately. "They that sow in tears shall reap in joy. He that goeth forth and weepeth, bearing precious seed, shall doubtless come again with rejoicing" (Psalm 126:5, 6).

Archibald Naismith of India stresses the importance of sowing the good seed of God's Word in the following story:

> A merchant, going abroad for some time, gave two of his friends each two sacks of grain to care for while he was gone. Years passed by. When he came back, he asked his friends for the sacks of grain. The first took him into his storehouse and showed him the two sacks as he had received them, now mildewed and worthless. The other led him into the country and showed him fields of grain growing and ripening, the produce of the two sacks he had used as seed.
>
> "Give me the two sacks," said the merchant to him, "and keep the rest."[10]

Christian, to you has been given the good seed of God's Word. What are you doing with it? Are you selfishly and sinfully hoarding it, indeed, protecting it, as if to spread it would destroy it? Or are you taking that good seed of God's Word and scattering it far and wide by means of Scripture portions, tracts, testimony, message, and missions?

Only those will be rewarded who have propagated the seed of God's Word.

FOR YOUR FURTHER STUDY

1. What is it that sets God's Word apart in a class by itself?
2. In the light of Jesus' teaching in Luke 8:4–15, why is it that the seed of God's Word does not produce a harvest in some hearts?
3. What is the missionary message involved in our consideration of God's Word as seed?

Mission Accomplished

The effort of the Church to preach Christ crucified will no more fail of its effect, than the rain will fail to water the earth, and cause the seeds that are sown in it to germinate.

—W.G.T. Shedd

Revelation, in its effect upon mankind, is like the rain and the snow in their effect upon the earth. The rain and the snow are sapped into the earth, and then incorporated in the grain, resulting in seed to the sower and bread to the eater. Similarly, the published Word, being assimilated into the human mind, fashions thought, moulds character, regenerates life; and, therefore, it does not return void to its Author.

—Harri Edwards

Rain softens and moistens the earth, and produces fruitfulness. The Word of God enlightens, impresses, alarms, convinces, and converts. It is the instrumental means of regeneration and holiness. Wherever it is received it produces these happy and delightful effects.

—Jabez Burns

God's Word is like the rain that falls
In soft, refreshing show'r;
It germinates the waiting seed
Through its inherent pow'r.

—Author Unknown

We all know how the rain softens the dry and hardened ground. Its drops go to the roots of the withering grass and the fading flowers, and soon new life appears everywhere. So it is when God's Word falls upon a human life. It makes the life fruitful. Sometimes it lies like snow on the earth, not melting for a time. The results of holy teaching do not always appear at once. But as at last the snows melt and fill streams and rivers, so God's Word in a life will some day find its way down into the human heart and bless it. Heavenly lessons have lain for scores of years, producing no effect; yet, at last, when the warm love of God touches the life it brought forth beautiful fruits.

—J.R. Miller

STUDY 4
God's Word Is Productive

Our Key Scripture—"As the rain cometh down, and the snow from heaven, and returneth not thither, but watereth the earth, and maketh it bring forth and bud, that it may give seed to the sower, and bread to the eater: So shall my word be that goeth forth out of my mouth: it shall not return unto me void, but it shall accomplish that which I please, and it shall prosper *in the thing* whereto I sent it" (Isaiah 55:10, 11).

Supplementary Scriptures—Deuteronomy 32:2; Job 14:7–9; Psalm 33:9; Isaiah 9:8; Amos 7:16; Colossians 1:5, 6; 1 Thessalonians 1:5–7; Hebrews 4:12 (see the word powerful, or energetic, effectual).

THERE can be no doubt that of all the promises regarding the influence of God's Word, the promise of Isaiah 55:10, 11 is the best known. How many missionaries, pastors, Sunday school teachers, Christian parents, Bible colporteurs, and tract distributors have claimed this blessed promise! But like so many promises of God's Word, this promise has suffered from detachment from its original context and disregard of its primary meaning. Before we suggest some general applications of the promise, let us take time to note the setting of this glorious declaration concerning the efficacy of God's Word.

The stirring message of Isaiah 55 was addressed initially by God to His people, the nation of Israel. They are looked upon in the chapter as backslidden and banished from God's presence. But because God is a God of grace, there is a call to repentance and return. This offer to pardon His people is completely contrary to man's ideas about God. God explains this in verse 8: "My thoughts *are* not your thoughts."

God has declared that His people shall return to Him. To this end His Word has been given, so that by its entreaties and encouragements the divine purpose for Israel may be accomplished. Accordingly, the word of verse 11 is God's revelation of His purposes for Israel. These purposes will be fulfilled.

That is the particular application of this great promise of Isaiah 55:10, 11. But having emphasized the initial scope of the promise, we may now extract from the promise a general application of all of God's Word, the Holy Scriptures. That application in brief is this: We are to take heart from the certain and ceaseless cycle of nature, inasmuch as the rain and snow in their effectual working mirror the successful Word of God.

BASIC OUTLINE

We may compare the Word of God and its effects to rain and snow in four ways: By considering, first, the *origin* of the Scriptures; second, the *objective* of the Scriptures; third, the *operation* of the Scriptures; and, finally, the *outcome* of the Scriptures.

Origin

Let us then compare the Word of God to rain and snow with regard to the *origin* of the Scriptures.

In our scientific age we are so accustomed to thinking of rain and snow as belonging to the realm of the natural that we overlook the fact that these precious gifts are divine as to their origin. The biblical writers constantly affirm their belief that God is the God of nature, and, consequently, He is the God of the rain and the snow. Here are just a few of the many verses that could be cited:

"Let us now fear the LORD our God, that giveth rain, both the former and the latter, in his season: He reserveth unto us the appointed weeks of the harvest" (Jeremiah 5:24). Eliphaz speaks of God as the One "Who giveth rain upon the earth, and sendeth waters upon the fields" (Job 5:10).

The psalmist speaks of God as the One—"Who covereth the heaven with clouds, who prepareth rain for the earth, who maketh grass to grow upon the mountains" (Psalm 147:8).

Many other verses could be added to these, all indicating that as far as the biblical writers were concerned, regardless of all other considerations, God is the Author of the rain and snow—that is, it is as a result of His creative and controlling power that these benefits are precipitated upon the earth.

Now when we turn to the Bible and ask the question, "What is the origin of the Bible?" we receive the same answer: "The Bible comes from God"—not in the naive sense that it came directly from Heaven, printed in English, and published with black covers—but in the sublime sense that it was God who chose, conditioned, and controlled the Bible writers, with the result that what they wrote is indeed the Word of God.

The key passage, of course, for this view of Scripture is 2 Timothy 3:16. Paul clearly and categorically affirms: "All scripture *is* given by inspiration of God." Likewise Peter states: "For the prophecy came not in old time by the will of man: but holy men of God spake *as they were* moved by the Holy Ghost" (2 Peter 1:21).

It is true that the Bible was written by men, written moreover in the languages of men, employing different literary styles, incorporating many idioms and figures of speech, each reflecting his background and environment; but in affirming the "humanity" of the Bible, we must never lose sight of its "divinity," that it is supremely the production of the Holy Spirit.

Objective

In examining the points of comparison between God's Word and rain and snow, we must think as well of the *objective* of God's Word. Just as the rain and the snow descend from heaven to earth upon a specific mission, so the Word of God comes to men with definite goals in mind. In Isaiah 55:10 the prophet affirms that the purpose of the moisture is to "give seed to the sower, and bread to the eater." Likewise the Word of God, which represents spiritual moisture for arid hearts, achieves various objectives.

Give Me That Book!

It will be helpful to review briefly what is said in the Bible concerning these objectives.

In 2 Timothy 3:15 Paul reminds Timothy of his priceless heritage: "And that from a child thou hast known the holy scriptures, which are able to make thee wise unto salvation through faith which is in Christ Jesus." What is the purpose of God's Word? Here it is defined as illumination—able to make wise unto salvation. Man is in the dark as to the way of salvation. The Bible is God's light to dispel that darkness and to guide man into the way of salvation, a salvation which is through faith that is centred in Christ Jesus.

But not only is the Bible the instrument of our illumination, it is also the instrument of our salvation. Thus James writes: "Receive with meekness the engrafted word, which is able to save your souls" (James 1:21). Here salvation must include the entire experience of the believer. The Scriptures are given in order that the believer may be saved from sin. By taking heed to their warnings, entreaties, promises, and exhortations, the believer is delivered from the chains of sin.

In his final message to the Ephesian elders Paul said: "And now, brethren, I commend you to God, and to the word of his grace, which is able to build you up, and to give you an inheritance among all them which are sanctified" (Acts 20:32). Here is the ability of God's Word to edify. That Word is able to "perfect, stablish, strengthen, [and] settle" us (1 Peter 5:10).

Here, then, in separate passages of God's Word, are set before us three objectives of the Scriptures: illumination, salvation, and edification. Other verses could be added, filling out the picture still more. But with these three aspects of the purpose of God's Word in mind, we may note that primarily God's Word is designed to accomplish a spiritual work in the hearts of men and women. As we have seen in previous studies, God's Word comes to us not as a history book, or a science text, or a psychology manual; it comes as a book for the heart, to bring us into contact with God, to work a spiritual transformation in our lives.

Operation

We have compared God's Word to rain and snow with regard to both its origin and its objective. Consider now the *operation* of God's Word and what we may learn from comparing the Holy Scriptures to the rain and the snow in their operation on earth.

First, we learn that, as in the case of the rain and the snow, there are aspects of the operation of God's Word which are visible, and there are aspects which are invisible. Our Saviour said concerning the action of the wind, "The wind bloweth where it listeth, and thou hearest the sound thereof, but canst not tell whence it cometh, and whither it goeth: so is every one that is born of the Spirit" (John 3:8). Likewise it may be said concerning the action of rain and snow: we see the rain falling and the snow descending, but we do not see all the mysterious processes of nature by which the seed in the ground is quickened and germinated.

In all our teaching of God's Word it is important to keep this aspect of the operation of God's Word in mind. We may ask a student to recite or to explain a passage of God's Word. But we see and hear only part of the total operation of God's Word. We do not see that divine Word at work in the secret recesses of the heart. That work of the Holy Spirit is carried on all unseen by men.

Here is both hope and encouragement for the teacher of God's Word—be he parent, Sunday school teacher, or pastor. You may be giving out God's Word daily or weekly without any apparent response to that Word. You may imagine that the Scripture is being shed "like water off a duck's back." But you must not forget the inward ministry of the Holy Spirit. It is He who employs that Word to accomplish His own work.

A.J. Gordon taught this truth in a beautiful illustration:

> I saw a sign-painter take a dish of gold dust and pour it over the board upon which he was working; but when he turned the board over all of it seemed to slide off. But no, not all; the lines where his brush had been drawn a few moments before with the adhesive preparation, these caught the glittering particles and held them firm. So, thought I, must the teachers of God now do. They must pour the golden sand of the Gospel over the whole congregation; and if it seems to slide off and get no hold upon their hearts, they must know that many a one who has been touched with the preparing grace of the Holy Spirit

will catch and hold fast the Word of life, and so the Word shall not return to God void.[1]

Second, we may learn in comparing the operation of God's Word to the operation of rain and snow that there are phases of the operation of God's Word which are vastly different from each other, and yet all are complementary to each other.

Let us explain. In its action the rain may be gentle, falling softly on the soil; on the other hand, it may descend in copious showers, deluging the ground. Likewise the snow may fall in tiny flakes, swirling about our feet; or it may blanket the ground, piling up in depth on garden and field. The rain and the snow come in a great variety of ways, but all for the same purpose: that the ground may be prepared for the seed and that the seed in turn may be germinated.

Likewise the Word of God comes to us in a variety of ways, but yet there is a unity in the midst of this variety. Think of the variety of preachers and teachers who have given us the Word of God! What variety there is in them! Sometimes the Word of God comes to us gently; at other times it comes to us like a blast of cold wind, bringing sleet and snow. Yet the purpose of that Word is ever the same—to meet our spiritual need.

With regard to rain, we may see an immediate effect: gardens that are parched and dry spring forth to life again. But with regard to snow, there may be no immediate effect. The snow may lie for weeks, and then slowly melt away. The actions of the rain and the snow are different but the aim is constant.

Again, we may compare the Scripture to the rain and the snow. Sometimes there is an immediate response to God's Word; at other times, there is a long delay while the "snow" of the Scriptures melts into hearts and softens hard attitudes.

It is in the pages of Christian biography that we see the diverse activities of the Word. All Christians experience the quickening power of God's Word, but all Christians do not experience that quickening power in the same way. We must be careful not to stereotype the Spirit's working. He is sovereign in the way He works.

Third, as in the case of the rain and snow, there are seasons when the operation of God's Word is greatly facilitated and furthered. There are seasons of the soul. There are seasons when the seed of God's Word lies dormant in the soil of the soul. But there comes a time when the voice of the Spirit says—

> Rise up, my love, my fair one, and come away. For, lo, the winter is past, the rain is over *and* gone; The flowers appear on the earth; the time of the singing *of birds* is come, and the voice of the turtle [dove] is heard in our land; the fig tree putteth forth her green figs, and the vines *with* the tender grape give a *good* smell. Arise, my love, my fair one, and come away (Song of Solomon 2:10-13).

That there are seasons of the soul is clearly indicated by the psalmist in Psalm 1. According to him the godly man brings forth his fruit in his season. Surely this implies that the moisture of God's Word may descend upon the heart, but there may be no immediate response or result. That moisture may be treasured up, and in the springtime of the soul, there will be all kinds of evidence that God's Word has been at work in the heart. Or we may have to wait until the autumn season of the soul, and at that time glean the precious fruit of the Spirit in our lives.

J.R. Miller assures us that summer will come to the soul:

> Men's hearts by nature are hard, like trodden fields. But even the hardest heart God's grace can soften. 'As the rain cometh down and the snow from heaven . . . so shall My word be.' We all know how the rain softens the dry and hardened ground. Its drops go to the roots of the withering grass and the fading flowers, and soon new life appears everywhere. So it is when God's Word falls upon a human life. It makes the life fruitful. Sometimes it lies like snow on the earth, not melting for a time. The results of holy teaching do not always appear at once. But as at last the snows melt and fill streams and rivers, so God's Word in a life will some day find its way down into the heart and bless it. Heavenly lessons have lain for scores of

years, producing no effect; yet, at last, when the warm love of God touched the life it brought forth beautiful fruits.[2]

Fourth, as in the case of the rain and the snow, the operation of God's Word needs the co-operation of other factors. It is not the rain and the snow alone that produce germination and growth. There must be suitable soil and adequate sunlight and prior ploughing and abundant fertilizer. Then the rain and the snow work together to produce a harvest.

It is no reflection upon the efficacy of God's Word to say that it alone does not produce a harvest. There must be an open heart. There must be the ministry of the Spirit. There must be the plowshare of repentance and faith. Then as the rain and the snow of God's Word fall upon the heart, "the word of the truth of the gospel" brings forth fruit (Colossians 1:5, 6).

Finally, we must note that, as in the case of the rain and the snow, the operation of God's Word issues in an abundant harvest. Commenting on this text W. Kay stated:

> "Every *word* that proceedeth out of the mouth of the LORD" has in it vital energy (Deuteronomy 8:3; Hebrews 4:12). Whence, indeed, but from the creative Word comes the productive power of the earth, the fertilizing properties of the rain, the germinating power of seed, the nutritive quality of the corn? So, too, must it be with His redemptive Word (see Isaiah 40:8). It shall cause "righteousness to bud" (45:8; 2 Corinthians 9:10). It shall quicken and sustain the life of the soul (see Isaiah 55:2).[3]

In a remarkable collection of expositions, W.G.T. Shedd, writing on Isaiah 55:10, 11, stated:

> The Scriptures warrant us in asserting that God is more profoundly concerned for the success of that body of truth which He has revealed to mankind in the Scriptures, than He is for the spread and influence of all other ideas and truths whatsoever. This is the only species of truth which He personally watches over, and accompanies with a divine influence. He leaves human knowledge to itself, to make its own way

without any supernatural aid or influence from Him; but the doctrines of the Bible are not dismissed from His hand with this indifference....

From the very depths of the depths of the divine Essence, there issues an energy that adds to the intrinsic energy of revelation, and makes it a two-edged sword, quick and piercing. Powerful as the Word of God is in itself, it would fail to touch and soften the flinty human heart, were it not that God personally watches over it, and effectually applies it....

This fact is clearly taught in the text. "My word," says God by His prophet, "shall not return unto me void, but it shall accomplish that which I please, and it shall prosper *in the thing* whereto I sent it." Here is personal interest and personal supervision. These doctrines relating to the salvation and destiny of man are not sent forth from Heaven as lonely messengers, to make their way as they best can. The third Person of the Trinity goes with them, and exerts an influence through them that is undefinable, but as almighty and irresistible, within its own sphere and in its own way, as physical omnipotence itself. For there is not a human heart upon the globe, whose hardness is impenetrable to the combined operation of the Word and Spirit of God. There is not a human will upon the planet, so strong and stubborn as to be able to overcome the union of the Scriptures and the Holy Ghost.[4]

Outcome

Our final point of comparison between the Word of God and the rain and the snow from heaven is the *outcome* of the divine Word. We have noted aspects of the outcome of God's Word in previous points, but we wish to stress this aspect in such a way that we will not be left in any doubt as to the achievements and accomplishments of Scripture.

First, like the rain and the snow, God's Word germinates the seed that has been sown. Here, we are presented with a paradox, for God's Word is both seed and moisture; that is, there are aspects of its working which correspond to both seed and moisture (see Study 2 for a discussion of God's Word as seed).

Second, like the rain and the snow, God's Word gratifies both the eater and the sower. Although this may not be strictly involved in Isaiah 55:10, 11, we suggest that God's Word provides spiritual bread for the eater and spiritual seed for the sower. It is part of the amazing qualities of God's Word that it both satisfies the hungry and equips the labourer in God's great field, which is the world.

Finally, like the rain and the snow, God's Word glorifies its Sender. In accomplishing the divine design, God's Word brings glory to its Author.

Let W.G.T. Shedd apply the promise of Isaiah 55:10, 11 to your heart:

> Go forth to evangelistic labour of any and every variety, with cheerfulness, with courage and with confidence. And when the vastness and difficulty of the work threaten to discourage and dishearten you, look away entirely from earth and man's misery, to God's throne, and recall His own Word which is settled in Heaven: "For as the rain cometh down, and the snow from heaven, and returneth not thither, but watereth the earth, and maketh it bring forth and bud, that it may give seed to the sower, and bread to the eater: So shall my word be that goeth forth out of my mouth: it shall not return unto me void, but it shall accomplish that which I please, and it shall prosper *in the thing* whereto I sent it."[5]

FOR YOUR FURTHER STUDY

1. What various forms of moisture are referred to by Moses in Deuteronomy 32:2? What did he intend to set forth by his comparisons?
2. In the light of Isaiah 55:10, 11 why is it necessary to defend and declare the divine inspiration of the Scriptures?
3. In addition to those aspects suggested under point 3, can you propose some other comparisons between the operation of God's Word and the operation of rain and snow?

Man Shall Not Live by Bread Alone

The Word of God may be likened to food as it is essential to the life of the soul.

—**Jabez Burns**

The Word of God is the Bread of Heaven; the more it is broken and given forth, the more it remaineth.

—**Bishop Jewel**

Bread nourishes, not when it is looked at, but when it is eaten.

—**Alexander MacLaren**

Bread is baked not for analysis, but for consumption.

—**G. Scroggie**

Let the whole soul be fed by the study of the whole Bible, so that there may be no irregularity of its parts or powers.

—**Dr. H. Bonar**

The man who only samples the Word of God occasionally never acquires a keen taste for it.

To get the most out of your Bible reading, eat it with plenty of prayer.

—**M.R. DeHaan**

Nothing will impart sinew and muscle to your piety like the thorough study and digestion of your Bible. A good sermon must be digested or it will be of little use to you, and your daily bread of the Bible must go through the same process in order that it may be assimilated and taken into your spiritual fiber.

—**T. Cuyler**

The Word of God is the food of the life of God. The Word of God, read, marked, learned, and inwardly digested, is essential to healthy spiritual life. …Think how the milk is fitted to the child, or the meat to the strong man; how each nourishes the whole system, turning into blood, bone, nerve, muscle; how each strengthens every organism: brain, heart, lung, eye, ear, hand. So the Word of God is fitted to the life of God within us, ministering to every spiritual faculty, invigorating all the graces of our new life.

—**Mark G. Pearse**

God feeds us through His Word.

—**Dr. J.R. Miller**

A little girl brought the following statement to her Sunday school teacher: "The Bible is a loaf, every chapter a slice, every verse a bite."

—**F.H. Wright**

STUDY 5
God's Word Is Nutritive

Our Key Scripture—"I have esteemed the words of his mouth more than my necessary *food*" (Job 23:12).

Supplementary Scriptures—Deuteronomy 8:3; Psalm 19:10; 119:103; Jeremiah 15:16; Ezekiel 2:8–3:3; 1 Corinthians 3:2; Hebrews 5:11–14; 1 Peter 2:2; Revelation 10:7–11.

IN Deuteronomy 8:3 Moses affirmed that, during the wilderness wanderings of his people, God desired to teach Israel the lesson that "man doth not live by bread only, but by every *word* that proceedeth out of the mouth of the LORD doth man live." In these words Moses indicated that what food is to man's physical life God's Word is to his spiritual life. This insight is basic to all those passages of Scripture which compare God's Word to food—whether bread, milk, meat, or honey. Enlightened by it, there is much that we can learn from the symbols that compare the Bible to food.

BASIC OUTLINE

In order to develop the rich teaching of our theme, we offer some *deductions*, some *distinctions* and some *directions*. We do not offer these three aspects as an exhaustive treatment, but rather as a suggestive approach to a very helpful and profitable study.

<u>Some Deductions</u>

Since the Bible is compared to food, we may make some basic *deductions* from that fact.

First, if the Bible is our spiritual food, then we may conclude that the Bible is essential for spiritual life. This is implicit in Moses' great affirmation, quoted already in full: "Man doth not live by bread only, but by every *word* that proceedeth out of the mouth of the Lord doth man live."

In His wilderness temptations, after He had fasted for forty days, our Lord Jesus faced Satan's subtle suggestion, "If thou be the Son of God, command that these stones be made bread." Our Lord met this assault of Satan by quoting the words of Moses, "Man shall not live by bread alone, but by every word...of God" (Matthew 4:3, 4).

God's Word, therefore, is essential to the maintenance of spiritual life. The late Dr. Donald G. Barnhouse wrote:

> The Word of God is the food of the Christian; every Christian needs a certain minimum of food from the Word of God to live his life day-by-day. If, in addition, he has special work to do for the Lord, he needs special feeding from the Word. The more his output, the more he must feed upon the Word. The greater his service for the Lord, the greater his need to consume at the table which God has laid .... Those who would advance in God must, like the prophet, say, "Thy words were found, and I did eat them" (Jeremiah 15:16).[1]

That great Christian doctor, Dr. Howard M. Kelly, gave his testimony to the absolute necessity of eating God's Word in this way:

> My own daily life is as full as that of any man I know, but I found long since that as I allowed the pressure of professional and other engagements to fill in every moment between rising and going to bed, the spirit would surely starve; so I made a rule, which I have since stuck to in spite of many temptations, not to read or study anything but my Bible after the evening meal, and never to read any other book but the Bible on Sunday.[2]

But from the fact that God's Word is compared to food, there is a second deduction we may make, namely God's Word is essential not only for the maintenance of spiritual life, but also for spiritual growth. Life is one matter; growth is another. There is no growth without adequate food. Peter urges us to desire the sincere milk of the Word that we may grow thereby.

In the presentation of deeper-life teaching, there may be a tendency to overlook the fact that Christian life is a growth. We speak often of the crisis of the victorious life; we tend to overlook the continuance of the victorious life. In the New Testament the goal that is constantly set before the believer is that of spiritual maturity—that is, we must pass through the stages of babyhood and childhood on to adulthood.

Now for growth the child of God needs food. There can be no progress, no advancement, no maturity without the vitamins of God's Word. If you are conscious of being but a babe in spiritual things, then you need to begin feeding in the Word of God.

The believer needs God's Word for life and for growth. A third deduction from the fact that God's Word is compared to food is that the believer needs the Word for spiritual health. We need to have life, but we must be healthy as well. We need to grow, but we need to grow healthfully, in a balanced manner. In the Word of God is found all that is necessary for spiritual health. Peter states that God's power has given to us all things that relate to life and godliness (2 Peter 1:3). To absorb the Word of God into our spiritual system will ensure protection against all kinds of spiritual disease, sickness, and deformity.

Dr. W.H. Griffith Thomas wrote:

> The reason why people are ill in body is because they are "below par," and they thereby become a prey to the microbes that come in their millions. If people are strong and vigorous, they may consume microbes by the thousand and suffer no harm. But if we are below our normal state of health, and the microbes enter and find something to attach themselves to in our body, the result is illness and disease.
>
> So it is in the spiritual life. God's Word is spoken of as food, milk, and honey—food to eat, milk to drink, and honey for "dessert." There is an entire meal in God's Word. If we eat God's Word we are strong, but if we do not, we become a prey to the microbes of temptation; they find us below spiritual "par," and the result is, we fail and become ill and diseased.[3]

Give Me That Book!

There is a fourth deduction we may make from the fact that the Bible is our food: We need it for spiritual strength: Life, growth, health, and strength. Writing to Christians, John the Apostle stated: "I have written unto you, young men, because ye are strong, and the word of God abideth in you, and ye have overcome the wicked one" (1 John 2:14). There is the relationship between God's Word and spiritual strength: We derive abounding strength from the Word.

We are familiar with the command: "Be strong in the Lord." How is this to be realized? Certainly one way is to permit the dynamic Word of God to be resident and reigning within our hearts.

Why, then, does the believer value the Word of God more than our necessary food? Because it contributes to spiritual life, growth, health, and strength. These are the deductions we may make from the fact that the Scriptures are symbolized as food.

Dr. Robert G. Lee points out that, according to Professor J.A. Carlson, "A bird can go nine days without food. A man twelve days. A dog twenty days. A turtle five hundred days. A snake eight hundred days. A fish one thousand days. Insects twelve hundred days." Dr. Lee then makes the application:

> There are some "turtle" Christians, who go five hundred days without much real Bible meat. And many "bird" Christians, who go more than nine days without food. And not a few "fish" Christians, who go one thousand days without eating much of the honey and meat and bread of the Bible. Classify yourself![4]

But what kind of Christian is he who can go a thousand days without eating God's Word?

J.S. Keiffer gives us the right approach to the Bible in these words:

> From age to age, the Word of God continues to be of unfailing and inexhaustible interest. It contains the most ancient history, the profoundest philosophy, the noblest morality, the sublimest poetry, which the world possesses. These, however, do not constitute its chief significance and interest; it is more

than history, or philosophy, or morality, or poetry, or all of these together; it is nourishing and strengthening food for the human soul. He deals most wisely with the Bible who reads it, not to gratify his curiosity, nor in order to find questions for philosophical discussion, or literary or artistic beauty to admire, but in order that he may obtain therefrom the food which will strengthen him for the doing of those things which he is therein required to do.[5]

Some Distinctions

The Bible is compared to food. That is a general description of the value of the Bible to us, but it is possible in studying the Bible as food to make some *distinctions*. This aspect of our study emphasizes the variety there is available for our spiritual diet. The Bible is compared to at least four different kinds of food: milk, meat, honey, and, by implication, bread.

Jabez Burns comments on the Bible:

> In it there is everything to enrich the sanctified imagination, to enlighten the understanding, to counsel the judgment, to purify the conscience, to exalt the affections and to meet all the spiritual desires of the soul. It contains food for every grade of character, for every age and condition, for all ranks and degrees and classes in the Kingdom of Jesus Christ. For the young and old; for the weakly and the strong; for pastors and teachers; for every member of the household of faith.[6]

Think of the Bible as bread. Again we quote the words of Moses: "Man shall not live by bread only, but by every *word* that proceedeth out of the mouth of the Lord doth man live." There is a clear implication here that God's Word constitutes man's daily spiritual bread. Perhaps we need to apply the words of the prayer taught to the disciples by our Lord to the matter of spiritual bread: "Give us this day our daily bread."

Consider God's Word as milk. There are two ways in which this symbol is used in the Bible.

First, Peter exhorts us to desire the sincere milk of the Word "as newborn babes." Here the emphasis is placed upon the intense desire that every one of us should have as believers for the pure and perfect Word of God. Peter is not necessarily describing his readers as newborn babes—that is, we need not understand that they have just become Christians. Rather, he is affirming that every child of God should be characterized by a thirst for the Word of God in the same way as a newborn infant desires milk—especially at two or three o'clock in the morning!

Peter describes the milk of the Word as the sincere milk of the Word, or, as it may be translated, unadulterated milk of the Word. Milk, as is well known, very readily becomes contaminated with micro-organisms, some pathogenic to man. Peter reminds us that it is possible for the pure Word of God to become contaminated with the theories and reasonings of man and for this adulterated mixture to harm the child of God.

The second way in which the symbol, milk, is used in the Scriptures is to draw a contrast between spiritual babyhood and spiritual maturity. This in no way contradicts the first use of the symbol. Each writer had a distinct purpose in employing the symbol.

Writing to the Corinthians Paul describes them as carnal, not spiritual (1 Corinthians 3:1). He then proceeds to state: "I have fed you with milk, and not with meat: for hitherto ye were not able *to bear it*, neither yet now are ye able."

The writer to the Hebrews concludes concerning his readers: "For when for the time ye ought to be teachers, ye have need that one teach you again which *be* the first principles of the oracles of God; and are become such as have need of milk, and not of strong meat. For every one that useth milk *is* unskilful in the word of righteousness: for he is a babe" (Hebrews 5:12, 13).

Putting the Corinthians passage together with the Hebrews passage, we learn that there is a stage of spiritual growth best described as spiritual infancy, and also that there is a form of spiritual food adapted to the needs of those who are spiritual infants. It is clear from Hebrews 5:11–6:3 that this spiritual pablum includes the elementary teachings of the Gospel—such as repentance from dead works and faith toward God. And while the milk of the Word is not for mature believers, it is absolutely essential that young converts be properly cared for by being fed the milk of the Word.

We are reminded of the little girl from a very poor home, where food was never plentiful and where a glass of milk had to be shared with her brothers and sisters, who was admitted into hospital. A nurse brought her a large glass of cold milk. The little girl took a sip, and then set the glass down again as if that was all she could drink. The nurse, understanding her background, encouragingly said, "Drink it all! It's all yours!"

So we say to young converts: Drink the milk of the Word! It's all yours! May your teeth be white with the milk of God's Word (Genesis 49:12)!

According to a newspaper report, when Mrs. Charles Smith of Phoenix, Arizona, gave birth to a son, he was found to be suffering from a rare ailment for which there is no known cure. When the baby is taken off human milk, burn-like blotches appear all over his body.

The disease, however, can be controlled by a combination of mother's milk and drugs called quinolines. Accordingly the mother of the ten-month-old boy was trying to set up a human milk bank to keep her child alive. It is difficult these days to find the increasingly larger amount of human milk he needs each day to keep free of the splotches.

When Peter counselled Christians, "As newborn babes, desire the sincere milk of the word," he was pointing them to the believer's milk bank. Here in the Scriptures we have a supply of milk, pure and rich in vitamins, that will produce growth in the believer, and will prevent the believer from becoming the victim of spiritual disease, whether personal sin or false teaching. There must be a daily appropriation of this divine supply if health and growth are to be maintained.

Bread and milk—but what about meat? We have seen that two passages of God's Word refer to the Scriptures as meat. By definition meat is composed essentially of muscle and connective tissue, and surely the meat of God's Word are those truths and doctrines which will build muscle into our spiritual system.

Perhaps two simple illustrations will make clear the distinction between milk and meat.

First, consider the books of the Bible. The "milk" stage involves learning the names of these books, their chapters, their authors, their circumstances, dates, etc. But the "meat" stage lies in the inner meaning and message of each book, the divine principles embedded in the histories and prophecies, the sublime spiritual truths taught in the types and symbols; in a word, the living messages of the books of the Bible.

Take another example—the doctrines of the Bible. We say Christ died—that is a basic fact. We need not be learning that all the time. That is the "milk" stage. But the "meat" of that particular biblical doctrine lies in the wonderful explanation of that historical fact given to us in various passages of the Bible—where we are taught that He died as our Substitute and as our Representative. We must seek to grow up to the stage where we are feeding daily on the "meat" of the Word.

The final form of food to which the Bible is compared is honey. The psalmist, in fact, claims that the Word of God is "sweeter also than honey and the honeycomb" (Psalm 19:10). Elsewhere the psalmist states, "How sweet are thy words unto my taste! *yea, sweeter* than honey to my mouth!" (119:103).

At this point we need to remind ourselves that the Bible was, for the most part, written in Palestine and reflects the eastern background of its writers. In Palestine honey was a prized food and occupied a more essential place in the human diet than it now does. It seems to have been natural for those living in Palestine to compare good words to honey: "Pleasant words *are as* an honeycomb, sweet to the soul, and health to the bones" (Proverbs 16:24).

Both Ezekiel (Ezekiel 3:3) and John (Revelation 10:10) found God's Word, when obediently received into the heart, to be sweeter than honey. Even from difficult passages of Scripture we may extract "honey out of the rock" (Psalm 81:16). "Eat thou honey," then, "because it is good" (Proverbs 24:13).

H.P. Barker once described three things he saw in a garden among the plants and flowers:

> The first object was a butterfly that alighted on an attrac-
> tive flower, sat for a second or two, then moved on to another,

seeing and touching many lovely blossoms, but deriving no benefit from them.

Then came a botanist with a large notebook and a microscope. He spent some time over each flower and plant and made copious notes of each. But when he had finished, his knowledge was shut away in his notebook; very little of it remained in his mind.

Then a busy bee came along, entering a flower here and there, and spending some time in each, but emerging from each blossom laden with pollen. It went in empty and came out full.

There are those who read the Bible, going from one favourite passage to another, but getting little from their reading. Others really study and make notes, but do not really get to know the teachings of the Scriptures. Others, like the bee, spend time over the Word, read, mark, and inwardly digest it; and it feeds their minds with wisdom and their lives with heavenly sweetness.[7]

Some Directions

We have made some *deductions* from the fact that the Bible is compared with food. We have offered some *distinctions* in that God's Word is compared specifically with bread, milk, meat, and honey. Now we offer some *directions* for those who desire to eat God's Word.

1. Eat God's Word according to a well-defined schedule. **The Radio Bible Class** calls its devotional booklet, *Daily Bread*. That is right to the point. We should feed upon God's Word daily. We should be consistent and systematic and regular in our eating of God's Word. Someone once remarked, "Seven days without prayer and Bible reading makes one weak." J.E. McKee stated emphatically: "A year of systematic study of the books of the Bible will bring more profits than a lifetime of grasshopper nibbling at its contents."[8]

Dr. R.A. Torrey recalls the following incident:

In one of my early pastorates I asked one of my parishioners how she was getting along in her Christian life.

She replied: "Very poorly. My life is a disgrace to me and to the church; it is a disgrace to Jesus Christ. I don't understand why it is."

"Do you study your Bible every day?" I asked.

"Oh no; but I study it occasionally, when I have time."

A little baby was lying in a baby carriage nearby, and I said: "Suppose you should feed that baby once in two hours today and once in six hours tomorrow, then let it go back and feed it every two hours the next day, and keep up that process, do you think the child would grow?"

"No," she said. "I think the child would die under that treatment."

"And yet that is just the way you are treating your soul."[9]

2. Eat, after asking God's blessings upon what you are to receive spiritually. M.A. Lathbury's great hymn is wonderfully suitable as a prayer hymn—we give one verse as an example:

Break Thou the bread of life,
Dear Lord, to me,
As Thou didst break the loaves
Beside the sea:
Beyond the sacred page
I seek Thee, Lord;
My spirit pants for Thee,
O living Word.[10]

3. Eat a variety of spiritual food. That simply means you should aim to read and study and appropriate all of God's Word. On one occasion, Charles H. Spurgeon was on a visit to Scotland. Browsing in a library, he came across a very old and much-worn Bible. As he examined the Bible, he noticed that a worm had eaten its way from cover to cover. "Lord," he

exclaimed, "make me a bookworm like that—from Genesis to Revelation it has gone clear through the Bible!"

Don't neglect familiar passages in your eating of God's Word. G.F. Allee tells us that in Kate Wiggins' story of Patsy there is a quaint incident of how one day Patsy brought her teacher an orange that bore every evidence of having gone through tribulation.

"Here's an orange I brunged yer," said Patsy. "It's been squz some, but there's still some more in it."[12]

That is true with regard to many a favourite portion of God's Word. Although generations of Christians have derived strength and inspiration from such passages, there is still some more in them!

A.E. Richardson tells us that one of the names given to the Methodists by their enemies was "Bible moths," because they were constantly "feeding upon the Bible as moths do upon clothes."[13]

4. Eat slowly, chewing your food well. This is what is meant by meditation in God's Word. According to Dr. James M. Gray:

> Holding the Word in your mind is like holding the food in your mouth. That is how to get the full taste of it. Prayer does in the one case what the saliva does in the other. Turning it round and round, thinking of it from this point of view and that, asking questions about it, taking it to your Sunday school teacher, your pastor, searching its meaning in a commentary, all these things correspond to the chewing that makes good digestion and assimilation.[14]

5. Eat only that which is nutritive, avoiding that which would spoil your appetite for God's Word. "To own a Bible," states one, "and to feed on newspapers and magazines is one way to be a lean, undernourished Christian."[15] Today Christians are enticed by a multitude of attractively produced magazines and books, most of which yield no nourishment for the soul.

6. Eat with joy, inviting others to share your discoveries with you. Jeremiah testified: "Thy words were found, and I did eat them; and thy word was unto me the joy and rejoicing of mine heart" (Jeremiah 15:16).

Give Me That Book!

We should be like a little African bird known as the honey guide which chatters loudly and guides people, especially woodchoppers, to bee trees, where it feasts upon the honey thus made available.

A Christian colporteur (book salesman) was seeking to sell a Bible to an owner of an orchard in northern Italy. But the owner was not ready to accept the Bible as the Word of God:

> "You tell me," he argued, "that your book is the Word of God, but you do not prove it so."
>
> "What fine looking pears," responded the colporteur, suddenly changing the subject, "but what a pity they are of such poor quality."
>
> "What!" exclaimed the orchard owner indignantly. "Of poor quality? It is plain that you have not tasted them. Pick one or two and try them!"
>
> The colporteur did as he was bidden, and began to eat.
>
> "Yes, sir, you are right," he said, smacking his lips, "the pears are excellent; but, sir, you must deal with my book as I have dealt with your fruit. Taste, and you will see that the Word of God is good."[16]

"O taste and see that the LORD"—and His Word—"*is* good" (Psalm 34:8).

7. Eat when you feel weak. Dr. A.J. Gordon said: "If then you ever get weary and languid for a moment, 'Taste the powers of the world to come,' and you will be refreshed and invigorated."

We have a beautiful illustration in the story of the sick soldier. He was given up to die, and his father hastened from a long distance to his bedside in the hospital. He lay half-conscious, and nothing that father or attendants could do could rouse him till the father said: "Here is a loaf of your mother's bread which I have brought you."

"Bread from home," said the dying man; "give me some." And from that hour he began to mend.

Bread from Heaven! Don't fail to eat it every day, O Christian. You are in the world, but not of it, and you will die if you eat the native food. Feed upon the Word of God; live upon the promises of God; satisfy your souls with the hope of God, which He has revealed to you in the Scriptures. "This is the bread which cometh down out of heaven, that a man may eat thereof, and not die."[17]

FOR YOUR FURTHER STUDY

1. With the symbol of food in mind, suggest the meaning of Paul's words in 2 Timothy 3:16, 17, "All scripture *is* ... profitable."
2. In describing our duty toward God's Word as food, Jabez Burns states that we should "thankfully receive it, believingly feed upon it, and constantly apply it."[18] Write a brief paragraph on each of his three points with reference to yourself.
3. Pinpoint some ways in which your own appetite for God's Word has been spoiled.

God's Mirror and You

We believe that men who are by nature sinners and lost can discover themselves in the mirror of the Scriptures.

—**Lawrence O. Richards**

Just go to the mirror and look at yourself
And see what that man has to say;
For it isn't your father, or mother, or wife,
Who judgment upon you must pass.
The fellow whose verdict counts most in your life
Is the one staring back from the glass.

—**Author Unknown**

If we are wise, we shall hold the mirror of God's Word before us every day.

—**H.P. Barker**

The only safe place to look is in the Word of God, which reflects all things as they are.

—**D.G. Barnhouse**

It is the mirror where I see
All the sins that blacken me;
Now for cleansing full and free,
O Lamb of God, I come.

The mirror of the Word is painfully clear.

—**R.E.O. White**

The faithful preacher should so hold up the mirror of truth before the very eyes of those whom he addresses, that they shall be constrained to behold their natural face in the glass and know what manner of men they are.

—**W. Hay Aitken**

We have to be as honest with the Bible as with the mirror. We have to clean up our lives until we can look our Bible in the face and our hearts shall not condemn us. If we used the Bible more, and learned to look it in the face more often, we would check our faults and mend our ways, and please Him, who made us for truth and grace and loveliness.

—**John MacBeth**

STUDY 6
God's Word Is Reflective

Our Key Scripture—"But be ye doers of the word, and not hearers only, deceiving your own selves. For if any be a hearer of the word, and not a doer, he is like unto a man beholding his natural face in a glass: For he beholdeth himself, and goeth his way, and straightway forgetteth what manner of man he was. But whoso looketh into the perfect law of liberty, and continueth *therein*, he being not a forgetful hearer, but a doer of the work, this man shall be blessed in his deed" (James 1:22–25).

Supplementary Scriptures—2 Chronicles 34; Psalm 1:2; 119:18; Jeremiah 36; 2 Corinthians 3:18.

THERE is a fable concerning a mirror equipped with properties so miraculous that it enabled the beholder to discover any object which he wished to see. The mirror thus enabled the beholder to detect everything above, below, behind, and before him.[1]

Though not magical, the Bible as God's mirror has qualities that are supernatural. As we behold ourselves in it, we see ourselves as God sees us, and we are directed to the Source of cleansing and transformation.

BASIC OUTLINE

But the Bible, God's mirror, is used in various ways. Let us trace seven possible ways of looking into the mirror of God's Word. We may look at it with a look that is *casual, curious, cynical, condemning, careful, convicting,* or *converting.*

The Casual Look

Some people give only a *casual look* at the Bible. They do not manifest ill-will toward the Bible; rather, they are characterized by indifference. In his letter James refers to a man who looks into the mirror, sees himself, and then moments later forgets what he looked like.

There are many who treat the Bible this way. Perhaps they refer to the Bible only on Sundays. From Monday through Saturday their Bible lies on the shelf, unnoticed and unread. Then there is a hunt on Sunday morning to locate their copy of God's Word. Dr. W.H. Griffith Thomas illustrated the point well when he wrote:

> In the course of a Bible reading some years ago, I ventured to make this assertion: I said that if there were five hundred people outside that church, and each one of them was a backslider, I would undertake to say, although they were all strangers to me, that every one had become a backslider through neglect of the Bible.
>
> After the meeting was over, a lady said to me: "I cannot understand how it is that every one of the five hundred should have become a backslider through neglect of the Bible."
>
> "Well, now," said I, "let us see. Have you got a looking glass in your bedroom?"
>
> She answered, "Yes."
>
> "Do you use it?" I asked.
>
> "Yes," she replied.
>
> "Suppose," I went on, "you did not use it for a week, would you be quite sure that your personal appearance would be such as you would like your friends to see?"
>
> "No," said she.
>
> "Now, in the Epistle of James," I remarked, "the Bible is spoken of as a mirror in which we see ourselves; and if we do

not open that Book, we cannot be sure of our spiritual appearance. 'In Thy light shall we see light.'

"As long as we keep the mirror before us in which we see ourselves, at the same time 'beholding as in a glass the glory of the Lord,' we become transformed."[2]

But the casual reader of the Bible never experiences this transformation. We do well to heed the advice of Amos R. Wells in his poem on Bible study:

> You who treat the crown of writings
> as you treat no other book —
> Just a paragraph disjointed, just a
> crude impatient look —
> Try a worthier procedure, try a
> broad and steadier view:
> You will kneel in very rapture when
> you read the Bible through.[3]

Mildred Cable and Francesca French stated the truth this way in their book on Christian growth:

> The Bible is a mirror which shows a man both what he is and what he may become, but anyone who only throws a casual and forgetful glance in its direction receives no benefit at all. It is the man who sees, acts, and obeys that receives the blessing, for only what is related to life finally counts.[4]

The Curious Look

Closely associated with the casual look is the *curious look* into the Bible—not to find its real message or to apply its teachings, but simply to discover what it's all about.

In the Book of Ezekiel we are introduced to one congregation which was very curious about the Word of the Lord, but which had no real intention of obeying that Word. We quote from Ezekiel 33:30–32:

> Also, thou son of man, the children of thy people still are talking against [or, about] thee by the walls and in the doors of

the houses, and speak one to another, every one to his brother, saying, Come, I pray you, and hear what is the word that cometh forth from the LORD.

And they come unto thee as the people cometh, and they sit before thee *as* my people, and they hear thy words, but they will not do them: for with their mouth they shew much love, *but* their heart goeth after their covetousness.

And, lo, thou *art* unto them as a very lovely song of one that hath a pleasant voice, and can play well on an instrument: for they hear thy words, but they do them not.

Curiosity concerning the Bible is not enough. To desire merely to understand the types of the Bible, or to interpret the prophecies of the Bible, is by no means adequate to save the soul. There must be a personal and practical application of the central message of the Bible to the reader's heart. Don't let curiosity strangle any real spiritual interest that you may have.

The Cynical Look

There are those who read and study the Bible with a *cynical look*. They approach the Bible with doubt and unbelief. They listen to its message, but they seek to deny its teachings by an attitude of scorn or by an appearance of scholarship.

King Jehoiakim of Judah stands as the arch-type of all those who treat the Bible with impiety and indignity. His story is found in Jeremiah 36.

As Jeremiah the Prophet dictated all the messages he had delivered to the people from the reign of Josiah until the reign of Jehoiakim, Baruch recorded them on a scroll. Later, Jeremiah's secretary read the prophecies in the Temple at Jerusalem. The outcome of that was a further reading of the messages in the royal secretary's chamber. Finally, the scroll was brought before Jehoiakim.

Concerning the scroll we read in the account that—

Jehudi read it in the ears of the king, and in the ears of all the princes which stood beside the king.

> Now the king sat in the winterhouse in the ninth month: and *there was a fire* on the hearth burning before him.
>
> And it came to pass, *that* when Jehudi had read three or four leaves, he cut it with the penknife, and cast *it* into the fire that *was* on the hearth, until all the roll *was* consumed in the fire that was on the hearth. Yet they were not afraid, nor rent their garments, *neither* the king, nor any of his servants that heard all these words (36:21–24).

That is an illustration of the cynical look. Jehoiakim doubted the truthfulness of Jeremiah's warnings, and burned the scroll as an indication of his attitude both toward the prophet and toward his God.

There are many who doubt the Bible's promises and prophecies. They look with disdain at its offer of eternal life. They are not prepared to accept its overtures of divine love. They treat it despicably and destructively. But as John Hus, a pre-Reformation martyr, said: "Fire does not consume truth. It is always a mark of a little mind to vent anger on inanimate and uninjurious objects."[5]

Archibald Naismith reminds us of the humorous poem with the refrain, "And the barber kept on shaving."[6]

It describes the visit of a young man who went to a barber shop in which there were samples of a taxidermist's work—some stuffed birds, and among them an owl. The youth, priding himself in his knowledge of ornithology, commenced a tirade on the work of the taxidermist, pointing out the faults in the owl's wings, legs, and the angle of its head. He continued for a few minutes in this strain till the owl surprised its critic by turning its head and winking, thus making him feel more of an owl than he had ever felt.

Many people mistakenly put the Bible, the living Word of God, on a par with the dead literature everywhere around, imagining it to be mere man's handiwork, when it is God's all the time. The young man in the poem vainly thought himself wise until one act of the living bird stultified all his babbling.

Writing on this aspect of our subject, A.J. Gordon explains why people have criticized the Bible as a book full of mistakes:

> An errant Bible is exactly what is demanded by errant youth. To a "man beholding his natural face in the glass" of Scripture, it is a vast relief to be assured, on scientific authority, that the glass is perchance considerably convexed, so that the sinful self seen therein, which has often been so troublesome, after all, may have been greatly exaggerated. Our plea is not, however, for war on the critics, but for watch over ourselves—that we let no day pass in which we do not turn the light of Scripture upon our lives, subject our hearts to its searching inquisition, and rejoice to be found out by it concerning those sins of which we have been willingly ignorant.[7]

The Condemning Look

The cynical look, as we have seen, easily becomes the *condemning* look. Jehoiakim scorned Jeremiah's scroll and ended up by consigning it to the flames.

People often condemn the Bible because of its realistic portrayal of their own lives. Dr. Harry Ironside used an amusing incident to drive this point home:

> An elderly gentleman, who was very nearsighted, prided himself on his ability as an art critic. While accompanying some friends through a large gallery, he sought to display his real or fancied knowledge of pictures to these friends.
>
> The man had left his glasses at home and was not able to see things very clearly. Standing before a large frame, he began to point out the inartistic features of the picture revealed there.
>
> "The frame," he began, "is altogether out of keeping with the subject, and as for the subject itself [it was that of a man], it is altogether too homely, in fact, too ugly, ever to make a good picture. It is a great mistake for any artist to choose so homely a subject for a picture if he expects it to be a masterpiece."

78

The old man was going on like this when his wife managed to get near enough to interrupt. She exclaimed, "My dear, you are looking into a mirror!" Her husband was quite taken back to realize that he had been criticizing his own face.

Dr. Ironside concludes: "The Word of God is such a mirror. It does not hide our deformities."[8]

We are told that the first Queen Elizabeth of England, when her wrinkles waxed deep and many, an unfortunate master of the mint incurred disgrace by a too faithful likeness of her cast on the shilling; the die was broken, and only one mutilated specimen of that coin is now in existence.

Further, the Queen's maids of honour took the hint, and were thereafter careful that no fragment of a mirror should remain in any room in the palace. In fact a magazine of the times stated that the Queen "had not the heart to look herself in the face for the last twenty years of her life!"[9]

Many people do not wish to know the truth about themselves. They would rather continue in their ignorance and iniquity than face what God's mirror shows them to be.

The Careful Look

What is needed with reference to the Scriptures is the *careful look*. That is the point James is making in James 1:22–25. He contrasts the individual who looks casually—even carelessly—into the mirror with the person who looks with attention and care. He bids us be those who look into the perfect law of liberty and who continue to remember what we saw. Then if we are doers of the work, we shall truly be blessed in our deed.

It is as we look into the mirror of God's Word that we see ourselves as we really are.

H.P. Barker tells us of a young Spanish prince who was smitten in early years with smallpox. He was cured, but permanently and badly scarred. His parents, thinking to spare him a good deal of self-depreciation, removed every mirror from the palace in which he lived, with the consequence that he grew up filled with self-importance. He became arrogant in the extreme.

Give Me That Book!

At last the servants thought of a way in which to cure him of his arrogance and his overbearing attitude to others.

One evening, when the prince had retired to his room, they put outside and opposite his door a large mirror. When the prince stepped out the next morning he had the greatest shock of his life. He who had heretofore thought of himself as some great one, to be admired and respected, discovered that he was in himself a most abhorrent creature.[10]

"If we are wise," comments Mr. Barker, "we shall hold the mirror of God's Word before us every day." Careful scrutiny of ourselves in that Word will disclose to us the ravages of sin in our moral and spiritual constitution.

J.D. Gilmore wrote:

When we see ourselves, as reflected in the holy law of God, we know that we have not merely acquired bad habits which may be stopped; but that we have a diseased, wicked, unclean, rebellious heart. Alas! how often men have looked into this mirror and yet remain "like unto a man beholding his natural face in a glass: for he beholdeth himself, and goeth his way, and straightway forgetteth what manner of man he was."[11]

The Convicting Look

The careful look will become the *convicting look*. In the reign of Josiah, king of Judah, the mirror of God's Word was scarce—so scarce, indeed, that even Josiah himself did not possess a copy of the law.

But in the providence of God, Hilkiah the Priest found a copy of the law of the Lord. When this book was read in the hearing of the king, and he had opportunity "to look into" the book, "he rent his clothes, and gave instructions to his servants to find someone who could explain the meaning of the law." We quote from 2 Chronicles 34:21: "Go, enquire of the Lord for me, and for them that are left in Israel and in Judah, concerning the words of the book that is found: for great *is* the wrath of the Lord that is poured out upon us, because our fathers have not kept the word of the Lord, to do after all that is written in this book."

Josiah's look into God's Word brought conviction. He applied the warnings of God's law to himself and to his people.

John Macbeath reminds us that, "the mirror tells the truth about us. It doesn't touch us up as a photograph often does. It gives the real likeness."[12]

"The sacred record," wrote Augustine, "like a faithful mirror, has no flattery in its portraits."[13] It is not like the mirror provided by a Belgium hairdresser for his customers:

> Hairdresser Louis Legrand of Brussels, Belgium, has found the perfect way to produce angelic expressions to go with his angelic coiffures. As the lady customer stares into the mirror to regard the finished hairdo, a halo gradually appears above her head in the reflection. "The mirror is wired to produce the halo when I press the right button," explained Legrand. "Even my most shrewish customers become angels with amused smiles when they see it appear."[14]

There is one mirror, however, that provides no halos to flatter men and women, and that is the Bible. It is James who compares God's Word to a mirror (see James 1:23–25). Rather than flattering us, the Bible mirror exposes us as we really are. The Bible pictures us neither as angels nor fiends but as sinners, needing cleansing. And along with its message of condemnation, it proclaims the divine provision for that restoration. It provides no halos, but it does provide the way of salvation.

Dr. Macbeath tells us, too, of a man who was once brought into court for doing something very wrong. His evil life had left its traces on his face, and the magistrate ordered a mirror to be brought into court; then he urged the man to take a good look at himself, and after that to leave the court. "It seemed to be punishment enough to let the man see what he was making of himself."[15]

Similar is the story told by Amos R. Wells:

> Once there was a judge in Chicago who kept a mirror in his court, and who, whenever a drunkard was brought before him, compelled the man to gaze at himself in the mirror and see what sort of man he had become. He believed that half of these victims of drink were cured by that sight of themselves as they really were.

And this is what the Bible does throughout its truthful, searching pages. In the clear mirror of its pure ideals it forces us to perceive how very far we have fallen short of the beauty and glory and holiness and strength that are possible for us. We turn away with loathing for what we are, and with determination to seek, in Christ's power, the life which He means for us.[16]

John Ruskin wrote:

Make sure, that however good you may be, you have faults; that however dull you may be, you can find out what they are; and that however slight they may be, you had better make some patient effort to get quit [rid] of them. If you do not dare to do this, find out why you do not dare, and try to get strength of heart enough to look yourself fairly in the face, in mind as well as in body.[17]

The Converting Look

The convicting look should lead to a *converting look*. As we gaze into the mirror of God's Word, we should begin to be changed and transformed. Paul Rader affirmed:

We must test ourselves by God's Word, looking into it to see ourselves, just as we see our faces in a mirror. This mirror is a very useful instrument .... Seek to see yourself in it. Have a good look at yourself. It will reveal to you your blemishes, your faults and defects. Let it speak to your heart. If you admit and confess, you will receive forgiveness, cleansing and power to engage in this tremendous world business of witnessing for Christ. This preparation is of the utmost importance.[18]

There was a mining camp far away in the bush, John Macbeath tells us, where for a long time the men had no mirror. Sometimes they helped one another to be tidy, but they never guessed how careless they had become about anything neat and clean. Then a new arrival carried a mirror in his baggage, and it soon became general property. Everybody used it, and a new look came over everything. The men looked like new. They mended their ways until the mirror's portrait of them showed a sweet and clean life.[19]

Perhaps we can give a few pointers on how to use the mirror of God's Word.

First, get a full-length mirror. Use both the Old and New Testaments. You need a whole Bible for the whole man. "The Bible is my mirror," wrote Martin Luther, "in which I see what I was in Adam before the Fall, what I became by the Fall, what I am, what I should be in Christ now, and what I shall be throughout eternity."[20]

Second, use the mirror daily. Don't permit your reading of the Bible to become spasmodic or intermittent. Have a schedule, and stick to it.

Third, take time before the mirror. Here's one place where you can afford to spend time. Every minute spent before the mirror of God's Word will mean more spiritual beauty and attractiveness for you. "In the reading of Holy Scripture," wrote Alcuin in the sixth century A.D., "lies the knowledge of true blessedness, for therein as in a mirror a man may consider himself and what he is and whither he goes. He who would be always with God ought frequently to pray and frequently to read, for when we pray we are speaking to God, and when we read God is speaking to us."[21]

Fourth, accept the verdict. Heed the words of Clarence E. Macartney:

> The man to look at is the man in the looking glass. So careful we are, so thoughtful or anxious, about the other man, about what he thinks or says; but the one to look at is thyself— the man in the glass. If the one staring back from the glass does not approve, if he does not say, "Well done," then the praise and recognition and approval of others mean nothing. Look, then, at the man in the glass, and see what he has to say.[22]

Dr. Bob Jones wrote:

> God's Word is a mirror. Look into it. It will show you just exactly what you are. Are you selfish? You will see this in the Bible. Are you filled with pride? You will find that spot on the face of your soul if you look in the Bible. That is the reason unregenerate men hate the Book. God, in the Bible, paints the picture of the sinner, and God never touches it up. He does

not take off any moles nor hide any scars. The Book reveals to a man just exactly what he is. It does not flatter anybody.[23]

Don't be like the African princess whose story is told thus in the records of missionary service:

A certain society in order to gain access for a missionary to some African tribes, sent down trinkets to be bartered with the natives. Among them was a package of those little hand glasses, such as ladies use.

The natives had never seen their own faces, except in the waters of some lake or stream, and the news of this wonderful instrument, by which people could see their own features, was spread abroad until the missionary was invited by tribe after tribe to visit them, with his hand glasses.

It happened that away in the interior there was a princess in one of the tribes, who had been told that she was the most beautiful woman in the tribe, and that her face was the most beautiful one on earth. When she heard of this instrument in which she might see what a beautiful creature she was, she sent for the missionary and bade him bring one of those mirrors.

But the truth was, the princess was the least attractive woman in the tribe. So she got the mirror, and went into the hut to take one good long delicious look at her beauty; but when she held up the glass and saw what a hideous creature she was, how ugly in every feature, she lifted up her royal fist and dashed the glass to pieces, banished the missionary, and made a law that no looking glass should ever be brought into the tribe.

Why did the princess hate the glass? She hated it because it told the truth about herself. The truth was not a pleasant one. She found that she was an ugly woman, and she did not like it.

Why do men slight the Bible? Because the righteousness of a man is as filthiness in God's sight. And when this Book, like a mirror, reveals man to himself; when the truth is seen in that mirror, with the light of the Great White Throne falling upon it, his hatred is aroused, and the Bible is smitten as the heathen princess destroyed the mirror, because it told the truth.

But she was just as ugly after she destroyed the mirror as before. And it remains true that, though man rejects the Bible and tramples it under foot, he is exactly the same sinner as before, and is moving on just as steadily toward eternity and the Great White Throne as before he rejected the Bible.[24]

Fifth, don't let the distorting mirrors of the world lead you to make wrong evaluations.

Dr. D.C. Barnhouse once wrote concerning one of the governors of Leeds Prison in England. This man was formerly the aide-de-camp to King Abdullah of Jordan. He told how the King had two mirrors which he used in the rooms where he entertained guests. One, which made the people look thin, was put in the room where the guests assembled before dinner. The other which made people look fat, was put in the salon, to which guests moved after eating.

We live in rooms of distorted mirrors and must never be taken in by things as they seem to be. There is great folly in outward appearances. There are those who look small to the world who are great for God. There are people who seem to be fruitful in activity who are barren in fruit. The only safe place to look is in the Word of God, which reflects all things as they are.[25]

Let John Macbeath summarize our study. "There is a Book," he wrote, "that acts like a mirror. It tells us what is wrong with our lives, what is wrong with the world, and it tells us how we can put away our evil and selfish ways, our bad tempers, our unfairness and unkindness, all that is nasty and wrong. It tells us how we can get a clean heart, and a clean heart is one of the best things in the universe."[26]

FOR YOUR FURTHER STUDY

1. List as many qualities of God's mirror, the Bible, as you can; for example, it is unbreakable.

Give Me That Book!

2. Why do men and women reject the Bible as God's mirror?
3. In addition to seeing ourselves in God's Word, what else may we see by persistent, patient "beholding"? See 2 Corinthians 3:18.

The Washing of Water in the Word

Through the Blood of Jesus Christ believers are saved from the guilt and penalty of sin, and through daily contact with the Word of God they are being sanctified and cleansed from the power and defilement of sin.

—Oscar Lowry

The Word is for cleansing as well as for instruction, and if it keeps going through you it will have a marvellous effect upon your mind and heart and life. It will cleanse and purify you and fit you to be a real worker for the Lord Jesus Christ.

—H.A. Ironside

The man who has come to Christ comes under the constant judgment of God. And the instrument of His judgment is His Word. The man who has really come to Christ submits to God's judgment upon everything in his life that cannot stand the light.

—Dr. Stuart Holden

As water is to the body, so is the Word of God to the soul. It cleanses.

—W.H. Griffith Thomas

He who obeys what the Lord says receives the purifying energy of the Spirit that abides in the Word. The Lord's instructions direct us to holiness, but we must obey those commands if we are to be sanctified. A command disobeyed cannot benefit but only condemn; a command obeyed removes the moral blemish against which it is directed or supplies the virtue lacking.

—G.H. Lang

Water is the symbol of the Word of God applied to the soul, in power, by the Spirit of God.

—John A. Trench

We come to wash our hands and feet,
Defiled each day by sin;
Be pleased Thy people here to meet,
And make us pure within.

—T.S.R.

STUDY 7
God's Word Is Purgative

Our Key Scripture—"Wherewithal shall a young man cleanse his way? by taking heed *thereto* according to thy word" (Psalm 119:9).

Supplementary Scriptures—Exodus 30:17–21; Psalm 24:4; John 13:1–17; 2 Corinthians 7:1; Ephesians 5:25–27; 2 Timothy 2:20–22; Titus 2:14; 3:5; Hebrews 10:22; Revelation 19:8.

IN the Old Testament dispensation Aaron and his sons, in order that they might serve as priests in the Tabernacle, underwent a ceremonial washing, or bath. In Exodus 29:4 we read that God gave instructions to Moses to bring Aaron and his sons to the door of the Tabernacle and wash—bathe them with water. But thereafter, before a priest could function in the Tabernacle ministry, he had to wash his hands and feet.

For this washing there was provided a laver of brass, described for us in Exodus 30:17–21. This laver, or basin, was placed between the Tabernacle of the congregation and the altar of burnt offering, and Aaron and his sons were to "wash their hands and their feet thereat" (Exodus 30:19).

This Old Testament type with its double aspect of initial and continual washing becomes normative for New Testament teaching. There we are encouraged to draw near to God, "with a true heart in full assurance of faith, having our hearts sprinkled from an evil conscience, and our bodies washed with pure water" (Hebrews 10:22), and to "cleanse ourselves from all filthiness of the flesh and spirit" (2 Corinthians 7:1).

The key to this teaching seems to be that the water referred to in various passages is typical of the Word of God applied efficaciously by the Holy Spirit to the heart of the one obedient to God.

BASIC OUTLINE

With the Old Testament type in mind let us look carefully at the Christian's experience of "the washing of water by the word" (Ephesians 5:26). We shall consider four aspects of this washing: *priestly, primary, perpetual,* and *preventive.*

Priestly Washing

Let us note first that the ceremonial washing of the Old Testament was a *priestly washing*—that is, it was in their character and capacity as priests that Aaron and his sons underwent washing. Their cleansing was not an end in itself, but a means to an end, and that end was service in the Tabernacle.

Aaron and his sons had been delivered from the bondage of Egypt. At Sinai they were formally inducted into the priesthood. They could not undertake the duties or enjoy the privileges of the priesthood without both the introductory washing and the incessant daily washing.

It is from this particular perspective that we must view the various references to the believer's cleansing in the Scriptures, especially in the New Testament. Believers have been made "kings and priests unto God" (Revelation 1:6). They are "an holy priesthood, to offer up spiritual sacrifices, acceptable to God by Jesus Christ" (1 Peter 2:5). They are "a royal priesthood" (2:9).

But before believers can function as priests there has to be a cleansing, a washing from defilement. This cleansing is essential both for the commencement of priestly service and for the continuance of priestly service.

It is instructive to learn that as a symbol of their purification before God the priests of the Levitical system were clad in white linen garments (see Exodus 28:40–43).

Primary Washing

Let us examine in more detail the primary washing of the priests and by application the *primary washing* of the believer.

Exodus 29:1 begins, "This *is* the thing that thou shalt do unto them to hallow them, to minister unto me in the priest's office." There follow various instructions that are related to sacrifice. Sacrifice and the shedding of blood, we know, formed the ground of the individual's acceptance before God.

Then in Exodus 29:4, we read: "Aaron and his sons thou shalt bring unto the door of the tabernacle of the congregation, and shalt wash them with water." Now this is evidently a further step in the induction of the priests. The agent here is not blood, but water. If blood for a priest was the ground of his acceptance before God, then water with its cleansing power was the ground for his activity for God in the Tabernacle. It is not the case that one is more important than the other; rather, both are important, although both did not do the same thing for the individual. Blood does not do what water does, and water cannot do what blood does.

What light is thrown upon New Testament teaching by these aspects of the Levitical economy? Let us glance at a number of New Testament texts.

In 1 Corinthians 6:11 Paul states concerning the Christians at Corinth: "But ye are washed, but ye are sanctified, but ye are justified in the name of the Lord Jesus, and by the Spirit of our God." Whether this be passive as in the *Authorized Version* or active as in the Williams' translation ("But now ye have washed yourselves clean," etc.), the important point for our consideration is that Paul alludes to a washing taking place at conversion. He speaks of some of the Corinthian Christians as having once been defiled by sin (see 6:9, 10), but they had washed away the defilement. Thus he is able to greet them in the opening part of his letter as those "sanctified in Christ Jesus, called *to be* saints" (1 Corinthians 1:2).

Before the sinner can serve God, therefore, he must be washed from the pollution of his sinning. Two matters in fact must be dealt with: the penalty of his sin and the pollution of his sin. The blood of Jesus Christ deals with the penalty, and the Word of God, received in repentance and faith, deals with the pollution of sin.

Other New Testament texts indicate likewise that there must be a primary washing of the sinner, a washing that can best be described as a complete bath.

In Ephesians 5:25–27 Paul states: "Christ also loved the church, and gave himself for it; That he might sanctify and cleanse it with the washing of water by the word, That he might present it to himself a glorious church, not having spot, or wrinkle, or any such thing; but that it should be holy and without blemish." Here is a total washing of the Church and of each member of the Church.

In Titus 3:5 Paul affirms that God "saved us, by the washing of regeneration, and renewing of the Holy Ghost." Here is a washing closely associated with regeneration. We may paraphrase Paul's words slightly in this way: "God saved us by the washing that is involved in regeneration, and renewing of the Holy Spirit." This, again, is the initial experience of the sinner who believes in Christ. He is washed thoroughly from the pollution of his sins.

This work of primary washing is presented in Scripture as being performed jointly by the Spirit and the sinner. Some passages emphasize the work of the Spirit; others emphasize the work of the sinner. Both aspects are brought together in 1 Peter 1:22: "Ye have purified your souls in obeying the truth through the Spirit." Here is clear explanation of what is involved in the cleansing of the sinner. Taught by the Holy Spirit, he responds to the Word of God as it judges him as a sinner, and by repentance and faith he removes from his life all that which offends a holy God.

This washing initiates the believing sinner into his ministry as a priest in God's service. Hence as priests we are urged in Hebrews 10:22 to draw near to God, "Having our hearts sprinkled from an evil conscience [that is, the Blood has dealt with the penalty of sin, the fear of which haunts the sinner], and our bodies washed with pure water [that is, the water, the Word, has dealt with the pollution of sin, which hinders the sinner from serving God]."

Perpetual Washing

We have learned that for Aaron and his sons there was a primary washing that qualified them to enter the office of priest. But there was also a *perpetual* or continual *washing* required. Here is Exodus 30:17–21:

> The LORD spake unto Moses, saying, Thou shalt also make
> a laver *of* brass, and his foot *also of* brass, to wash *withal*: and

thou shalt put it between the tabernacle of the congregation and the altar, and thou shalt put water therein. For Aaron and his sons shall wash their hands and their feet thereat: when they go into the tabernacle of the congregation, they shall wash with water, that they die not; or when they come near to the altar to minister, to burn offering made by fire unto the LORD: So they shall wash their hands and their feet, that they die not: and it shall be a statute forever to them, *even* to him and to his seed throughout their generations.

This passage informs us that before a priest could minister acceptably in the Tabernacle he had to wash his hands and feet. He had been bathed at his induction; in his daily service he had but to wash hands and feet.

What did this mean for the Levitical priest?

It meant that before he could serve at the altar of burnt offering he had to cleanse his hands and feet.

It meant that before he could attend to the lampstand in the holy place he had to wash his hands and feet.

It meant that before he could arrange the loaves on the table for shewbread he had to diligently wash his hands and feet.

It meant that before he could approach the altar of incense he had to obey the divine directions and wash his hands and feet.

We may reduce all this in summary form to: no washing, no working; no ablutions, no activities; no cleansing, no communion with Jehovah in the Tabernacle. There had to be purity on the priest's part before there could be performance of his duty.

In Psalm 24:3, 4 the psalmist states: "Who shall ascend into the hill of the LORD? or who shall stand in his holy place? He that hath clean hands, and a pure heart." Isaiah exclaims, "Be ye clean, that bear the vessels of the LORD" (Isaiah 52:11).

In its typical form this perpetual washing reminds us that even those who have been regenerated by the Holy Spirit do daily contract defilement in thought, word, or deed, and therefore need the daily cleansing of God's living Word in order that they may not be disqualified from service.

This is taught in various New Testament passages. Writing to the same people as he had on a former occasion (and at that time, he had said concerning them that they had been washed), Paul gives the following appeal: "Having therefore these promises, dearly beloved, let us cleanse ourselves from all filthiness of the flesh and spirit, perfecting holiness in the fear of God" (2 Corinthians 7:1; cf. 1 Corinthians 6:11).

Here is the duty of the believer-priest. He must continue daily to cleanse himself from all that which defiles. This filthiness may be of the flesh (that is, it may be associated with activities of the body) or it may be of the spirit (that is, it may be attitudes of the spirit). The result of this diligent cleansing of himself will be an increase in the holiness which is the goal of all Christian living.

Amy L. Person reminds us that "according to Greek mythology, when Achilles was a baby, his mother dipped him in the river Styx, holding him by his heel, to make him invulnerable to injury. He grew up to become a mighty warrior who did many brave deeds, but finally he was killed by an arrow that pierced his heel, the spot where the water had not touched."[1]

How many a Christian, engaged in fighting against the forces of evil, has been defeated because the water of God's Word had not touched every part of his body? In coming to God our hands and our feet must be completely cleansed. There must be no part of us where the water does not touch.

While in the upper room, as recorded by John, the Lord Jesus taught His disciples concerning the necessity of daily washing. When Peter remonstrated with Jesus and refused the Master-turned-Servant as He sought to wash Peter's feet, the Lord Jesus said, "If I wash thee not, thou hast no part with me" (John 13:8).

To this, Peter said, "Lord, not my feet only, but also *my* hands and *my* head."

Jesus responded by emphasizing a principle: "He that is washed [or bathed] needeth not save to wash *his* feet, but is clean every whit: and ye are clean, but not all" (John 13:10, 11).

It has been customary to explain these words in terms of the customs associated with the Roman baths. In the public bath an individual could wash himself completely, bringing refreshment to his tired body. But on the way home from the bath the individual, wearing open sandals, might defile his feet in the dust of the road. Consequently upon entering his house he required that his feet be washed in a basin.

This interpretation is most helpful in understanding the words and actions of the Lord Jesus, and if we keep in mind the additional teaching of the Old Testament type, we learn that for spiritual service there must be daily cleansing of feet that have been defiled. In contracting this daily defilement the believer does not lose the benefits of that initial bath that he experienced at conversion, but, rather, he is disqualified from undertaking service for God.

A salesman in a jeweller's store, noticing that his hands were some-what soiled, said: "This is very trying to me. Of all persons, I should have soft and clean hands. It is awful to offer a diamond or pearls of any sort to a possible customer when my hands are not perfectly white and tidy. It makes a repulsive background for the piece of jewellry."[2]

In all our service for God we should have clean hands and a pure heart. In offering the jewels of God's Word and the diamonds of His grace to others, we should manifest in ourselves that purity which is part of our message. We who bear the vessels of the Lord should be holy.

Preventive Washing

In the account of the laver (Exodus 30:17–21) it is made quite clear that Aaron and his sons were required to wash hands and feet lest God's judgment fall upon them. "When they go into the tabernacle of the congregation, they shall wash with water, that they die not; or when they come near to the altar to minister, to burn offering made by fire unto the LORD: So they shall wash their hands and their feet, that they die not" (30:20, 21).

While it may be difficult for us to pinpoint the way in which this type is fulfilled in its antitype, we call attention to the fact that to disregard the ceremonial washing in the Old Testament economy brought the individual priest under severe divine judgment. To minister unwashed was considered a capital offense against Yahweh, King of Israel.

Give Me That Book!

The New Testament records that at the beginning of the new dispensation divine judgment fell upon various people: Ananias and Sapphira, for example, in seeking to serve the Lord with unclean hands, came under that divine judgment. Various members of the church at Corinth died because they partook of the Lord's Supper in an unworthy manner, and thus brought judgment upon themselves (see 1 Corinthians 11:29–32).

The abiding teaching of Exodus 30:21, 22 seems, then, to be that God is displeased with any who serve Him with unclean hands and an impure heart. While the penalty is not now administered publicly as it was in the early days of the New Covenant, the pattern of God's judgment upon sin is clearly set forth in Scripture. Surely these records are given to us in order to show us that, if "every transgression and disobedience received a just recompense of reward," then God's judgment would fall now upon those guilty of seeking to serve in an unwashed condition. The washing of hands and feet on the part of the priests was a preventive washing.

Once while speaking in London, Dr. W.H. Griffith Thomas affirmed that most Christians become backsliders through neglect of the Bible. After the service, a woman questioned him with regard to his sweeping statement:

"Do you have soap and water in your house?" asked Dr. Thomas.

The woman smiled and said, "Yes."

"Suppose you did not use it for a week, would you be quite sure of your personal appearance, especially if you live in London?"

"No," replied the woman.

"Now," said Dr. Thomas, "in the Epistle to the Ephesians, the Word is called 'water.' As water is to the body, so the Word of God is to the soul. It cleanses. If we do not practise cleansing, we cannot be clean."[3]

So taught Dr. Thomas. He was also ready to affirm that, "as long as we use the water of God's Word for the cleansing of our inner life, it will be absolutely impossible for us to backslide, while it will be blessedly possible for us to go on from grace to grace, and from strength to strength."

In the last century a woman was once seen standing on the bank of a river with what looked like a square sieve. The sieve contained an object. She was seen lowering the sieve into the water, and allowing the water to pass through it.

As she went through this process, a minister of the Gospel approached her and asked her what she was doing. Surprised, she looked up into his face and said, "Oh, sir, I am glad to see you."

It was now the minister's turn to be surprised. "I don't know how you can be glad, since I am a stranger in this part of the country, and I was not aware that I was known."

"Well," replied the woman, "I heard you preach many years ago, and your sermon was a real blessing to my soul. I have been a different woman ever since."

"I am thankful to hear that," said the minister, "and what was the text?"

"I'm sorry, sir, I don't remember your text."

"But," replied the minister, "it is very curious that a sermon should have been blessed to your soul, and yet you cannot remember the text."

"Well, sir, it's like this," was the woman's reply. "I have got some wool in this sieve, and my mind is very much like the sieve, which is full of holes. The water runs through the sieve, but as it runs through, it cleanses the wool.

"Now that text of God's Word went through my mind, and though it did not stop there long enough for me to remember it, yet as it went through it cleansed me, and I have been a different woman ever since."[4]

That is the cleansing action of God's Word, and believer-priests need to avail themselves constantly of its purifying power.

FOR YOUR FURTHER STUDY

1. How is God's Word as a mirror related to God's Word as water?
2. What condition of cleansing is set forth in Psalm 119:9? Rearrange the following outline in its proper order: heeding God's Word,

honouring God's Word, hearing God's Word, and hiding God's Word (see Psalm 119:1-11).

3. What did our Lord mean when He prayed the words of John 17:17?

The Christian's Golden Shield

The shield is not for the defence of any particular part of the body, as almost all other pieces are: helmet for the head; plate designed for the breast; and so others, they have their several parts, which they are fastened to: but the shield is a piece that is intended for the defence of the whole body.

—**William Gurnall**

The particular use of a shield is to ward off a blow from any part of the body that may be menaced; and to that end it is to be applied in every direction as occasion may require. Now Satan strikes sometimes at one part, and sometimes at another, according as the different parts may seem most open to his attack. And the temptations with which he makes his assaults are as fiery darts, which fly with incredible velocity, and are calculated to inflame the soul with their deadly poison.

—**Charles Simeon**

> There is a golden shield divine,
> A shield that's seven-ply;
> Behind that shield we need not fear
> To heed the battle cry.

That which we must oppose to all perils is the truth, or Word of God; so long as we keep that, and ward off darts and swords by that means, we shall not be overcome.

—**David Dickson**

Double armour has he who relies upon the Lord. He bears a shield and wears an all-surrounding coat of mail—such is the force of the word 'buckler.' To quench fiery darts the truth is a most effectual shield, and to blunt all swords it is an equally effective coat of mail. Let us go forth to battle thus harnessed for the war, and we shall be safe in the thickest of the fight.

—**C.H. Spurgeon**

Are you learning to make the Word of God your shield on which you catch and quench the fiery darts of the wicked?

—**A.W. Pink**

STUDY 8
God's Word Is Protective

Our Key Scripture—"He shall cover thee with his feathers, and under his wings shalt thou trust: his truth *shall be thy* shield and buckler" (Psalm 91:4).

Supplementary Scriptures—Genesis 15:1; Deuteronomy 33:29; 2 Samuel 22:3; 1 Kings 14:25–28; Psalm 3:3; Proverbs 30:5; Isaiah 21:5; 22:6; Ezekiel 27:11; Ephesians 6:10.

ACCORDING to a Greek myth, Perseus was tricked by the evil king Polydectes into going after the head of the Gorgon Medusa. Since her gaze turned all who looked at her into stone, Perseus realized that he would not be able to look directly at Medusa. Accordingly he went armed with winged sandals, a special helmet and sword, and a shiny shield. When he approached Medusa, Perseus guided himself by her reflection in the shield, and thus beheaded her as she slept. The shining shield was the means of his victory over his enemy.[1]

If, as we believe, Psalm 91 represents Moses' charge to Joshua, then in verse 4, there is reference made to the equipment that Joshua, as a soldier in the Lord's army, needed to carry into battle. "His truth," affirmed Moses, "*shall be thy* shield and buckler."

Truth in this verse may refer to truthfulness or faithfulness; that is, Moses may be referring to the faithfulness of the Lord to fulfill His Word and thus to save and keep His own. Truth, on the other hand, may refer here to God's Word itself—that is, to the very promises that the faithful God has given in the Scriptures. Interpreted in this way, the reference to truth in Psalm 91:4 would be equivalent to Joshua 1:8, where we have another charge of Moses to Joshua: "This book of the law shall not depart out of thy mouth; but thou shalt meditate therein day and night, that thou mayest observe to do according to all that is written therein."

Joshua's shield, therefore, was to be the Word of God, "the book of the law." And that shield is more valuable and vital than the shield of Athena given to Perseus.

BASIC OUTLINE

With this interpretation before us, let us examine first the *attributes* of our shield, its *advantages*, its *achievements*, and, finally, its *appropriation*.

Attributes

First, let us carefully examine the *attributes* of our shield, the Word of God. The ancients loved to describe in glowing terms the shields of their mighty warriors. Homer, for example, describes the shield of Achilles, made for him by Vulcan, in these words:

> With five folds Vulcan had fortified it;
> two were brass;
> The two interior were tin;
> the mid-most gold.[2]

A craftsman once made a wonderful shield and worked his name into it so that it could not be removed without destroying the shield.[3] Even so it is with the Bible; God's name is written into it on every page. We cannot remove the divine element without destroying the whole Book.

In describing our shining shield, we begin by emphasizing that it is divine. It is the truth of the Lord that is to be our shield, and our Saviour Himself said, "Thy word is truth" (John 17:17). Implicit in this fact that our shield is divine is a remarkable comparison between the Lord our shield and the Word of God our shield. The same symbol is used to describe both the Lord Himself and His Word.

To Abraham God said: "Fear not, Abram: I *am* thy shield, *and* thy exceeding great reward" (Genesis 15:1). To Israel Moses said: "Happy *art* thou, O Israel: who *is* like unto thee, O people saved by the LORD, the shield of thy help, and who *is* the sword of thy excellency!" (Deuteronomy 33:29).

King David, the mighty warrior, testified: "The LORD *is* my rock, and my fortress, and my deliverer; The God of my rock; in Him will I trust: *he is* my shield, and the horn of my salvation, my high tower, and my refuge, my saviour; Thou savest me from violence" (2 Samuel 22:2, 3; cf. Psalm 18:2). Again he testified: "*As for* God, his way *is* perfect; the word of the LORD *is* tried: he *is* a buckler to all them that trust in him" (2 Samuel 22:31).

It is in the Book of Psalms that the shield symbol finds its most extensive use. Reference is made to God as a shield in the following passages: Psalm 3:3; 5:12; 18:35; 28:7; 33:20; 59:11; 84:9; 84:11; 115:10, 11. The same symbolism is used in Proverbs 30:5.

It is really because God is our shield that His Word, too, becomes our shield and provides protection for us.

Arising from the relationship in which the Word of God stands to God Himself is the fact that the attributes of our shield are diverse.

Is God *holy*? Then our shield, the Word of God, is also holy. We remind ourselves of this each time we refer to the Scriptures as the "Holy" Bible.

Is God *indestructible*? Then is our shield, the Word of God, also indestructible.

Is God *trustworthy*? Then our shield, the Bible, is preeminently trustworthy.

Commenting on Psalm 91:4 with its reference to truth, Alexander Maclaren insists that "it is not the body of revealed words" (that is, the Bible) that is in view, but, rather, "a certain characteristic of the divine nature."[4] Maclaren is technically correct, but by the principle of extension, surely we may say of God's Word itself that it is true and, therefore, faithful and trustworthy.

Charles Hodge wrote:

> Truth is, so to speak, the very substratum of deity. It is in such a sense the foundation of all the moral perfections of God, that without it they cannot be conceived of as existing. Unless God really is what He declares Himself to be; unless He means what He declares Himself to mean; unless He will

do what He promises, the whole idea of God is lost. As there is no God but the true God, so without truth there is and can be no God.[5]

What Dr. Hodge has said about God Himself we may say about the Bible. "Truth is, so to speak, the very substratum of the Word of God." All other attributes hinge on the truthfulness and dependability of the Scriptures. We are not called upon to go into battle with a toy shield, or a flimsy buckler. The shield of God's Word is true and faithful. We are to hold fast "the faithful word" (Titus 1:9). Well do we pray with Frances:

> Thy light and truth forth-sending
> From Thy own radiant side,
> Be Thou our Guard and Guide!
> On Thee alone depending,
> No darkness can affright
> Thy shield of Truth and Light,
> Clear-flashing through the night,
> Is all-defending.[6]

Advantages

But let us turn now to discuss the *advatages* of God's Word as our shield for conflict. Other shields are being offered to us today to protect us in the spiritual conflict in which we are engaged, but the shields of philosophy, science, and psychology are not part of the divine panoply. As for ourselves, we take the Word of God to be our buckler in battle.

First, as we list the advantages of God's Word as our shield, in the conflict of the ages the Word of God gives the clearest identification of us as soldiers in the army of the Lord. "Significant devices on shields," we are told, "are of great antiquity. Each Roman soldier had his name inscribed on his shield."[7]

Let us not be ashamed of the Word of God. Let us boast in the fact that God's truth is our shield and buckler. Let our enemies see clearly and constantly the Cross of Christ emblazoned on our shield, for the Bible witnesses from cover to cover to the atoning death of Christ.

In the ancient world, great honour was attached to the shield. A Spartan mother once said to her son, "Either bring back this shield, or be brought back upon it."[8]

"It was natural enough," writes one commentator, "for a man, when escaping, to desire to disencumber himself of such a burden and encumbrance as the larger kinds of shields were: and, therefore, the sentiment of honour was brought in, and made it disgraceful to lose the shield under any circumstance."[9] David apparently alluded to this sentiment in 2 Samuel 1:21.

Let the man, therefore, who casts away his shield, the Word of God, come under dishonour. Let no man retreat shamefully from the battlefield, casting his shield from him.

Some are ready to cast away their shield because of the thrusts of the enemy. We are told that the shield we carry is obsolete and worn-out. It is ridiculed and held up to scorn. But take courage, brother; the shield you carry is the Word of God, and it will outlive its critics and its adversaries.

Second, God's Word as a shield gives complete protection. In Psalm 91:4 there is a double figure: one taken from the farmyard, the other taken from the battlefield. States Moses: "He shall cover thee with his feathers, and under his wings shalt thou trust: his truth *shall be thy* shield and thy buckler."

The first figure is that of the mother hen protecting her chickens under her wings. The second figure is that of the shield protecting the soldier as he engages in battle. The first figure throws light on the second figure, and reminds us that God's protection of His children is complete. As a shield God's Word gives us completest protection from the attacks and assaults of our enemies.

In Ephesians 6:16 Paul exhorts us in these words: "Above all, taking the shield of faith." Writing on the words "Above all," Dean Howson comments:

> The words in which the *Authorized Version* introduces the shield are again (I conceive) inadequate, or, at least, obscure. "Above all" conveys the impression of "especially," as though the Apostle were now about to mention what is most important.

And perhaps "the shield of faith" is, in fact, the most important of all the defences of the Christian soldier. But I think the Greek words mean simply "over all," "on the outside of all."

The great Roman shield referred to here was very different from the small bucklers which were used in some kinds of ancient warfare. It covered and protected the whole body; and whatever weak points there might be in other parts of the armour, this supplied their deficiencies.[10]

In the same way God's Word, our shield, when appropriated by faith, grants the completest protection to the Christian engaged in spiritual warfare.

As we study the advantages of taking God's Word as our shield, we discover that God's Word withstands the strongest opposition. How many battlefields there have been and still are where the enemies of God's Word have found that they could not penetrate the shields of God's people! "A fiery shield is God's Word," said Martin Luther; "of more substance and purer than gold, which, tried in the fire, loses naught of its substance, but resists and overcomes all the fury of the fiery heat; even so, he that believes God's Word overcomes all, and remains secure everlastingly, against all misfortunes; for this shield fears nothing, neither Hell nor the Devil."[11]

The swords of civil power, the arrows of hatred and venom, the spears of hostile criticism have not availed to break through the ranks of God's people when they have stood shoulder to shoulder armed with the shield of God's Word. Surely we may say of God's Word what Isaiah said about the people of Israel: "No weapon that is formed against thee shall prosper; and every tongue *that* shall rise against thee in judgment thou shalt condemn" (Isaiah 54:17).

Finally, we note that God's Word as a shield survives the test of time. Concerning the Roman shield, Captain P.N. Corry states:

When studying Ephesians 6, I searched many museums to find one of these shields, but no Roman shields of this pattern have survived, and the reason was not far to seek. They were made of a double layer of boards, fastened together with glue and linen, the outside surface being covered with calf-skin bound at the edges with a framework of metal to enable the shield to withstand sword blows. The wood soon decayed and only the center plate or boss of metal which helped to strengthen the shield, and on which the various badges of the legions were engraved, has survived.[12]

But our shield, the Word of God, is not like the shields of the Roman legions. Our shield has withstood the ravages of time, and "liveth and abideth forever" (1 Peter 1:23).

As you go on in the conflict against Satan and his hosts, consider well the advantages of taking God's Word as your shield. Let it give you constant, complete, and certain protection.

Achievements

Concerning the mercenary soldiers of Tyre, it is written that "they hanged their shields upon [the wall of Tyre] round about" (Ezekiel 27:11). These shields were symbolic of victories won, and they were hung up in public in order that all might know of the conflicts in which the bearers of the shields had been triumphant.

Consider, then, some of the *achievements* of God's Word as a shield. Indeed, we may single out some texts, which by themselves have acted as shields for God's people when "pressed by the foe."

There's a shield hanging on the wall of the past. It is from 1 John 1:7. Engraved on the shield are the words: "The blood of Jesus Christ his Son cleanseth us from all sin."

Here's the victory that this shield commemorates.

On one occasion, Martin Luther had a dream in which he stood, on the Day of Judgment, before God. Satan was there to accuse him; when the books were opened, he pointed to transgression after transgression of which Luther was guilty. Luther's heart sank in despair.

Then he remembered the Cross, and turning upon the devil, he said, "There is one entry which thou hast not made, Satan."

"What is that?" asked the devil.

"It is this," answered Luther: " 'The blood of Jesus Christ his Son cleanseth us from all sin.' "[13]

The force of Satan's accusations and attacks is blunted when we meet them with the shield of God's Word.

Here is another golden shield from the divine armory. On it are written the words: "Lo, I am with you alway, even unto the end of the world."

It is 1896, and Glasgow University has just conferred upon Dr. David Livingstone the degree of Doctor of Laws. He rises to speak to the student audience. They listen to the veteran missionary and explorer in respectful silence. Livingstone stands before them, a living testimony to God's keeping power. He tells the students that, in spite of physical weakness and weariness, he is returning to Africa. He adds:

> Would you like me to tell you what supported me through all the years of exile among a people whose language I could not understand, and whose attitude toward me was always uncertain and often hostile? It was this: "Lo, I am with you alway[s], even unto the end of the world." On these words I staked everything, and they never failed.[14]

That was Livingstone's shield, and it protected him as he carried the battle to darkest Africa.

And so we could continue through the pages of Christian biography, noting the part that God's shield, the Word of God, has played in the defence and protection of God's children in their fight against sin and Satan.

In the light of the achievements of God's Word we may well ask ourselves: Have I a particular portion of God's Word that I have used over and over again as a shield against the attacks of the enemy? Do I know what it is to hide behind some massive Scripture that gives me complete protection? Are there any shields hanging on the walls of my past Christian experience, proof of past victories and pledge of future triumphs? Do I recognize the truth of Edwin Hodder's words:

> Thy Word is like an armory,
> Where soldiers may repair,

And find for life's long battle-day,
All needful weapons there?[15]

Appropriation

Having studied the attributes, the advantages, and the achievements of our shield, the Word of God, we ought at this point to consider what is involved in the *appropriation* of our shield.

We would like to call attention to a number of references to shields in the Bible, and although the primary interpretation of these references is to actual shields, we may derive help from them by relating them to God's Word, either in its entirety or in part.

The first of these references is found in Jeremiah 51:11, where we read: "Gather the shields." In context these words were spoken to the Medo-Persian soldiers as they prepared for battle against Babylon. The shields had to be gathered together, ready for the soldiers.

Let the Christian soldier learn from this appeal to gather together those portions and passages of Scripture that he can use as shields in the heat of the battle. This can be done both by memorization and by meditation. While all Scripture is inspired of God, and all Scripture is profitable, Scripture is not all equally profitable. There are some verses that serve as better shields than others.

The second reference is found in Isaiah 22:6, where we learn that certain soldiers "uncovered the shield." When not in use, the shield of the ancient soldier was protected by a leather covering. But immediately prior to battle, the leather covering was removed. The removal of the covering signified the readiness of the soldier to engage in conflict.

It is not sufficient for the soldier in the army of the Lord to gather together various passages from God's Word to serve as shields; he must understand those passages. Perhaps the removal of the covering can suggest this truth to us. There is a covering of familiarity that often has to be removed before the shield of Scripture shines out with all its pristine glory.

The third reference is found in Isaiah 21:5, where we read: "Arise, ye princes, *and* anoint the shield." Before soldiers entered battle, they often anointed or oiled their shields, so that they would shine brighter, and also more readily deflect the blows of the enemy.

To the Christian soldier this would suggest that his employment of any portion of God's Word as a shield must be in the power of the Holy Spirit. His shield must shine with the Spirit's blessing and be strengthened through the Spirit's power.

Gather the shields—uncover the shields—anoint the shields: these three commands to soldiers of a forgotten era may remind us of our responsibilities with regard to the Word of God.

Failure to appropriate and employ God's Word as our shield will result in total failure.

Proverbs 7 gives us the picture of an unsuspecting young man becoming the victim of a prostitute. He is enticed by her into her house, and seduced through her allurements. Comments Solomon: "With her much fair speech she caused him to yield, with the flattering of her lips she forced him. He goeth after her straightway, as an ox goeth to the slaughter, or as a fool to the correction of the stocks; Till a dart strike through his liver" (7:21–23).

In symbolic language Solomon is telling us that this young man had no shield, or did not use the shield he had. The dart of his seducer met with no opposition and inflicted a serious wound in the young man's emotional life.

In light of the illustration given by Solomon, we can understand the wisdom of his counsel given in the opening verses of the chapter:

> My son, keep my words, and lay up my commandments with thee. Keep my commandments, and live; and my law as the apple of thine eye.
>
> Bind them upon thy fingers, write them upon the table of thine heart. Say unto wisdom, Thou *art* my sister; and call understanding *thy* kinswoman: That they may keep thee from the strange woman, from the stranger *which* flattereth with her words.

This is one illustration of many which could be given. It is practical, related to the basic problems of life, and the way to victory is clearly outlined. It is by using moral instructions—especially that given to us in the Bible—as our constant shield that we find protection from evil.

In light of the importance of God's Word as our shield, we must never permit the Bible to be downgraded in our eyes. It is the golden shield of the Spirit, given to us to be employed in the fight against Satan and his armies.

There is a tragic incident in the history of Israel, recorded for us in 1 Kings 14:25–27. There we read that during the reign of King Rehoboam, Shishak, King of Egypt, attacked Jerusalem. As a part of the tribute that he exacted, the treasures of the Temple and the King's palace were taken away. Included among these treasures were shields of gold which Solomon had made. Impoverished and weakened by military defeat, Rehoboam could not replace the shields of gold; accordingly he made shields of brass in their place.

From gold to brass—that is a degeneration we must never allow when we think of God's Word as our shield. We must cling to the Bible as the Divine Word, "all of gold." There are those who would take away from us the shields of gold and put in their place shields of brass. But we must resist all such attempts, and put our confidence in the inspired Word of God.

Let Richard Crashaw's words, initially written concerning a prayer book, assure our hearts as to the protective value of God's Word:

> It is an armoury of light;
> Let constant use but keep it bright,
> You'll find it yields
> To holy hands and humble hearts
> More swords and shields
> Than sin hath snares, or hell hath darts.[16]

FOR YOUR FURTHER STUDY

1. We have given some examples of attributes common both to God and to His Word. Can you list more of them?

2. Are you able to identify some temptations which are best met with the shield of God's Word?

3. What is the connection between Psalm 91:4 and Ephesians 6:16?

There Is None Like It

What the sword is to a warrior, the Scriptures are to a child of God.

—Charles Simeon

Then said Mr. Greatheart to Mr. Valiant-for-Truth, "Thou hast worthily behaved thyself; let me see thy sword." So he showed it to him. When he had taken it into his hand and looked thereon a while, he said, "Ha, it is a right Jerusalem blade."

Then said Mr. Valiant-for-Truth, "It is so. Let a man have one of these blades, with a hand to wield it, and skill to use it, and he may venture upon an angel with it. He need not fear its holding if he can but tell how to lay it on. Its edge will never blunt. It will cut flesh and bones, and soul and spirit and all."

— John Bunyan

It is God's Word which does the work of saving souls and of elevating the Church. Instead of the wooden swords of modern thought, let us take the good old Jerusalem blade.

—C.H. Spurgeon

A regular feature of the *Reader's Digest* is a quiz entitled, "It Pays to Increase Your Word Power." The caption certainly represents a truth for Christians. It is an advantage to be familiar with the Word of God. This is the sword of the Spirit which we must learn to wield with dexterity and skill.

—A. Skevington Wood

The Word of God in wise and skillful hands is a weapon sure and deadly.

—R.E.O. White

Oh, come! Let us turn from the feeble and false substitutes—the man-made garden sticks of modernism and human philosophy—and let us preach the Word, parry with the Word, pound with the Word, persuade with the Word, and prevail with the Word. Oh, let us be mighty in the Scriptures and with the Scriptures!

—Evangelist John G. Ridley

STUDY 9
God's Word Is Defensive

Our Key Scripture—"Take … the sword of the Spirit, which is the word of God" (Ephesians 6:17).

Supplementary Scriptures—Judges 7:18; 2 Samuel 23:10; Song of Solomon 3:8; Hebrews 4:12; Revelation 1:16; 2:12; 19:11–16, especially verse 15.

IT is recorded that during the coronation of Edward VI, after various ceremonial swords had been brought to him, the king said to his nobles: "There is one sword yet lacking, the sword of the Spirit, which is the Word of God. Without that sword we are nothing and we can do nothing."[1] It is our purpose in this study to examine—in order that we may employ—that sword without which we are nothing and can do nothing.

BASIC OUTLINE

With regard to the sword of the Spirit it is essential for the Christian to *know* it, to *trust* it, and to *use* it.

Know Your Sword

It is essential, first, that each believer should *know* the sword of the Spirit. That may seem to be a very trite and threadbare statement to make, but nevertheless it needs to be emphasized. Whatever else we may know, we must know the Scriptures.

We come to know the Scriptures, the sword of the Spirit, by various exercises.

We come to know the Bible by reading it. Charles Spurgeon was once asked how a Christian could obtain a thorough Bible knowledge. The great preacher replied: "There are three rules to follow in order to have a deep understanding of the Word of God. First, read the Bible. Second, read the Bible. Third, read the Bible."[2]

Professor Richard Moulton once wrote concerning the attitude of Christians toward the Bible:

> We have done almost everything that is possible with these writings. We have overlaid them, clause by clause, with exhaustive commentaries; we have translated them, revised the translations, and inspiration, and suggested textual history with the aid of coloured type; we have mechanically divided the whole into chapters and verses; and we have sought texts to memorize and quote .... There is one thing left to do with the Bible—simply to read it.[3]

The Bible, indeed, does not need to be rewritten, but to be reread.

But we may come to know our Bibles, too, by memorizing portions of God's Word. That great missionary-doctor of Labrador, Sir Wilfred Grenfell, gave his testimony in the following words:

> To me, the memorizing of Scripture has been an unfailing help in doubt, anxiety, sorrow, and all the countless vicissitudes and problems of life. I believe in it enough to have devoted many, many hours to stowing away passages where I can neither leave them behind me nor be unable to get at them.
>
> Facing death alone on a floating piece of ice on a frozen ocean, I have found that the comradeship it afforded me supplied all I needed. It stood by me like the truest of true friends that it is. With my whole soul I commend to others the giving of some little time each day to secure the immense returns it offers and insures.[4]

When Nansen, the explorer, went to the Arctic regions, he took with him a phonograph into which he had his wife, a most accomplished musician, sing her sweetest songs, and into which also his little children had talked a message to him; and, when he was in the frozen seas of the north, and the nights were dark, and his heart was almost broken because of a sense of loneliness, he would start the phonograph and hear again and again the music of his home, and his heart would rejoice.[5]

The Word of God, memorized, recorded as it were on the disk of memory, can do for us what Nansen's recording did for him—and more. Wherever we find ourselves, we can turn on the Word of God with its messages of peace and promises of blessing.

We may come to know God's Word by reading it and by memorizing it. But it is important, too, that we come to know the sword of the Spirit by studying it. We should know all about its handle, shaft, edges, and point.

We should study its history. This will enable us to grasp the vast panorama of its chapters, outlining as they do the history of man from Paradise lost to Paradise regained.

We should study its prophecy. What challenging themes are here dealt with—the future of Israel, the fate of the nations, the founding of God's Kingdom, the focus of history! All these and more are presented in the word of prophecy.

We should study as well its theology. In the pages of Scripture we have basic teaching concerning God, man, sin, redemption, holiness, and many other fundamental topics.

As we come to know the sword of the Spirit through reading, memorization, and study, we are constrained to say what David said concerning the sword of Goliath, the Philistine superman: "*There is none* like that; give it me" (1 Samuel 21:9). We should pray daily with Edwin Hodder, who expressed his desire with regard to God's Word in these lines:

> Oh, may I find my armour there,
> Thy Word my trusty sword;
> I'll learn to fight with every foe
> The battle of the Lord.[6]

In his book, *Among Many Witnesses*, Evangelist M.B. Williams recounts the thrilling story of Martius, the Roman soldier:

> Once during the early days of the Church, there was a young Roman soldier named Martius, who had been converted

to Christianity. The centurion of his band died and upon Martius his mantle was to fall; but he who stood next beneath the fortunate young aspirant, knowing of his faith, through jealousy, made known his secret to the emperor. The penalty was death, and Martius was summoned to appear before him. When the emperor looked upon his stalwart, manly form, he hesitated to deprive the state of so good a soldier. "Are you a Christian?" he asked.

"I am, sire," answered Martius.

"I will give you until tomorrow morning to reconsider," returned the emperor, and Martius was led away.

Theotecnes was then Bishop of Rome, and hearing of the young man's sad plight, sought him out in his confinement. He brought with him a beautiful centurion's sword, with glittering blade and jewelled hilt, and, laying by its side a roll of Scripture, said, "Son, I know of your unhappy lot; now"—pointing to the book and sword —"choose for yourself."

For a moment, the young man looked longingly upon the glittering blade and thought how well his strong right arm could wield it in the fight, in leading his band to victory. Then he looked upon the Book and thought of all the comfort it had brought, of all the precious promises it bore, and of its Christ, who died that he might live. "Choose," said the Bishop.

"He that findeth his life shall lose it; and he that loseth his life for my sake shall find it." As he read the words, the young man's eyes were filled with blinding tears that trickled down his sunburned cheek. Then reaching out his hand he drew the precious volume to his heart. "I choose," he said, in solemn tones.

"And thou hast chosen well," replied the Bishop, "for before the setting of tomorrow's sun thou shalt be with thy Lord." The emperor died and passed away, but Martius still lives, and for eighteen hundred years has been singing the praises of his

King. Fear not them who destroy the body, but God, who has power over body and soul.

These are days when the glittering blades of pseudo-science and philosophy tempt us as we first begin to think for ourselves; but a second glance at the old Book touches our hearts with tender thoughts and sweetest memories. May the Good Spirit help us in our choice for Christ's sake.[7]

Trust Your Sword

We must know the sword of the Spirit. We must also *trust* our divine sword.

E. Paxton Hood recalls the children's story of the magic sword. This mysterious sword had in its construction a kind of life of its own. It was put in the hand of a coward in order to cure him and to develop courage on his part. When he tried to run away, the sword kept him right up to the front of the battle. Whenever he attempted to fling it from him, it clung to his hand. Whenever he sought to slink out of sight and to hide the bright blade in the folds of his uniform, by itself it would leap from the scabbard and begin smiting the first foe it could find.

Gradually the coward learned to put confidence in his sword. He realized he could never be beaten as long as that invincible blade was in his hand. Such a weapon is the sword of the Spirit. It will fight by itself, it will conquer by itself, and in the end defend and deliver every brave man who trusts it.[8]

We must trust our sword as being divine. It is pre-eminently the sword of the Spirit of God. King Arthur's legendary supernatural sword Excalibur was wrought by the lonely Maiden of the Lake in nine years.[9] But the supernatural sword the Christian soldier wields was formed and fashioned by the Holy Spirit during the course of many centuries. It is divine in its origin. "The sword we are to wield," affirmed George F. Pentecost, "is 'the sword of the Spirit, which is the word of God' (Ephesians 6:17), that Christian's 'Excalibur,' which makes him who wields it invincible."[10]

Like the Lord Jesus Christ, who is the living Word of God, the written Word has a two-fold nature: it is both human and divine. We dare not say it is merely human; we cannot say it is solely divine. It is a fusion of both the human and divine elements.

Early in his experience as an evangelist Dr. Billy Graham had doubts about the Bible. In August of 1949 things came to a crisis. He tells of walking down a mountain trail, almost wrestling with God.

> I dueled with my doubts, [he writes] and my soul seemed to be caught in the crossfire.
>
> Finally, in desperation, I surrendered my will to the living God revealed in Scripture. I knelt before the open Bible and said: "Lord, many things in this Book I do not understand. But Thou hast said, 'The just shall live by faith.' All I have received from Thee, I have taken by faith. Here and now, I accept the Bible as Thy Word. I take it all. I take it without reservations. Where there are things I cannot understand I will reserve judgment until I receive more light. If this pleases Thee, give me authority as I proclaim Thy Word, and through that authority convict me of sin and turn sinners to the Saviour."

Shortly after that, Dr. Graham began the Los Angeles crusade. Concerning his preaching in those days, he has written"

> I felt as though I had a rapier in my hand and, through the power of the Bible, was slashing deeply into men's consciences, leading them to surrender to God. Does not the Bible say, "For the word of God *is* quick, and powerful, and sharper than any twoedged sword, piercing even to the dividing asunder of soul and spirit, and of the joints and marrow, and *is* a discerner of the thoughts and intents of the heart" (Hebrews 4:12)?[11]

"Too many preachers," said Dr. A.T. Pierson in one of his early sermons, "are not content with using the plain sword of the Spirit, which in its naked simplicity thrusts deep and cuts quickly. Scholars, instead, forge for themselves swords of gold, diamond-hilted, that are brilliant but have neither point nor edge."[12]

We must constantly keep in mind that the Bible is the sword the Spirit employs in His attack upon the citadel of human reasonings and arguments. When Saladin saw the sword which Richard Coeur de Lion carried in battle and with which he had fought so valiantly, he marvelled that so common a blade should have wrought such mighty deeds on the field of battle. "It was not the sword," replied one of the English officers, "it was the arm of Richard."[13] Let the Christian soldier give similar testimony to the Bible; it is because the Holy Spirit wields it that it is such a great force. We do well to pray:

> Thou sword of the Spirit,
> Put error to flight,
> And banish the forces
> Of darkness and night![14]

We must trust our sword as being divine. We must trust it, too, as being dependable.

Ralph C. Norton, who once served as the director for personal work in the Chapman-Alexander missions and as director of the Belgian Gospel Mission, was talking with some friends about the supreme task of winning men one by one to Christ.

When they noticed the almost exclusive place he gave to the Bible in personal work, one asked him: "What do you do, Mr. Norton, in cases where the unsaved man does not accept the Bible as having any authority?"

"Well," replied Mr. Norton, "if I had a fine Damascus sword with a keen double-edged blade, I would not sheathe it in a fight just because the other man said he did not believe it would cut."[15]

"Because of the strength and sharpness of its steel," Allan Poole informs us, "Hereward, the Wake called his sword 'Brainbiter.' Sharper than the keenest sword, more searching than radium, more penetrating than the X-ray, the Word of God pierces to the deepest recesses of the mind, and searches the innermost secrets of the soul."[16]

Our sword is divine and it is dependable. We must also trust it as durable. Hebrews 4:12 describes the sword of the Spirit as living, and as a living Book it survives the ravages of the centuries and the ravings of its critics. It is not the Book of the month; it is the Book of the ages. It is the living Word of the living God. All other books are dead books in comparison with this living Word.

Shortly before his death, the Rev. Thomas Taylor, an English minister, preached a sermon in which he expressed his wish that he might die as an old soldier with his sword in his hand. After his death James Montgomery wrote a poem in tribute to him, part of which reads:

> His sword was in his hand,
> Still warm with recent fight;
> Ready that moment at command
> Through rock and steel to smite.
>
> It was a two-edged blade
> Of heavenly temper keen;
> And double were the wounds it made
> Where'er it smote between.
>
> 'Twas death to sin; 'twas life
> To all that mourn'd for sin;
> It kindled and it silenced strife,
> Made war and peace within.[17]

William Pettingill once told Richard H. Seume the following story about the last days of Dwight L. Moody and C.I. Scofield.

> Those two men shared many hours together in walks among the trees at Northfield, Massachusetts. On one occasion, Scofield turned to Moody and said, in jest, "D.L., I have your sermon subject ready should you precede me in death."
>
> "What is it?" said Moody, and Scofield replied, "It is that text in Scripture, 'And...the beggar died' (Luke 16:22)!"
>
> "Well, that is strange," retorted Mr. Moody, "for I have your subject ready should you precede me." Scofield may well have expected a jest in return, but in a much different tone Mr. Moody said, "It is that other text, 'And his hand clave to the sword' (2 Samuel 23:10)!"[18]

Use Your Sword

We must know the sword of the Spirit. We must trust it as well. And, above all, we must *use* it. G. Woods prayed, "O Word of power, of pure design, help me Thy sword-thrusts well to use."[19]

In the Wakefield Tower of the Tower of London there is to be seen a jewelled sword of state. It is one of the most beautiful and valuable swords in the world. Emeralds and diamonds, sapphires and rubies, along with other precious stones, encase it so thickly that the gold setting beneath can hardly be seen.

Yet, strange to say, during the reign of Queen Victoria, this sword was lost for some decades. Packed away in an old box that closely resembled an ordinary gun case, it got pushed aside, and was only accidentally found at the back of a disused cupboard. It is hard to imagine how such a treasure could be treated so carelessly. And yet there are many people who treat the sword of the Spirit in the same way.[20]

"The sword is useless," Henry Melville reminds us, "so long as it is confined to the scabbard; and the Bible is useless if it rests idle in the intellect."[21]

Alexander Maclaren claimed that there are some Christians whose hands are too nerveless or too full of worldly trash to grasp the sword they have received, much less to strike home with it at any of the evils that are devastating their own lives or darkening the world. The feebleness of the Christian conflict with evil, in all its forms, whether individual or social, whether intellectual or moral, whether heretical or grossly and frankly sensual, is mainly due to the feebleness with which the average professing Christian grasps the sword of the Spirit.[22]

Writing on *The Sword in Warfare*, T.H. McGuffie comments: "The sword is obsolete in warfare. Those glittering blades carried on guard-duty or in royal processions by certain mounted squadrons of the Household Cavalry are merely picturesque military survivals, as useless in modern battle as the plumes or great shining boots."[23]

That may be so in the military world, but in the spiritual world the sword of the Spirit is still effective. It is not only alive, according to Hebrews

4:12, but it is powerful—energetic and effectual. It is still to be employed in the conflict of the centuries.

"I will fight you," said a hard-fisted, hard-hearted man to a godly Christian.

"Very well," said he, quietly taking his Testament from his pocket, "just wait till I get my sword."[24]

> Flash out from its scabbard
> The Spirit's bright sword;
> And pierce your dread foe
> With "Thus saith the Lord."[25]

Use the sword of the Spirit as did the Lord Jesus, who, when He was tempted by the Devil, used the sword of the Spirit three times over. Watch Him in the wilderness as He duels with Satan. He grasps the sword, wields it in faith, and puts the Devil to flight. Christ knew and trusted and used the sword.

Use the Spirit's sword like Paul the Apostle, whom J.H. Jowett described as a "most excellent swordsman."[26] Paul knew where to find the exact word of the Spirit for every emergency, and he knew how to wield the sword in conflict.

Use the sword of the Spirit like Martin Luther, who wrote: "A Christian must be well-armed, grounded, and furnished with sentences out of God's Word, so that he may stand and defend religion and himself against the Devil—in case he should be asked to embrace another doctrine."[27]

Use the sword like Dr. Caesar Malan of Geneva. On one occasion he was travelling to Paris and fell into conversation with a man who began to reason with him about Christianity. The doctor answered every argument with a quotation from the Bible, not venturing a single remark or application. Every quotation his companion sought to evade, only to be met by another passage.

At last Malan's companion could stand it no longer. "Don't you understand?" he remonstrated. "I don't believe your Bible. What's the use of quoting it to me?"

The only reply was another thrust of the Spirit's sword: "If ye believe not that I am *he*, ye shall die in your sins."

Some years later, Dr. Malan received a letter in an unfamiliar handwriting. The letter was in the form of a testimony. "You took the sword of the Spirit," claimed the writer, "and stabbed me through and through. And every time I tried to parry the blade and get you to use your hands and not the heavenly steel, you simply gave me another stab. You made me feel I was not fighting you, but God."

As he read on, Dr. Malan recognized that the letter was from his Paris-bound companion of years before. The sword of the Spirit had done its work.[28]

Use the sword of the Spirit, then, like Evangelist John Ridley of Australia, who gave his testimony in these words:

> This sword was drawn from its sheath at my conversion to the Lord Jesus Christ, and I have been fighting with it ever since. It is the one weapon that wins in the stern struggle with Satan and sin. I say this with all confidence, because the Bible is profuse with illustrations of its own victories, and human experience confirms it on every side.[29]

And then that veteran warrior in the Lord's army exhorts us, "If we would be valiant for God as our Captain was, then we must use His weapon."[30]

Let preachers especially use the sword of the Spirit, but let them be careful how they wield it. A.J. Gordon wrote:

> The Lord would not have told Simon to put up his sword, if it had been the sword of the Spirit that he was wielding. The sword of the Spirit lays open the heart, while the sword of the flesh only cuts off the ears. Now there has been a long succession of Petrine apostles, valiant swordsmen of the faith, whose principal ministerial trophies are severed ears, and not converted hearts; who have preached with such two-edged severity as to alienate their hearers when they should have won them. The Lord has not called us to be theological gladiators,

to win applause from the crowd by our skill in cutting and
slashing....[31]

Use the sword of the Spirit as Eleazar used his sword. Concerning him
it is written that when in battle "his hand clave unto the sword: and the
Lord wrought a great victory that day" (2 Samuel 23:10). Let the sword
of the Spirit be in our hands, and that Scripture will be fulfilled which
says,"*Let* the high *praises* of God *be* in their mouth, and a twoedged sword
in their hand" (Psalm 149:6).

We have read of the way in which the grey heron defends itself when
attacked. When confronted by an eagle or falcon, the heron stands quiet
and firm, using its bill as a kind of sword. The heron simply waits for its
enemy to pierce itself through in the violence of its attack.[32]

The Christian's method of defence is very similar. We have the sword
of the Spirit. When attacked by the enemy, let us stand firm, displaying
our sword. The more fiercely the foe attacks, the more surely will he pierce
himself through, Henry Thorne assures us:

> Spiritual victories—the subjugation of the heart to God,
> the humbling of the proud spirit, the reconciliation of the
> alienated mind—can only be won by a spiritual instrumental-
> ity. Such an instrumentality we have in God's precious Word.
> This Word was Spirit-breathed, and in its spirituality we find
> its strength and its charm. It can search out the conscience as
> no carnal weapon can. A famous sword which Mohammed
> often carried with him to the field of battle was called Dhul
> Fakar, which means the Piercer; but that famous weapon
> couldn't pierce the human spirit as does the Word of God.

> Quick and powerful is the Word,
> Sharper than a two-edged sword;
> Wielded by the Spirit's hand,
> Nothing can its force withstand.[33]

Do you remember the legend of Excalibur, King Arthur's great sword?
In the yard of a London church stood an anvil, and thrust into the anvil was
a sword. Around the sword, in letters of gold, these words were written:

"Whoso pulleth out this sword from this stone is righteous king of all England." That sword, symbol of the royal power, was so deeply embedded in the anvil that not one of the knights of England could remove it. This feat was finally accomplished by the chivalry, strength, and courage of Arthur, who was thereby proclaimed King of England.[34]

There is a sense in which the power of the Bible as the sword of the Spirit will not yield itself to any except those born into the royal family, the household of God. It is to those who are the children of God that Paul says, "Take the sword of the Spirit, which is the Word of God."

In the Middle Ages there was a unique ceremony called the Vigil of Arms. Before a young man was permitted to enter into the knighthood, he had to spend one night in a chapel clad in his armour, kneeling on the cold stones with his sword in his hands lifted up before the altar.[35]

Should there not be something comparable from time to time in our own experience? Before we go out to battle for the Lord, should we not get away into some quiet place, clad in the armour of God, with the sword of the Spirit in our hands, to dedicate ourselves and our armour to God, the Lord of armies? Then we would be able to cry with Sir Galahad:

> My good blade carves the casques of men,
> My tough lance thrusteth sure.[36]

FOR YOUR FURTHER STUDY

1. Study the attributes of the Spirit's sword as they are given to us in Hebrews 4:12.
2. What does the statement in Revelation 1:16 mean—that is, "Out of his mouth went a sharp twoedged sword"?
3. Take Gideon's motto of Judges 7:18, "*The sword* of the LORD, and of Gideon," and apply it to the sword of the Spirit. What truths would his words now suggest to you?

For the Healing of the Nations

The Bible is God's doctor's book, to show people how to get rid of soul-sickness. You must diligently consider its diagnosis of soul-diseases, and its methods of cure, if you want soul-health.

—Samuel L. Brengle

Remember, dear souls, if you are sick, that the medicine that is to reach your case is somewhere between the covers of this Book. There is something in here for every sin-sick soul that seeks it.

—Charles H. Spurgeon

Nathaniel Hawthorne wrote a weird tale of a professor who brewed a strange elixir, and when some drops of the mysterious fluid fell upon a stunted plant that was about to die, the plant sprang into new and luxuriant life. The Bible is like that strange elixir, for it has power to revive a drooping heart, to lift up a fallen soul, and to bring back a broken life.

—Selected

The Bible reveals the divine recipe for our salvation. It makes known the one great and infallible remedy. It announces the one Physician, the one catholicon [i.e., panacea] for all moral diseases of mankind.

—Jabez Burns

There is only one medicine that can possibly help in connection with the great social crisis that grips our world right now. It is the medicine God furnishes in His Word, the Holy Bible. Here we meet Jesus, and here we have the opportunity to bow in faith before Him.

—Joel Nederhood

The Word's a balm to heal (Psalm 107:20)
The broken heart (Psalm 147:3)
New life and strength and zeal (John 6:63)
It doth impart (1 Kings 18:1).

— F.E. Marsh

STUDY 10
God's Word Is Curative

Our Key Scripture—"He sent his word, and healed them" (Psalm 107:20).

Supplementary Scriptures—Psalm 6:2; 38:3; 41:4; 67:2; 147:3; Proverbs 3:7, 8; 4:20–23 (see marginal reading of verse 22); 15:4; Isaiah 58:8; Jeremiah 8:22; 17:14; 30:12, 13; 46:11; Hosea 5:13; 3 John 2.

CONCERNING the tree of life referred to in Revelation 22:2, it is written: "The leaves of the tree *were* for the healing of the nations." The Bible itself is such a tree of life; its multitudinous leaves have supernatural medicinal properties that bring healing to sin-sick men and women. When any verse of God's Word is received by faith into the heart, it comes to pass that "the leaf thereof [shall be] for medicine" (Ezekiel 47:12).

BASIC OUTLINE

To consider God's Word as medicine for sin-sick hearts is to study a most important aspect of the Bible. There are those who treat the Bible as a souvenir, rather than allowing the Bible to treat them as patients. But the Bible is not for the museum; it is for the hospital! It has come to minister to needy hearts.

Study with us the following aspects of God's curative Word: its *appropriateness*, its *ability*, its *abundance*, its *administering*, and its *acceptance*.

Its Appropriateness

"He [God] sent his word, and healed them." Think of the *appropriateness* of God's curative Word.

Give Me That Book!

God's Word addresses itself to men as those who are sin-sick. It announces that there is a remedy available for those who recognize how serious is their condition before God. It does not tantalize sinners; it treats them with a view to healing. When people ask for medicine, God does not mock them by offering them a band-aid. Their problem is more than skin deep; their cure must also reach to the heart. In this regard God's Word is appropriate to the sinner's need. It recognizes that the heart of man's trouble is the trouble of man's heart.

How fortunate we are that the Bible is not a book on philosophy! The Bible contains principles of true philosophy (philosophy by definition is the love of wisdom), but it is not a systematic presentation of various human philosophies. How many people would have been unable to read the Bible if it had been such a volume!

How glad, too, we should be that the Bible is not a book on psychology! That it enunciates true principles of psychology none can deny, but it makes no attempt to systematize all the views of psychology.

How glad we should be that the Bible is not a book on science! It is our conviction that whenever the Bible touches on matters of science, it speaks with accuracy and authority, but the Bible is not in and of itself a book dealing with science.

How glad we should be that the Bible is not a book on history! There is a sense in which it is "the history of redemption," but it does not claim to be a history of mankind.

The Bible deals with man as sick with a terminal sickness. It announces to him that sin issues in death— not only physical death, but spiritual and eternal death. It does not gloss over the seriousness of man's problem.

The Bible deals with man as being unable to cure himself. He is both hopeless and helpless. What God said to Israel may be said concerning every sinner: "Thy bruise *is* incurable, *and* thy wound *is* grievous. *There is* none to plead thy cause, that thou mayest be bound up: thou hast no healing medicines" (Jeremiah 30:12, 13).

The Bible deals with man as being unable to receive help from any other source than God. We are like the nation of Israel in Hosea's time. "When

Ephraim saw his sickness, and Judah *saw* his wound, then went Ephraim to the Assyrian and sent to king Jareb: yet could he not heal you, nor cure you of your wound" (Hosea 5:13). Healing is only obtainable when we come to God with these words on our lips: "Come, and let us return unto the LORD: for he hath torn, and he will heal us; he hath smitten, and he will bind us up" (Hosea 6:1).

The Bible deals with man in all of these ways, but supremely the Bible deals with man as being able to be healed. Thus the Bible is both pessimistic and optimistic. It is pessimistic as it considers man in himself—sick, impotent, hopeless, and helpless. It is optimistic when it relates man to the curative Word of God. Man need not die from his sickness; there is hope, but that hope is only in Christ.

Some years ago, relates W.M. Tidwell, people were selling various wares at a fair. Among them was a woman selling medicine and a man selling Bibles. Some wicked young men came to the woman and jestingly said, "Do you think your medicine will cure us?"

To this she replied, "What is the matter with you?"

They sarcastically replied, "Oh, we have the devil in us."

The woman replied, "No, my medicine will not cure you." Then pointing to the man selling Bibles, she said, "He has the medicine that you need, and it will cure you."[1]

In *Our Daily Bread*, monthly devotional booklet published by **The Radio Bible Class**, Grand Rapids, Michigan, Dr. Richard W. DeHaan once wrote:

> While reading some of the mail received in response to *Day of Discovery*, our television program, I came across the following letter: "I would like to receive a copy of *Our Daily Bread*, the daily *medication* booklet mentioned on the telecast." What a difference "c" in the place of "t" makes! Actually, this error in typing was not a bad one. Even though this devotional guide contains daily meditations, it is also a daily medication booklet. Based upon God's Word, it is filled with preventive, curative, and palliative medicines for the spiritual ills of man.

Here is *preventive medicine*: "Thy word have I hid in mine heart, that I might not sin against thee" (Psalm 119:11). Here is *curative medicine*: The world is sin-sick and "the wages of sin is death." Life, however, is offered to those who take God's cure. Through faith in the Lord Jesus Christ, the sinner is born again, given new life, and this is accomplished through God's Word. Peter tells us that we are "born again . . . by the word of God" (1 Peter 1:23). And, finally, here is *palliative medicine*: The psalmist said, "The word . . . *is* my comfort in my affliction" (Psalm 119:49, 50).

Yes, think of *Our Daily Bread* as a daily *medication* booklet. As a dispenser of God's Word, it can make you spiritually healthy and immune to the epidemics of evil which threaten the soul. For this reason we urge you to read the suggested Scripture lesson with every article. Otherwise you are omitting the most important ingredient on these pages—the true "daily medication." Did you take yours today? God's Word is certainly appropriate to our daily need.[2]

Its Ability

"He [God] sent his word, and healed them." We must now consider the *ability* of God's curative Word. God's Word accomplishes its purpose. It is not only appropriate to our need; it is able to cure our sickness. We find its accreditation in its accomplishments.

God's Word, then, is no quack medicine. It makes no boastful, extravagant claims that it cannot fulfill. It does not advertise itself as being an infallible remedy, only to bring disappointment to those who try God's cure-all.

Ours is a day when we must be on guard against all quacks and charlatans. Cults by the score and isms whose name is legion offer "get-well-fast" prescriptions to poor, deluded souls. Such people are like the woman in the Gospel record of whom we read that she "had suffered many things of many physicians, and had spent all that she had, and was nothing bettered, but rather grew worse" (Mark 5:26). Such dupes of the devil need to hear that word first spoken to Babylon: "In vain shalt thou use many medicines; *for* thou shalt not be cured" (Jeremiah 46:11).

God's remedy is free; the remedy of the quacks is costly. God's remedy is simple; the remedy of the quacks is complex and confusing. God's remedy is available to all; the remedy of quacks is often esoteric.

Walter B. Knight tells us that on one occasion a woman of nervous temperament visited the world-renowned physician, Dr. Howard A. Kelly. The cares of life threatened her physical strength, and even her reason. Having given her symptoms to the physician, she was greatly astonished at his prescription: "Madam, what you need is to read the Bible more!"

"But, Doctor—" began the bewildered woman.

"Go home and read your Bible an hour a day," the great man reiterated with kindly authority, "then come back to me a month from today."

At first, the woman was inclined to be angry. But she reflected with a pang of conscience that she had neglected the daily reading of God's Word, and "the secret place of the most High," where formerly she communed with her Lord. In coming back to her God, and His Word, the joys of her salvation returned.

When she presented herself to the doctor a month later, he said, "Well, I see you have been an obedient patient. Do you feel as if you needed any other medicine now?"

"No, Doctor, I feel like a different person. But how did you know what I needed?"

Taking up his own worn and well-marked Bible, he said, "If I would omit my daily reading of God's Word, I would not only lose my joy, but I would lose my greatest source of strength and skill .... Your case called not for medicine, but for a source of peace and strength outside your own mind. My prescription, when tried, works wonders!"[3]

This is but one illustration of many that could be given to show the ability of God's Word to heal. Here is T.H. Darlow's interesting account of the history of the "Treacle Bible" as well as his application of it:

> The first English printed Bible, published in 1535, is sometimes known as the "Treacle Bible" — on account of the

sentence in Jeremiah 8:22, "*Is* there no balm in Gilead," which Coverdale rendered thus: *There is no more Triacle in Gallad.*

Now the derivation of our word treacle goes as far back as the Greek *Therion*, a venomous creature, the adjective from which, *theriakos*, meant anything appertaining to venomous creatures. Thus, in pharmacy, *theriaka* or "triacle" came to denote the antidote for snake-bite; and on the principle that "like cures like," it was believed that the *theriaka* must contain something of the *therion*. So Jeremy Taylor observes: "We kill the viper, and make treacle of him."

In Coverdale's time this word "triacle" had come to mean any balsam or sovereign remedy. Indeed, "Venice treacle," compounded of something viperine with other ingredients, lingered on in the British Pharmacopoeia as late as the eighteenth century; and our familiar sweet syrup received the name treacle because in appearance it resembled that once famous balsam. Thus the quaint epithet "Treacle Bible," at any rate, suggests the healing potency of Scripture, which contains God's sovereign anecdote for the evil that is in the world.[4]

Its Abundance

"He [God] sent his word, and healed them." Let us rejoice, too, in the *abundance* of God's curative Word. "God . . . loved the world," and in His love He made ample and adequate provision for all men.

Suppose a brilliant doctor discovered a cure for cancer. How criminal he would be if he kept that secret to himself, or sold it only to those who could pay great sums of money for it! But the Church has often failed to share the remedy of God's Word with sin-sick souls. It has kept the glorious secret to itself; it has limited the cure to a minority of the world's peoples. We need to see with conviction and clarity that God's curative Word is for all men.

Walter Shepard, missionary to Africa, discusses the abundance of God's remedy:

The element of the completeness, or sufficiency, of the Holy Scripture is . . . important to the missionary. It is indeed good to know that not only is the book God's Book, but that it contains "the whole counsel of God, concerning things necessary for His own glory, man's salvation, faith and life."

Here we have the assurance that our missionaries, all who go as witnesses of the Gospel, carry not only the right medicine but enough of that precious medicine, enough to restore the sickest soul to the most abundant life.

I remember how shocked I was to discover in the attic of one of our Congo hospitals a rather large quantity of an antimalarial drug and to learn that it was reserved for therapeutic treatment of the disease among the African populace and not made available for prophylactic prevention. "Why not go ahead and use these pills, as long as they will last, to prevent a disease instead of waiting to cure it when it develops?"

The answer was amazingly simple. There was just not enough of the drug to permit prophylactic doses for everybody (and nobody knew when we would ever get any more once the attic supply was gone), so that it was better to leave undisturbed the natural immunity and resistance, which the majority of the population enjoyed, rather than to make them become dependent on a drug which just wasn't available in adequate amounts!

Because the Holy Scripture is sufficient, containing the whole counsel of God, we need have no fear of running in short supply for the spiritual illnesses of man. There is enough for all to eat and be filled, and be healed forever.[5]

But not only is there an abundance for all men, there is an abundance in God's curative Word to bring healing for all kinds of soul-sickness. There is no malady of the soul for which there is not a corresponding medicine in the Bible.

When the soul feels guilty before God, there is a prescription in the Bible. "Though your sins be as scarlet, they shall be as white as snow; though they be red like crimson, they shall be as wool" (Isaiah 1:18).

When the soul feels lonely, there is a prescription in the Bible. "He hath said, I will never leave thee, nor forsake thee. So that we may boldly say, The Lord *is* my helper, and I will not fear what man shall do unto me" (Hebrews 13:5, 6).

When the soul feels weak, there is a prescription in the Bible. "My grace is sufficient for thee: for my strength is made perfect in weakness" (2 Corinthians 12:9).

When the soul feels gloomy and sorrowful, there is a prescription in the Bible. "The joy of the LORD is your strength" (Nehemiah 8:10).

When the soul feels tempted, there is a prescription in the Bible. "We have not an high priest which cannot be touched with the feeling of our infirmities; but was in all points tempted like as *we are, yet* without sin. Let us therefore come boldly unto the throne of grace, that we may obtain mercy, and find grace to help in time of need" (Hebrews 4:15, 16).

There is, in short, a plenitude in the Bible that points to its divine origin, an abundance that meets the need of every human heart. The inspired Word is indeed "profitable for doctrine, for reproof, for correction, for instruction in righteousness" (2 Timothy 3:16).

Its Administering

"He [God] sent his word, and healed them." God's Word must be dispensed to needy hearts. Thus we must think of the *administering* of God's Word.

Those who dispense God's Word must do so with definiteness. They must know man's condition, and they must announce the remedy with assurance.

They must also dispense it with discernment. They must be able to diagnose the patient's problem and to prescribe the exact remedy.

Thomas Ken describes the ideal pastor in these words:

> In God's own Word and Sacred Learning versed,
> Deep in the study of the heart immersed,
> Who in such souls can the disease descry,
> And wisely fair restoratives supply.[6]

We must take care lest they become like the quack doctor reported by a missionary:

> Once the camel driver of a medical missionary caused a lot of tabloid medicines to be thrown from the camel's back and scattered over the sands. They were all mixed up, could not be separated, and so were left lying on the ground.
>
> But one of the quack native doctors gathered them up, and some years later, the medical missionary called on him and found on a shelf a large bottle labelled "Assorted Pills." "These," said he, "are more sought after than any of my drugs. I give them only to patients whose cases I do not understand."[7]

We must not go to our Bibles as that native doctor went to his bottle of "Assorted Pills." The Bible is a complete pharmacopoeia. It contains a cure for every ill. But we must know in detail its contents, and be able to prescribe with discernment.

Amos R. Wells wrote this allegory to drive home this point:

> Once upon a time there was an apothecary, the only drug seller in a certain country neighborhood. He was a lazy fellow, and, as he had bought the establishment from another druggist, he had actually never looked over his stock to see what it contained. He was acquainted with a few of the bottles, and when the farmers came in for their remedies, if he did not know where to find what was asked for, he would persuade them to take their doses from one of the bottles he knew about. That community, therefore, got pretty well dosed with quinine and camphor and ipecac and a few other drugs, and the doctors grumbled, and the people died.
>
> Well, one day the apothecary's oldest son was taken suddenly and violently ill, and the doctor that was called in

declared, with a very sober face, that nothing on earth could save the lad's life except a certain rare medicine. There was some of it in the stock of the late druggist, he was sure, and he had no doubt it had not been used up; but where was it? Almost frantic, the foolish apothecary turned his store upside down, fairly throwing the bottles here and there in his anxiety to hit upon the right one.

And while he was hunting, his boy died.

You think there never was so foolish an apothecary? Probably not. But there are just as foolish men and women by the hundred thousand. For the Bible is our pharmacy, crammed by the Great Physician with whatever is needed for a sick soul going down to death. And how few of us have even read it clear through to find out what is in it, to learn, as it were, the names on the outside of the bottles, so that, for a case of doubt or sorrow or of trouble of any kind, we can put our hands at once upon the right remedy! Alas, how few![8]

In dispensing God's Word we should be like the pastor referred to by Walter B. Knight:

During World War II, a fine Christian girl was engaged to a serviceman who was overseas. One morning she received a telegram from the War Department, whose opening words ominously said: "We regret to inform you . . . ." Something snapped in the girl's mind. She lapsed into unconsciousness, which lasted for days. A faithful pastor cooperated with doctors and stood faithfully by, doing his best to bring the girl out of her dazed condition. As he prayed, this thought came to him: "I'm going to read the Word of God to her, whether she can hear me or not." He began to read comforting, reassuring verses and chapters.

Suddenly the pent-up sorrow and emotions of the girl burst forth into a profusion of tears. Her tears presently ceased. She said to her mother, "It's all right now!"

In relating what occurred when the pastor began to read God's Word, she said, "At first his voice sounded far away and unreal. Then, as I listened to the familiar passages, the words came closer and closer. Finally they seemed to reach my heart!"[9]

Its Acceptance

"He [God] sent his word, and healed them." We have considered the appropriateness, the ability, the abundance, and the administration of God's curative Word. But we must also consider the *acceptance* of God's curative Word.

God has given us His Word to cure us of the sicknesses of the soul, but that Word must be accepted. It is not enough to admire God's remedy; it must be applied. It is not enough to praise it; we must also prove it.

The Bible introduces to us Naaman, five-star general of the Syrian army. We are told that he was a "great man with his master, and honourable . . . *but he was* a leper" (2 Kings 5:1). His greatness was overshadowed by his grief, his position by his problem.

When God's Word came to Naaman, he objected to the terms of Elisha's instruction. He refused to accept the remedy proposed by the prophet. Elisha told him to dip in the Jordan river seven times.

Here's how the Bible describes Naaman's reaction: "But Naaman was wroth, and went away, and said, Behold, I thought, He will surely come out to me, and stand, and call on the name of the LORD his God, and strike his hand over the place, and recover the leper. *Are* not Abana and Pharpar, rivers of Damascus, better than all the waters of Israel? may I not wash in them, and be clean?" (2 Kings 5:11, 12).

Many people in our modern society are like Naaman. They suffer from the dread disease of sin. They want to be cured—at least, with reference to its outward manifestations. But they object to the simplicity of the plan of salvation. They have all kinds of "thoughts" as to what should be done in their case. They want an impressive miracle to be worked. But when they are faced with a cure that simply demands faith and obedience, they are disgusted and become infuriated. They are not prepared to accept God's way of salvation, God's cure for sin.

It is at such times that people turn to other alternatives. Naaman thought the rivers of his own land were vastly superior to the muddy Jordan.

Some people when they are faced with God's demands turn to good works as an alternative. Others turn to religion. Some try education. Some try morality. But these alternatives are totally inadequate and insufficient. No healing can be obtained from them. It is only as we come to Christ that we receive healing.

G. Franklin Allee tells us that some years ago in Galveston, Texas, Shott's Drug Store celebrated the fact that their doors had not been closed by night or by day for a period of twenty-six years. Huge stacks of prescriptions, hundreds of thousands that had been filled during that period of years, were on display, and above them a sign that read, "TRUSTED ONE MILLION TIMES."[10]

What would be the number if we placed a similar sign over the Bible? God's curative Word has brought healing of soul to millions of people down through the centuries. The Bible can be trusted.

"He [God] sent his word, and healed them." Are you receiving daily healing through daily heeding of God's Word?

FOR YOUR FURTHER STUDY

1. From the standpoint of the Bible what is wrong with modern man?
2. What is wrong with modern man's diagnosis of himself?
3. Can you list ten sicknesses of the soul for which there is a remedy in the Bible?

Wise Words as Goads

The sacred writings of Israel are endowed with a deeply penetrating power, in distinction from all worldly literature, which can only produce a superficial impression, and is incapable of stirring the deepest depths of the mind and the heart.

—F.W. Hengstenberg

"The words of the wise are as goads." Goads were the sharp, pointed sticks used to urge on the lagging cattle while ploughing. Such are the words of God when brought home by the Holy Spirit to the hearts and consciences of men—piercing, penetrating to the inmost depths the most secret recesses of man's nature, and laying his whole soul bare before God.

—Frederick Whitfield

The purpose of goads is to prod the sluggish to action. God's proverbs do that. They bear in them power to give a mental and spiritual stimulus.

—H.C. Leupold

A goad is a stick with a spike on the end, used to induce the oxen to go a little faster. Wise words are stimulating. Our preaching must result in action. Wise words are never pointless; they are sharp and stimulating. Sometimes they prick the conscience and cut the heart, resulting in hatred and opposition; such preaching cost Stephen his life. Sometimes the stimulation results in conversion, sometimes in spiritual progress.

—Ron Jordahl

There is no other volume which so stimulates the mind and enlightens the intellect.

—Bob Jones, Jr.

There is no part of the Word of God that does not bring refreshment, power, and stimulus into your lives.

—A.F. Schauffler

STUDY 11
God's Word Is Stimulative

Our Key Scripture—"The words of the wise *are* as goads" (Ecclesiastes 12:11).

Supplementary Scriptures—1 Samuel 13:21; Acts 9:5; 26:14.

"THE words of the wise *are* as goads." So wrote Solomon, the man to whom God gave "a wise and an understanding heart" (1 Kings 3:12). As one endued with wisdom Solomon coined three thousand proverbs (1 Kings 4:32). Since God's Word is a book of wisdom, we may rightly apply Solomon's simile to the Scriptures. "The words of the wise"—and of this blessed Book — "*are* as goads."

A goad, of course, is a pointed stick used by farmers to urge on an ox or a donkey that is loathe to get moving or is tempted to slow down. It is most interesting to learn that the English verb *to stimulate* comes from a Latin word to goad on, to incite, to spur on as with a goad.

With the etymology of the word *stimulate* before us, we may describe the Word of God as being stimulative. God's Word comes to us not merely as good advice, but as authoritative counsel, demanding action on our part, rousing us to respond to God's directions.

Before we examine this capacity of God's Word, we should note that there are current today other stimulants—philosophies and ideologies—that excite the minds and hearts of men. These other stimulants generally vie with the Bible, and drive men and women to seek goals that are detrimental to their spiritual well-being. The most subtle of these false stimulants is that which employs the words of Scripture, but which at the same time empties those words of their true meanings and exploits them for purposes which in actual fact are contrary to God's will.

BASIC OUTLINE

Considering now the words of the Bible as goads, we propose to examine three aspects of the stimulative power of the Scriptures: The words of the Bible stimulate us to seek *salvation, sanctification,* and *service.* These three aspects, in a sense, are comprehensive of the believer's life. Christian life begins with personal salvation; it is vitally related to sanctification, and it is made manifest in service.

Salvation

The words of the Bible stimulate us to seek *salvation.* The sharp point of the Scriptures arouses us to call upon God for His help in our plight.

In both personal and professional evangelism today it is popular to approach the sinner on the ground of what the Gospel can do for him. The Gospel is offered not as initially condemning him but as marvellously complementing him. The sinner is offered "love, security, peace, purpose, and eternal destiny" (from a tract).

While it is true that the Gospel does indeed offer to the sinner a solution to his problems, it seems to us that one major emphasis of the New Testament is upon awakening man to his real condition and his present condemnation by the law of a holy and just God.

The Bible, in other words, stimulates man to seek salvation by putting before him simply and solemnly the true nature of his state before God. The words of the Bible become sharp goads in the hands of the Holy Spirit to startle sinners into a realization of their terrible condition in God's sight. The presentation of man and his need may not be popular, but surely we neglect it to our own loss.

Various writers have drawn attention to the importance of presenting what the Bible teaches about man and his plight.

E.A. Stuart wrote:

> There can be no real awakening and permanent results without the presentation of doctrine. There is an evangelism

prompted by the lust of numbers that plays upon emotionalism for its success. Such evangelism thinks more of statistics than spirituality. It is like a bunch of burning shavings; it blazes up for a moment, and is soon out. It lacks support; it has no bones; it is weak, and soon drops by the wayside. Paul was the greatest of evangelists and theologians. His letters are heavy with doctrine. The abiding evangelism not only stirs but establishes.[1]

In his book, *The Revival We Need*, Dr. O.J. Smith quotes J.H. Lord as affirming:

There is another gospel, too popular in the present day, which seems to exclude conviction of sin and repentance from the scheme of salvation; which demands from the sinner a mere intellectual assent to the fact of his guilt and sinfulness, and a like intellectual assent to the fact and sufficiency of Christ's atonement; and, such assent yielded, tells him to go in peace, and to be happy in the assurance that the Lord Jesus has made it right between his soul and God; thus crying peace, peace, when there is no peace.

Flimsy and false conversions of this sort may be one reason why so many who assume the Christian profession dishonour God and bring reproach on the Church by their inconsistent lives, and by their ultimate relapses into worldliness and sin. The whole counsel of God must be declared. "By the law is the knowledge of sin." Sin must be felt before it can be mourned. Sinners must sorrow before they can be comforted.[2]

We must use the words of the Bible, therefore, as goads to awaken men and women to a realization of their terrible predicament.

We must use, for example, the Bible's teaching about sin as *disobedience*. Man has not failed in an honest attempt to please God; he has failed because he has been disobedient to the divine command. In Adam we have a very clear example of disobedience. Commanded to abstain from the fruit of the tree of the knowledge of good and evil, Adam responded to his wife's enticement and partook of the forbidden fruit. His partaking was an expression of an inner attitude toward God; the essence of his sin was direct disobedience to God.

We must also use as goads the words of the Bible with regard to sin as defiance. Man is disobedient, but he is not repentant. He raises his fist in the face of God. He defies the authority of God and goes on resisting God's appeals to him to be reconciled.

In Saul of Tarsus we have one whose latent antagonism to God and His moral standard had broken out into direct defiance against God. When he was struck to the earth as he rode toward Damascus, he exclaimed: "Who art thou, Lord?" And the Lord answered: "I am Jesus whom thou persecutest: *it is* hard for thee to kick against the pricks" (Acts 9:5).

We are nowhere told precisely what these pricks were. The illustration is drawn from agriculture. Saul was acting like an obstinate ox harnessed to the plough. The goad was being used on him, and he was kicking out wildly at the goad and at the wielder of the goad.

Was the goad the Old Testament, and were the pricks the impact of God's Word upon the conscience and heart of Saul as he opposed the Lord Jesus? Had Saul been stung wide awake by various passages of the Old Testament that pointed to Jesus of Nazareth as being the Messiah? And was Saul lashing out in anger and in prejudice against the Holy Spirit?

The same idea is found in Acts 2:37. After Peter's message on the Day of Pentecost, we read that when the audience heard his defence of Jesus as the Messiah, "they were pricked in their heart, and said unto Peter and to the rest of the apostles, Men *and* brethren, what shall we do?"

The words of Peter were as goads, and pierced the hearts of his hearers. In their case they responded positively and asked for further instruction. In Saul's case he lashed out at the words of the Gospel.

We must show to men that sin is disobedience and defiance. We must also show to them that sin is defilement. Sin contaminates. It pollutes. It blackens. It defiles. This is the uniform teaching of the Scriptures. But God is pure and holy, and cannot permit that which is defiled to come into His presence with favour. The defiled sinner is the damned sinner.

"The words of the wise *are* as goads." We are wise, therefore, when we employ the words and concepts of the Bible to present to man his plight and predicament. The facts of his condition, driven home by the Holy Spirit, will force him to cry out to God for mercy and pardon.

Sanctification

The words of the Bible act as goads to drive us to seek salvation. They also drive us to seek *sanctification*.

The words of the Bible goad us into seeking sanctification of life in three ways.

First, the Bible gives us exhortations, commands, warnings, entreaties, and appeals. From cover to cover there are words of wisdom arousing us to cleanse ourselves from all filthiness of the flesh and of the spirit.

Whatever other reasons we may be able to list for the believer's sanctification, this one surely tops the list. It is because God has commanded us in His Word. Here's how Peter states the case: "But as he which hath called you is holy, so be ye holy in all manner of conversation; Because it is written, Be ye holy; for I am holy" (1 Peter 1:15, 16).

Those words, quoted by Peter from Leviticus 11:44, are a goad to the believer, providing motivation for him to be holy.

It is not our purpose here to give a list of Scripture passages which act as goads for the believer in the matter of sanctification. The Holy Spirit is not shut up to a human list of such passages. He may take a passage and use it as a goad in the life of one believer that is never so used in the life of another believer.

But, on the other hand, it is absolutely necessary for us to be exposed constantly to the teaching—and the prodding—of the Holy Spirit in the Word of God.

But the Holy Spirit uses examples, as well as exhortations to arouse in us a desire to purify ourselves. All of us probably have one or two "favourite" Bible characters, from the record of whose lives we draw inspiration and instruction. It may be Abraham, or David, or Jeremiah, or Paul. As we read their biographies, we hear them saying, "Brethren, be followers together of me" (Philippians 3:17).

I have read that a member of the English House of Lords was accustomed to pass through an art gallery on his way to work. One day his son asked him why he visited this art gallery daily. The father asked his son to accompany him. When they reached the painting of the statesman's mother, he stopped and said to his boy, "I come here every morning and look into the face of my mother that I may receive the stimulus and inspiration that come from a consideration of her wonderful life. After seeing her picture I cannot think ignoble thoughts or do ignoble deeds."[3]

And shall we not go into God's art gallery every day and look at the portraits of the great cloud of witnesses? Shall we not receive inspiration and stimulation from a consideration of their lives?

Finally, we must note that the Holy Spirit employs the encouragements of His Word as goads in the life of the believer. The promises of the Word become prods to get us moving faster in the way of holiness.

Here again is how Peter explains the provision and purpose of the divine promises:

> Grace and peace be multiplied unto you through the knowledge of God, and of Jesus our Lord, According as his divine power hath given unto us all things that *pertain* unto life and godliness, through the knowledge of Him that hath called us to glory and virtue: Whereby are given unto us exceeding great and precious promises: that by these ye might be partakers of the divine nature (2 Peter 1:2–4).

The divine promises are given for daily progress in sanctification. In 2 Corinthians 7:1 Paul exhorts believers in these words: "Having therefore these promises, dearly beloved, let us cleanse ourselves from all filthiness of the flesh and spirit, perfecting holiness in the fear of God."

There is one caution that we must give with regard to the appropriation of God's promises. While our application of the Bible must be based upon the principles of hermeneutics (that is, the laws of interpretation), we must not, on the other hand, starve ourselves because we apportion out everything to other people and leave nothing for ourselves.

The wife of John Fletcher wrote an account of her life from childhood, and in that account she said:

> I was not, I believe, above ten years old, and can recollect many comfortable moments in reading the Word of God. The promises in Isaiah were in a particular manner applied to my soul: and I hardly ever opened the Bible but there was something for me: till one day I heard a person make the remark that "many people take promises to themselves which do not belong to them." Of some, she observed, they belonged to the Church, others to the Jews, and such to the Gentiles, etc., and then began to blame the presumption of those who apply them to their own souls!
>
> Such a thought never entered my heart before. I knew the words were primarily spoken on particular occasions; but the Lord had led me to believe that His Word was written to every soul so far as they were willing to receive it by faith. But from the above conversation I was unhinged. I knew not what to choose or what to refuse; so that, being cast into reasonings, I lost all my love for reading the Scriptures and sank into a very cold and lifeless state.[4]

It is said that Mrs. Fletcher did not recover from this shock to her simple faith in God's Word for many years.

We like what that great preacher of a past generation wrote about the understanding of God's promises. T. DeWitt Talmage said:

> Put down all the promises of the Bible on a table for study and put on one side of the table a man who has never had any trouble or very little of it and pile upon the table beside him all the encyclopedias, and all dictionaries, and all archaeologies, and all commentaries; and on the other side of the table put a man who has had trial after trial, disaster upon disaster, and let him begin the study of the promises without the

lexicon, without commentary, without any book to explain or help, and this latter man will understand far more of the height and depth and length and breadth of these promises than the learned exegete opposite, almost submerged in sacred literature.[5]

Service

God's Word acts as a goad to spur us on to seek salvation, sanctification, and, of course, *service*.

It is not stretching the truth to say that an entire volume could be written outlining the influence and impact of specific passages of God's Word on the hearts of His people, constraining them to undertake service for Him. Here, too, it has been proved that "the words of the wise *are* as goads."

Such texts as Matthew 28:18–20; Luke 9:62; Romans 1:16; 10:13–15; 12:1, 2; 2 Corinthians 5:14–21; and many other passages have been used by the Holy Spirit to constrain believers into becoming submissive yoke-fellows with the Lord Jesus Christ.

Such texts have served a two-fold purpose; they have encouraged believers to commence serving the Lord and have encouraged believers to continue serving the Lord.

First, God often employs His Word as a goad to encourage reluctant believers to commence serving Him.

Take Romans 12:1 as an example of such a verse. Paul writes: "I beseech you therefore, brethren, by the mercies of God, that ye present your bodies a living sacrifice, holy, acceptable unto God, *which is* your reasonable service." How many consecration messages have been based upon this passage! And how often has the Holy Spirit employed it as a goad in His hands to bring a foolish believer to his senses and to produce submission to His will!

But God's Word has also acted as a goad in the hearts of His people that they might continue serving Him.

It is easy for the ox pulling the plough to be distracted by sights and sounds that lie outside the sphere of his owner's work. On the other hand, the animal may become tired and refuse to continue pulling the plough. At such times the master may use the goad to compel the animal to continue.

Many illustrations could be given of the stimulative power of verses of Scripture in the lives of Christian workers and missionaries.

Matthew 28:20 with its promise of Christ's presence with His own until the end of the age, has been a tremendous stimulus to those working in hard places. James Gilmour, for example, a missionary among the nomad Mongols, found that verse to be immensely encouraging. In his lonely task he wrote:

> Companions I can scarcely hope to meet, and the feeling of being alone comes over me till I think of Christ and His blessed promise, "Lo, I am with you alway, *even* unto the end of the world."
>
> No one who does not go away, leaving all and being alone, can feel the force of this promise; and when I feel my heart threatening to go down, I betake myself to this companionship, and, thank God, I have felt the blessedness of this promise rushing over me repeatedly when I have knelt down and spoken to Jesus as a present companion, from whom I was sure to find sympathy.[6]

That is the stimulative power of God's Word, constraining His lonely, weary, and discouraged servants to continue at their task.

Is God prodding you with some verse of His Word? Is he goading you in order to awaken and arouse you? Then be not as the rebellious ox or ass. Do not kick against the pricks. Rather, submit to Him whether it be for salvation, sanctification, or service.

FOR YOUR FURTHER STUDY

1. Are you able to give any passage of Scripture that God has used as a goad in your life?
2. What reasons might there be in our lives for God to use His Word as a goad?
3. How should we respond when God employs His Word as a goad in our lives?

A Nail in a Sure Place

The words of the wise are "as nails fastened"—fastened in the memory, like nails driven home with the mighty power of a master hand. When used by the Holy Spirit, they pierce like the "goads," and are fastened in the memory like nails.

—Frederick Whitfield

Pithy sentences are like sharp nails which force truth upon our memory.

—Denis Diderot

If God makes use both of words which stir the mind and words which steady it, we may be sure that you and I have need of both.

—W.M. MacGregor

Read the Bible, and read it again, and do not despair of help to understand something of the will and mind of God, though you think they are fast locked up from you. Neither trouble yourself, though you have not commentaries and expositions; pray and read, and read and pray; for a little from God is better than a great deal from man; also, what is from man is uncertain, and is often lost and tumbled over by man, but what is from God is fixed as a nail in a sure place.

—John Bunyan

As a young preacher, Dr. Harry A. Ironside visited the aged Alexander Fraser and listened enthralled as one truth after another was opened up from God's Word by Mr. Fraser. Finally the young preacher could constrain himself no longer and cried out, "Where did you learn these things?"

"On my knees on the mud floor of a little sod cottage in the north of Ireland," replied Mr. Fraser. "There, with my Bible open before me, I used to kneel for hours at a time, and ask the Spirit of God to reveal Christ to my soul and to open the Word to my heart."

In one of his sermons Charles H. Spurgeon offers a prayer that could well be used as a pattern for every preacher before proclaiming God's Word: "O Thou great Master of assemblies, make our words as goads to the conscience, and fasten them as nails in the memory!"

STUDY 12
God's Word Is Penetrative

Our Key Scripture—"The words of the wise *are* as goads, and as nails fastened *by* the masters of assemblies, *which* are given from one shepherd" (Ecclesiastes 12:11).

Supplementary Scriptures—Judges 4:21; 5:26; Ezra 9:8; Isaiah 22:23, 25; 41:7; Jeremiah 10:4; Zechariah 10:4; Colossians 2:14.

FOR the want of a nail, a shoe was lost; for the want of a shoe, a horse was lost; for the want of a horse, a rider was lost; for the want of a rider, a battle was lost; for the want of a battle, a kingdom was lost.

All because of a nail! We learned the saying in our childhood, and we have never forgotten the importance of a nail, insignificant as a nail may be.

In our previous study we found that the words of God's Book, the Bible, may be compared to goads which stir and stimulate. In the same verse from which the goad symbol is taken, we learn that they may also be compared to nails. Thus by the double symbol the power of God's Word both to stimulate and to strengthen is brought before us.

BASIC OUTLINE

Let us consider simply how the words of God maybe compared to nails by studying the *form*, the *function*, the *fastening*, and the *fidelity* of a nail.

Its Form

Consider, first, the *form* of the nail. Nails vary in shape and size, but basically each nail has a point, a body, and a head.

Give Me That Book!

God's Word may be considered as a box filled with "nail" verses, and it is most helpful to keep in mind the form of a nail.

First, each of these "nail" texts has a point. The Bible is full of "pointed" exhortations, appeals, warnings, and cautions. These hortatory passages are sharp, and penetrate the heart when hammered in by the hand of faith. On the Day of Pentecost, after Peter had preached, we read that his hearers "were pricked in their heart." Through the power of the Spirit Peter had hammered his words home into the hearts of his audience.

Here is a definite word for the preachers and teachers of God's Word. You must employ the sharp nails of Scripture in your ministry. Your preaching must not be "pointless" (no reference here to homiletic outlines!). We refer, of course, to the fact that your preaching must use the sharp words of God that pierce and penetrate the heart.

G.B.F. Hallock tells of a sailor who had just returned from a whaling expedition. Wanting to attend church on the Sunday, he asked a friend where he should go to hear a good sermon. His friend directed him to one of the large churches in the town.

Afterward the sailor was asked by his friend how he liked the sermon. "Not much," replied the whaler. "It was like a ship leaving for the whale-fishing—everything shipshape: anchors, cordage, sails, and provisions all right, but there were no harpoons on board!"[1]

How many sermons are like that whaling-ship. They reflect all the principles of homiletics. They contain outline, illustrations and exposition. But they have no harpoons on board. They have no piercing power. They never stir the congregation out of slumber. They never catch souls for Christ.

But, in addition to a point, a nail must have body. This reminds us that every exhortation of Scripture has a proper contextual meaning. There is "body" to every point in Scripture.

The preacher, then, must be careful in his application of God's Word to make sure that he is giving to his text its proper meaning. One mark of Spirit-filled preaching is that the preacher is able to relate his text and its context to the immediate needs of his audience. The preacher has so meditated in the passage that he has understood the relevance of the whole passage to his hearers.

A sermon is not an oration, or an essay, or a lecture; it is a message, and the preacher must learn to apply the truth of his text to the hearts of his congregation. This will inevitably involve getting at the body of the truth in the passage from which his text is chosen.

All of us have had the frustrating experience of trying to hammer in a little nail that has so little body to it that we cannot grasp it in our fingers. It has point, but too little body. We have also listened to preachers who were attempting to hammer home a point, and their message was filled with exhortation, admonition, and warning, but their sermon obviously had too little body to it, and they were not able to get the point of their text driven home.

But each nail also has a head. Point is good, body is better, but head is best! The head is that which takes the blows of the hammer. It is the strongest part of the nail. Without a head the body of the nail might bend or be broken. The head provides strength for the penetration of point and body.

Likewise with regard to the preacher's text: there is a point, there is a body, and there is a head. The head of each text of the Bible is the Bible doctrine which the preacher must hammer home. The preacher must hit the nail on the head. He must explain the basis of his appeal. He must demonstrate that the message of the body of his text is in direct agreement with the teaching of the Bible on the subject he has chosen. "Exhortation without doctrine," stated C.H. Spurgeon, "is like powder without shot."[2]

This means for the interpretation and application of any one text of the Bible the preacher must know the whole Bible. Without an adequate presentation of the Bible's teaching the nail of truth may bend or buckle. Our nails must have heads!

Its Function

We can learn spiritual truth from the form of a nail; the *function* of the nail also helps us to understand Solomon's saying: "The words of the wise *are* ... as nails."

First, nails are used to hold things together. This is the aspect of strength.

Give Me That Book!

In a passage of high sarcasm Isaiah pictures an idol being made. "So the carpenter encouraged the goldsmith, *and* he that smootheth *with* the hammer him that smote the anvil, saying, It *is* ready for the sodering: and he fastened it with nails, *that* it should not be moved" (Isaiah 41:7). Even the idol-maker knows the value of a nail.

Let the preacher not be outwitted by the **idol-maker**! Nails hold things together, and in a day when things are falling apart morally and spiritually the preacher should be hammering in the nails of God's Word.

It is God's Word of wisdom that holds the **individual** together. Many a life is falling apart because of the constant storms of suffering and pain and temptation. Let the man of God repair such lives with words of wisdom, spoken in love and discernment. There are nails in the Bible for the individual.

It is God's Word that holds **families** together. In his counselling let the pastor employ the nails of Scripture to bring together husband and wife, parent and child, brother and sister. In the Bible are words of counsel that will bring ruptured relationships back into harmony, and fractured lives into a condition of wholeness and beauty.

It is God's Word that holds **churches** together. How prone churches are to fall to pieces! How many are in a state of disrepair. Division has marred the fellowship of God's people in many places, and there is need for one of God's "carpenters" to bring separated Christians together in the fellowship of the Gospel.

It is God's Word that holds **nations** together. Let a nation build its national structures using God's Word as the nails with which to bind the diverse factors and factions together, and there is hope of national unity and cohesion. Let a nation reject God's Word and the principles of righteousness and morality set forth therein, and that nation will fall apart at the seams.

Charles Edwards wrote:

> Nails are very common things, but they are sharp and short, bright and useful, safe and sure; so are Bible truths, and the practical qualities of the nails will illustrate the spiritual

force of the Word of life. Good nails clench and hold and make our work secure, so there are words of love that stick and hold and fix our hearts to God for eternal life when they have been driven home by the hammer of the Word, and by the power of the Holy Spirit.[3]

How nails help to hold things together! But they also help to hold things up! This is the aspect of support. Most commentators agree that when Solomon refers to nails, he has in mind actually tent pegs. Those who have struggled with a tent in a gale know exactly the function of such tent pegs. They provide essential support for the tent. And woe betide the person who neglects to hammer the tent pegs well into the ground.

There are many aspects of the Church's ministry that need to be strengthened by the nails of Scripture.

In Isaiah, we read: "Enlarge the place of thy tent, and let them stretch forth the curtains of thine habitations: spare not, lengthen thy cords, and strengthen thy stakes" (Isaiah 54:2).

It was William Carey who saw in this text a message for the church concerning its missionary responsibility. In his famous missionary sermon he enunciated two great principles from this verse: "Expect great things from God; attempt great things for God."[4]

But note that when the church expands her missionary program, she must "strengthen her stakes." May we suggest that this involves a deeper understanding of and greater commitment to the church's mission and message. The preacher must carefully instruct the members of his church with regard to the church's missionary obligation, and he must use the nails of scriptural teaching in his endeavour.

There is the Bible nail of truth concerning the lostness of all men apart from salvation in Christ Jesus. There is the nail concerning the church's commission to go into all the world. There is the nail concerning making disciples and establishing churches.

Using these Bible nails, the pastor can enlarge the program of his church, at the same time strengthening the stakes.

Give Me That Book!

Years ago, William Luff appealed to all Christian workers to use the Bible nails:

> You workers with the Carpenter, within this box behold
>
> The nails you need: sharp-pointed nails, and nails with heads of gold;
>
> The truth their point—their golden heads, the brightness of His grace,
>
> Who is the one true shining Nail fixed in God's holy place.
>
> Would you hang pictures on the wall of human heart and mind?
>
> Take hence your choice; God-guided, you the needed nails will find.
>
> Would you secure some cedar beam, or train some vagrant vine,
>
> Or fasten down some secret thing, some chest of wealth divine?
>
> Would you slay Sisera again, the modern foe of truth?
>
> For lowly work, or highest dome; for manhood, age, or youth,
>
> The nails are here—and blood-stained nails, that tell the old, old tale.
>
> Go work with these; drive these well home; such work will never fail.[5]

Its Fastening

In our study we have considered the form and the function of a nail; it will be profitable to look also at how a nail is to be *fastened*.

We suggest three simple steps.

First, the nail must be selected. A carpenter, skilled in his trade, knows exactly which type of nail will best do the job he is working at. Expertly he selects the kind of nail which will be the most fitting.

A man of God should know his Bible better than the carpenter knows his nails. The preacher should be able to select the precise text needed for a particular need. He should be so at home in the Bible from Genesis to Revelation that the Holy Spirit will guide him to the passage best suited to meet the needs of his hearers.

Imagine a carpenter not knowing what kind of a nail he should use! Surely such a tradesman would be considered inept and unqualified. The preacher who is constantly selecting texts of Scripture not related to the needs of his flock is surely no less unqualified.

But, second, the nail must be aimed. The experienced carpenter knows how to hold the nail, and how to aim it so that it will do the most good. Ah, preacher, here is the challenge for you! Are you aiming your text properly? Amateur carpenters know the frustration of trying to hammer in a nail that has not been aimed right to begin with! Oh, the disappointment (and embarrassment) of raising the board and discovering that the nail has never come through at all, but has been deflected due to a poor aim!

If, then, our texts are going to be driven home, they must be aimed right as we commence the message. The listener must understand from the beginning that the preacher intends to apply the truth of his text directly to his heart. The preacher is not in the pulpit to expound on the composition or the manufacture of the Bible nail he has selected. He is not there merely to deliver an oration on the qualities of the Bible. He is there to aim the truth of his text at his hearer's heart.

Finally, a nail must be driven into the board. This requires force and action.

With regard to hammering in the nail, Prairie staff member Ron Jordahl shares this insight:

> In working with carpenters I picked up an excellent expression. One man with a hammer in hand will place a board in the approximate position. Another man will measure

or sight the accuracy of placement and advise, "Up a fraction," or "Down a hair." When it is just right, he says, "Nail it!"

To me this is a meaningful expression. It means more than, "You now have the board in the proper position." It means that decided action can be taken; as if the workman were to say, "I will stand on this decision. With the nail in it, the board records my judgment for the foreman's inspection and the homeowner's pleasure."

As preachers and teachers we are not to be side-stepping and skirting issues. When we have come to a conclusion, the writer of Ecclesiastes here says, choose your words well and nail the truth. Drive it home, sink it in, make an end of it.[6]

Here is Paxton Hood, as quoted by C.H. Spurgeon, on this very point:

Some preachers expect too much of their hearers; they take a number of truths into the pulpit as a man might carry up a box of nails; and then, supposing the congregation to be posts, they take out a nail, and expect it to get into the post by itself.

Now that is not the way to do it. You must take your nail, hold it up against the post, hammer it in, and then clinch it on the other side; and then it is that you may expect the great Master of assemblies to fasten the nails so that they will not fall out.[7]

An unknown poet has captured the truth in the following words:

It should have in it many an ardent prayer,
To reach the heart, and fix and fasten there;
When God and man are mutually addressed,
God grants a blessing, man is truly blessed.

It should be closely, well applied at last,
To make the moral nail securely fast;
Thou art the man, and thou alone will make
A Felix tremble and a David quake.[8]

Its Fidelity

It is profitable to consider the analogies that exist between God's Word and the carpenter's nails. In our study we have traced these analogies with regard to the form, the function, and the fastening of a nail. Our final thought relates to the *fidelity* of the nail when hammered into place. Herein lies the real value of the nail; it is as the nail remains fastened and fixed that it accomplishes its purpose.

As the preacher employs Bible nails in his message, he has a number of assurances that God's Word will remain faithful to its task.

First, the Bible is the product of the Spirit's inspiration. In our key text we read: "The words of the wise *are* as ... nails fastened by the masters of assemblies, which are given from one shepherd." In the light of the total teaching of the Scriptures, who can that one shepherd be, but the Lord Jesus Christ, "the chief Shepherd" (1 Peter 5:4)? Let the preacher be conscious that he is giving the words of Christ, and his confidence in those words will be greatly increased.

Paul thanked God that the Thessalonian believers received the word of God "not *as* the word of men, but as it is in truth, the word of God, which effectually worketh also in you that believe" (1 Thessalonians 2:13).

Second, the preacher has the assurance that the Bible is the instrument of the Spirit's work. The Bible is the sword of the Spirit (Hebrews 4:12). As the preacher employs what God has provided and commanded to be used, he can look to God to bless that Word.

Third, the preacher has the assurance that the Bible is the reflection of the Spirit's nature. "Thy testimonies," affirmed the psalmist, "*are* righteous and very faithful" (Psalm 119:138). As the preacher uses the nails of Scripture to do God's work, he knows that God's Word will remain fixed in the hearts of his hearers.

We bring our study to a close by quoting once again that prince of preachers, C.H. Spurgeon:

> There is a story told—though I will not vouch for the truth of it—of a certain countryman, who had been persuaded by some one that all Londoners were thieves; and, therefore, on

coming to London for the first time, he tried to secure his watch by putting it into his waistcoat pocket, and then covering it all over with fish-hooks.

"Now," he thought, "if any gentleman tries to get my watch, he will remember it!"

The story says that, as he was walking along, he desired to know the time himself, and put his own hand into his pocket, forgetting all about the fish-hooks. The effect produced upon him can better be imagined than described.

Now it seems to me that a sermon should always be like that countryman's pocket, full of fish-hooks, so that if anybody comes in to listen to it, he will get some forget-me-not, some remembrancer, fastened in his ear and, it may be, in his heart and conscience. Let him drop in just at the end of the discourse, there should be something at the close that will strike and stick. As when we walk in our farmer friends' fields, there are certain burrs that are sure to cling to our clothes; and brush as we may, some of the relics of the fields remain upon our garments, so there ought to be some burr in every sermon that will stick to those who hear it.[9]

A good motto, then, for every preacher and teacher of God's Word would be: Every text a nail! Those engaged in the ministry of the Word should study how to drive home their text so that their preaching will strengthen and stabilize God's people in a day of storm.

FOR YOUR FURTHER STUDY

1. What must the preacher do before it can be said of him that he "hit the nail on the head"?
2. What did C.H. Spurgeon mean when he said: "Exhortation without doctrine is like powder without shot"?
3. Using the analogy of a nail, show how Paul discusses various aspects of the Bible's ministry in 2 Timothy 3:16.

The Power of God's Word

The Word of God to those that hug their sin can only be as fire, a hammer, and a sharp, two-edged sword.

—F.B. Meyer

Does any one ask how the genuine Word of God may be recognized? The answer is that it is like fire, consuming all dross of thought, all habits of evil, all empty, religious forms. What though they have made their faces "harder than a rock"? There is no rock so hard that God's hammer cannot break it in pieces.

—H. Elvet Lewis

The warnings and invitations, the threatenings and promises of God's Word are the hammers by which God makes the heart contrite and the spirit broken, so that it may become good soil in which to receive and grow the seed of eternal life.

—Hugh Macmillan

God's Word is like a hammer. So that, whenever a minister has the Gospel to use, this simile should teach him how to use it; with his whole might let him strike with it mighty blows for his Lord. Hammer away, then, brethren, hammer away, with nothing but the Gospel of Christ. The heart that is struck may not yield even year after year, but it will yield at last.

—C.H. Spurgeon

Watch the stonemason at his work. One blow; ten blows; twenty; thirty; forty; nothing happens. He strikes the forty-fourth time, and, lo, the stone cleaves in two. Yet it was not that last blow that did it. Rather, it was the cumulative power of the entire forty-four, under which the molecules gradually loosened their grip upon one another and readjusted themselves for the final cleavage. So is God's Word like a hammer. Keep on prayerfully using it.

—Norman B. Harrison

Look not at the hardness of the human heart, but look at the hammer and the fire that break it in pieces.

—W.G.T. Shedd

STUDY 13
God's Word Is Destructive

Our Key Scripture—"*Is* not my word like as a fire? saith the LORD; and like a hammer *that* breaketh the rock in pieces?" (Jeremiah 23:29).

Supplementary Scriptures—Jeremiah 1:10; 5:14; 20:7–9; 23:9–40; 2 Corinthians 10:4, 5; James 3:5.

LIKE as a fire...like a hammer—involved in this two-fold figure may be many and varied points of comparison with the Word of God; its primary significance, however, seems to be the destructive capacity implicit in both symbols. As a fire God's Word devours; as a hammer it destroys. Such is the tremendous power of the Scriptures. Whatever other points of resemblance, therefore, may be put forward in explanation of these two significant symbols, it is our intention in this study to develop the destructive capacity of God's Word.

Before we examine the points of resemblance between God's Word and a fire and a hammer, let us look carefully at the setting of Jeremiah 23:29. In this chapter (especially verses 9–40) a contrast is being drawn between "the words of his holiness" (that is, Jehovah's), referred to in verse 9, and the words of the false prophets, who were deceiving God's people. In verse 28 the Lord asks: "What *is* the chaff" (that is, the message of the false prophets) "to the wheat?" (that is, the message of the true prophet). This first is lifeless and worthless; the second is living and profitable.

What, then, will happen to the words of the false prophets? What is in store for their messages of deception and falsehood? Jeremiah 23:29 is the answer to that question: "*Is* not my word like as a fire? saith the LORD; and like a hammer *that* breaketh the rock in pieces?" God's Word, we are being told, will devour and destroy the words of the false prophets.

BASIC OUTLINE

In order to elucidate this double figure we want to consider first the fact that God's Word is *powerful* in its working; second, that it is *patient* in its working; and third, that it is *purposeful* in its working.

<u>Powerful</u>

First, then, remember that God's Word is *powerful* in its working. "*Is* not my word like as a fire? saith the LORD." What can withstand the advance and appetite of fire? "Behold, how great a matter a little fire kindleth!" (James 3:5). "*Is* not my word…like a hammer *that* breaketh the rock in pieces?" Under the pounding of a great hammer the hardest stone will crack wide open.

It may be, as Bishop Samuel Wilberforce maintained, that Jeremiah's double figure reflects the mode of highway construction of his time. If the roadbuilders were hindered in their work by a large rock, they first kindled a fire and heated the rock. Then they took hammers and broke the rock in pieces.[1]

A more recent illustration of the same method is supplied for us in this quotation:

> A friend some time ago told me how his father broke the old boulders on his farm in New England. He said his father would build a fire of hardwood around the great stones and keep it burning until he had heated them through and through, and then with a few blows from the sledge hammer, they would fall to pieces. How often God's Word, when it lodges in the heart, burns like a fire and breaks the stubborn will in pieces! God's Word is powerful in its working against natural reasonings. According to Paul in 2 Corinthians 10:4, 5, "(For the weapons of our warfare [Ephesians 6:17 informs us that the Word of God as the sword of the Spirit is one of these weapons] *are* not carnal, but mighty through God to the pulling down of strongholds;) Casting down imaginations, and

every high thing that exalteth itself against the knowledge of God, and bringing into captivity every thought to the obedience of Christ."[2]

Let Christians employ the burning fire and the mighty hammer of God's Word. Let us have faith in our tools. With them we can build a highway for our God in the hearts of men and women.

God's Word is powerful in its working against false hopes. This was the word of the Lord to Jeremiah in Jeremiah 23. Concerning the false prophets, the Lord said: "*They are* prophets of the deceit of their own heart" (verse 26). It was primarily concerning these men that Jehovah asked: "*Is* not my word like a fire? saith the LORD; and like a hammer *that* breaketh the rock in pieces?"

When he was appointed to the prophetic office, Jeremiah was informed by the Lord that his task was "to root out, and to pull down, and to destroy, and to throw down, to build, and to plant" (Jeremiah 1:10). Here is both a destructive ministry and a constructive ministry. How did Jeremiah fulfill this ministry? How did he root out and pull down and destroy and throw down? He did it by preaching the Word of God, that is both by the fire and the hammer. Jeremiah preached against the deceptive teachings of the false prophets. He scathed and scorched them by the burning Word of the Lord (see Jeremiah 5:14). He pounded and pulverized them with the hammer of God's truth. (See Jeremiah 23:9–40 for the proof of this.)

God's Word is powerful in its working against rebellious hearts. Indeed, the prophet himself found this to be true. He tells us (Jeremiah 20:7-9) that in the midst of persecution because of his preaching, he decided to resign his calling. "Then I said, I will not make mention of him, nor speak any more in his name. But *his word* was in mine heart as a burning fire shut up in my bones, and I was weary with forbearing, and I could not *stay*." Jeremiah's heart became like a volcano, and he simply could not keep back the burning lava of God's Word. That Word incinerated all his rebellion and reluctance, and compelled him to preach once again the message of God.

Preacher friend, be careful about trying to bottle up God's Word in your heart. It can't be done. God's Word will consume you and crush your flimsy excuses for resigning God's service. God will fight the fire of your self-will with the fire of His Word. And in that battle you have no hope of victory!

Concerning the power of God's Word as a hammer, Dr. Alexander Stewart wrote:

> A hammer that is wielded by an arm sufficiently strong will shatter the hardest rock, and the divine message has a similar effect on the obduracy of the unregenerate heart. In the hand of the Spirit of God it will break down the most obstinate resistance, and lay low the most boastful pride. However securely entrenched a man may be in spiritual insensateness and defiance of God, it needs but a touch of the divine hammer to shatter his self-complacency and bring his arrogance to the dust. It is the judicial function of the Word of God that is specially indicated by his figure of the hammer.
>
> The heart breaks asunder, though hard as a stone,
> When God speaks in thunder, and makes Himself known.[3]

Dr. Hugh Macmillan calls attention to the fact that no prayer was—

> . . . more frequently upon the lips of that great scientific man, Michael Faraday, than this. He used often to conduct the humble service of the small sect of Christians, called Sandemanians, to which he belonged, in their little church. Putting aside altogether on such occasions his great scientific fame and knowledge, he would pray fervently that the Word of God might be as a hammer, breaking the hard rock of man's heart in pieces, and bringing every proud and high thought into subjection to the rule of God. And the answer to the prayer in his own case tended to foster the childlike humility and meekness which was one of the most beautiful ornaments of his character.[4]

Patient

God's Word is powerful in its working. It is also *patient* in its working. This aspect is brought out particularly by the symbol of the hammer, and has a special message for all those engaged in the ministry of the Word of God.

When we become impatient, we are to remember that God's Word operates like a hammer. It does its work blow upon blow.

A preacher once came to the place where, because of his apparently fruitless toil, he decided to resign his ministry. But he dreamed that he was hired to break stones. After hitting away, he discovered that the stones would not break. He gave up in disgust and despair.

But then his employer called to him, "Did I not hire you to hammer stones?"

"Yes," the labourer replied.

"Then go and hammer them."

The labourer did, and after a while the stones cracked and broke.

At that point the pastor awoke, and so forcibly had God spoken to his heart in the dream that he cried out, "O God, I will go back to my hammering!" He did, and soon stony hearts began to break, and there was a wave of blessing.

Accordingly, when we become discouraged, we are to remember that God's Word is like a hammer in its activity.[5]

Sidney Collett encouraged us in this way:

> Some hearts are very hard, and need all the spiritual strength of the true workman, if he is to wield this hammer successfully. The work at times may seem to be slow, and the results uncertain; but let us not be discouraged. It is the steady, regular blows that tell in the end.
>
> A Christian was once reasoning with an infidel; the latter continually protested that, as he did not believe the Bible, it was a waste of time to quote passages of Scripture to him. The Christian, however, continued to wield his hammer by quoting texts, until at length the hammer did its work, and the infidel's heart was broken.[6]

Give Me That Book!

We have already noticed that Jeremiah employs a double figure to set forth the destructive power of God's Word. If it is possible to draw a distinction between two figures, fire and hammer, we suggest that in the fire we have the destructive power of God set forth in its sudden or rapid character, and in the hammer we have the destructive power of God set forth in its persistent and persevering character.

With regard to some people who hear the Word of God, the response is immediate. Like fire the Word of God swiftly consumes all opposition and burns up all dross. But in the case of others, the Word of God is more like a hammer, gradually reducing all opposition to pieces. "As a hammer," wrote Jabez Burns, "it breaks in pieces the obduracy of the heart, the impenitence of the heart, the unbelief of the heart, and the apathy of the heart. It produces conviction of sin, contrition for sins, and separation from sin."[7]

We are to keep in mind the patience and persistence of God's Word when we are tempted to be faithless and unbelieving.

There is a tiny rock plant, known to gardeners as saxifrage—meaning "rock breaker." This plant is so small that it can be crushed between finger and thumb. And yet this plant, by its gentle, persistent growth, is capable of splitting rocks in order to obtain a larger place for growth.

Let us take heart, then, for let but one word of God fall into a hard, stony heart, let that Word of God sink its roots down into heart and conscience, and soon that heart will be cracked wide open.

Dr. Macmillan wrote:

> A broken and contrite heart is a pleasing sacrifice to God, and till you yield it to Him, He will keep beating at your heart with the hammer of His providence and grace. Yield at once, and the hammer will be converted into the ploughshare, and you will, under God's gentlest dealings, in the fine soil of your heart, produce the peaceable fruits of righteousness to the praise of the glory of His grace.[8]

Purposeful

God's Word is powerful and patient in its working. It is also *purposeful* in its working. God's Word is fire, but it is controlled fire; it is a hammer, but it is in the hands of One who knows what He is doing.

The purpose of God's Word is to shatter the heart of the natural man—in other words, to produce conviction of sin.

Writing years ago, H.P. Buddicum stated that—

> When a mass of ore is to be submitted to the fire that its metal may be extracted, it is beaten small with hammers, then carried to the kiln, and finally to the furnace.

> Take the case of one whom the Word of salvation has never influenced, who is alienated from God, and who has no other principle of affection or action than his own unsanctified reason, or his own unrenewed desires. Here, then, is the rock. But let the law of God speak to his soul in its power; let it show him the perfection of the Lawgiver, the spiritual character of the law, the withering curse pronounced against "every one that continueth not . . . ." Let it moreover display his utter inability to do the will of the Being who charges even His angels with folly, by letting him into the secrets of his own fallen nature, and proving that he is carnal, sold under sin. What will be the consequence? The rock, hard it may have been as the nether millstone, will be bruised and beaten to pieces.[9]

But God's Word has a further purpose. It is designed to produce conviction; it is designed also to produce conversion.

Jabez Burns wrote:

> In every age God's Word has proved itself as a hammer breaking the rock in pieces . . . . The history of modern missions confirms the truth of the text. The hammer has been exerted on every grade and character of human beings . . . . Everywhere it has been as a purifying fire, and as a hammer . . . breaking the rock in pieces.[10]

Finally, we note that God's Word is designed to produce conformity to Christ. God's Word is like fire that refines; it is like a hammer that shapes the red-hot metal into objects of usefulness.

J.B. Courtenay wrote—

> The Word is the instrument which God always uses, and none other, wielding it like a hammer, to smite the human heart. If you went into the forge of a blacksmith, you would see him, with strong arm, beating a piece of heated iron with a hammer or sledge, in order to form it into some particular shape, either of a nail, a horseshoe, or a ploughshare. If you went into a shop of a carpenter, you would see him driving home nails into wood with a hammer, as he makes some article of furniture or of utility.
>
> Now in the same manner the Holy Spirit uses the hammer of the Word in order to fashion the hearts and characters of the saints, employing particular passages of Scripture for this purpose, by shedding upon them a light, which, when reflected into the soul, causes them to be felt and experienced in power. He uses the hammer of the Word in order to drive home truth as nails fastened by the masters of assemblies, which are given from one shepherd.[11]

We read once an account of the cutting of a diamond. "Pen and ink," we are told, "trace lines of cleavage on the surface of the rough diamond. After weeks of study, the stone is grooved to receive a mallet tap at the likeliest spot. A slight mistake may cause a gem to fly into a hundred bits. An unsuspected flaw will do the same. Upon a mallet tap hangs a diamond's future."[12]

Ah, child of God, you are being fashioned by the heavenly Lapidary to adorn the Saviour's crown. He it is who wields the mallet. With infinite wisdom and patience and skill He will form in you the image of Christ. The hammer is in His hands, and He will lovingly work with you until His whole design is accomplished.

Is God's Word like a fire and like a hammer? Does God's Word consume and crush sinners in their defiance and rebellion?

Then let us be persistent in our use of God's Word. Jabez Burns reminds us:

> However excellent in itself, or adapted to save the soul, it is powerless unless it is brought to bear upon the hearts of men. The hammer is adapted to break the rock, but it must be lifted up and made to fall with power upon it. The Word of God is adapted to save the soul, but the hand of the servant of God must bear it, and smite with it the consciences of sinners.[13]

Then let us be prayerful in our use of God's Word. A preacher was once watching a marble cutter at work. As he saw the chips flying, the preacher exclaimed, "I wish I could deal such clanging blows on stony hearts!"

"Maybe you could," replied the workman, "if, like me, you worked on your knees."[14]

Finally, let us be prepared in our use of God's Word. We should know how to use the fire and the hammer. It is easy to consume that which God would not have us to consume, and to destroy that which God would not have us to destroy. We must know how to apply God's Word to specific situations. We need the discernment of the Holy Spirit in our teaching and preaching of God's Word.

FOR YOUR FURTHER STUDY

1. In our study of God's Word as fire we have stressed the destructive aspect of fire. What other features of God's Word are suggested by the symbol of fire?
2. "The prince of darkness grim—we tremble not for him. His rage we can endure, for, lo! his doom is sure: one little word shall fell him." What did Martin Luther mean by these words?

Woe Is Me if I Preach Not . . .

From the very commencement of his ministry Jeremiah had met with opposition and persecution, and at times he was tempted to give it up; but he was compelled by a powerful internal impetus to persevere in the path of duty.

—E. Henderson

Because of that burning fire, which he could not contain, Jeremiah kindled a lamp in the Temple of Truth which still shines with undimmed flame. He lost the praise of his age, and gained the regard of the ages. He lost the ear of Jerusalem, and gained the ear of the world.

—H. Elvet Lewis

We have sometimes seen a little steamer, like the *Maid of the Mist* at the foot of the Falls of Niagara, resisting and gaining upon a stormy torrent, madly rushing past her. Slowly she has worked her way through the mad rush of waters, defying their attempt to bear her back; calmly and serenely pursuing her onward course, without being turned aside, or driven back or dismayed. And why? Because a burning fire is shut up in her heart, and her engines cannot stay, because impelled in their strong and regular motion.

Similarly, within Jeremiah's heart a fire had been lit from the heart of God, and was kept aflame by the continual fuel heaped on it.

—F.B. Meyer

As water becomes steam, so does every capacity become living energy when the fire of God lays hold of His servant. He needs no stimulus of human appreciation, nor encouragement of visible success. He cannot fight against the divine Spirit, who urges him to faithfulness. But how few of us who would fain speak with burning words are willing for cleansing by fire in our own secret lives!

—J. Stuart Holden

STUDY 14
God's Word Is Compulsive

Our Key Scripture—"*His word* was in mine heart as a burning fire shut up in my bones, and I was weary with forbearing, and I could not *stay*" (Jeremiah 20:9).

Supplementary Scriptures—Psalm 45:1; Jeremiah 1:6-9; Amos 3:8; Acts 4:20; 1 Corinthians 9:16.

IN the previous study, we examined the symbol of fire as found in Jeremiah 23:29 and suggested that in that verse the destructive capacity of God's Word is being emphasized by the Lord. As fire, God's Word consumes the teachings of false prophets.

But in Jeremiah 20:9 it is another aspect of the power of fire that is being utilized and underlined. Jeremiah tells us that in a particular set of circumstances he found God's Word in his heart to be like a burning fire, compelling him to take a certain course of action. In other words, we suggest, Jeremiah is telling us that God's Word is compulsive—compelling His servants to proclaim its message.

It will be helpful, therefore, to determine precisely the circumstances Jeremiah faced and why he described God's Word as a burning fire shut up in his bones.

BASIC OUTLINE

We can best understand Jeremiah's reference to God's Word as fire by studying the entire passage, Jeremiah 20:7-9. We may group the material in five sections: first, the *derision* Jeremiah faced; second, the *diagnosis*

Jeremiah attempted; third, the *decision* Jeremiah reached; fourth, the *discovery* Jeremiah made; and fifth, the *duty* Jeremiah undertook.

The Derision Jeremiah Faced

To understand Jeremiah's reference to the compelling character of God's Word, we must be clear as to the *derision* he faced. Jeremiah tells us about this aspect of his ministry in Jeremiah 20:7, 8: "I am in derision daily, every one mocketh me. For since I spake, I cried out, I cried violence and spoil; because the word of the LORD was made a reproach unto me, and a derision, daily."

Note Jeremiah's specific references to being derided and mocked and scorned by his fellow citizens. His daily experience was to be taunted by the people of Jerusalem. Whenever he appeared in the streets he was made the object of scorn and derision.

What was the explanation of this derision? Jeremiah answers that question most clearly. Jeremiah suffered derision because of the Word of the Lord. He was mocked because he was a prophet of Jehovah, a messenger of God's Word. There was no other reason for the daily derision.

As a young man Jeremiah was called by the Lord to be a prophet to the nations (cf. Jeremiah 1:6–9). The main subject of Jeremiah's message was the judgment of Jehovah upon Judah and Jerusalem. With minor variations that was the theme of his message as found in thirty-nine chapters of his prophecy.

But the people of Judah were not prepared to accept such a message. Their own prophets assured them of peace and continuance in the land (Jeremiah 14:15). Accordingly, when Jeremiah repeatedly predicted the invasion of the land by the Babylonians, the people reacted against him and ridiculed his message.

What, then, was the expression of this derision that Jeremiah faced? In Jeremiah 20:7, 8 Jeremiah intimates that this derision was expressed verbally. "I am in derision daily" stated the prophet, "every one mocketh me."

We have examples of this mockery in other chapters of Jeremiah. In 17:15, for instance, we read: "Behold, they say unto me, Where *is* the word of the LORD? let it come now." The people taunted Jeremiah with the apparent fact that his message of doom was never fulfilled. "Where *is* the word of the LORD?"—that is, where is the fulfillment of that word of judgment you have been predicting for these many years? "let it come now"— let us see the fulfillment of that message.

That was the kind of mockery Jeremiah faced as he sought faithfully to preach the message God had given him.

But the derision Jeremiah faced was not only verbal; at times, it broke out into actual physical violence. Indeed, the chapter from which our key Scripture for this study is taken begins by telling us that because of having delivered a message of judgment in the court of the Lord's House (see Jeremiah 19:14, 15), the Prophet Jeremiah was apprehended by the Temple police and placed in the stocks overnight. At the same time Jeremiah was beaten up by Pashur, the chief of police for the Temple.

Various chapters recount the persecutions of Jeremiah the Prophet. His own relatives plotted his death (Jeremiah 11:18–12:6). On one occasion, the priests, the prophets, and the people condemned him to death, and but for the intervention of certain rulers of Judah, they would have lynched him on the spot (Jeremiah 26). Later during the siege of Jerusalem he was accused of being a quisling and arrested by the captain of the guard (Jeremiah 37:13, 14). This earned Jeremiah the hatred of the princes of Jerusalem and they attempted to snuff out his life by imprisoning him in a disused well where he would surely have died but for the timely help of Ebed-melech the Ethiopian (Jeremiah 38:1–13).

It is with this background of scorn and suffering in mind that we must read Jeremiah's testimony to the compulsive power of God's Word.

The Diagnosis Jeremiah Attempted

This leads us to consider the *diagnosis* Jeremiah attempted while he was in the hot water of his undesirable circumstances. While it is not absolutely certain, it is at least possible that Jeremiah voiced the words of Jeremiah 20:7–18 at different times throughout the long night while he was in the stocks. It's amazing how much diagnosing of our circumstances we can do when we are under pressure. And Jeremiah, who was intensely human, tried to analyze his career while he was sitting in the stocks, the object of scorn on the part of passers-by.

Give Me That Book!

What did Jeremiah think about his plight? In Jeremiah 20:7 we read: "O Lord, thou hast deceived me, and I was deceived: thou art stronger than I, and hast prevailed." There it is, and how shockingly frank! Here is a prophet of the Lord speaking to the One who had called him and commissioned him, and he is accusing that One of deception and the use of superior strength with a view to the embarrassing of His prophet.

It is most instructive to set alongside these accusations of Jeremiah the account of his call as given to us in Jeremiah 1. Here are selected verses from that chapter.

> Then the word of the Lord came unto me, saying,

> Before I formed thee in the belly I knew thee; and before thou camest forth out of the womb I sanctified thee, *and* I ordained thee a prophet unto the nations.

> Then said I, Ah, Lord God! behold, I cannot speak: for I *am* a child.

> But the Lord said unto me, Say not, I *am* a child: for thou shalt go to all that I shall send thee, and whatsoever I command thee thou shalt speak.

> Thou therefore gird up thy loins, and arise, and speak unto them all that I command thee: be not dismayed at their faces, lest I confound thee before them.

> And they shall fight against thee; but they shall not prevail against thee; for I *am* with thee, saith the Lord, to deliver thee (Jeremiah 1:4–7, 17, 19).

In his diagnosis of his circumstances, Jeremiah was selective and, therefore arrived at a conclusion that was distorted and twisted. He was giving expression to how he felt, not to what he really knew.

When Jeremiah stated so crudely, "O Lord, thou hast deceived me, and I was deceived: thou art stronger than I, and hast prevailed," he was recalling the day of his appointment, but rather than that memory bringing inspiration and strength, it brought bitterness and despair. Jeremiah was really saying something like this: "The only reason why I am a prophet is that You, O Lord, deceived me by Your promises. Reluctantly, I accepted Your call on the basis of Your promise, 'I am with you to deliver you.' But look at me. Here I am in the stocks. I am a prophet for no other reason than that You are stronger than I am, and coerced me into this ministry."

But in this moment of extreme pessimism Jeremiah had become one-sided in his diagnosis. He was thinking only of his present distress, not of his future deliverance. As it turned out, Jeremiah's persecutors suffered during the siege of Jerusalem, but Jeremiah was wonderfully protected and granted the freedom of the country by the Babylonian invaders. Sitting in the stocks, complaining to God, Jeremiah had no knowledge of what still lay before him.

It is dangerous, then, to try to diagnose our circumstances and our condition when we are suffering from lack of faith in God's promises and power. We will most certainly come to wrong conclusions. With the smog of unbelief hanging over us our view of God will be partial, distorted, and even erroneous.

The Decision Jeremiah Reached

We have sought to sketch in the background of Jeremiah's testimony with regard to the compulsive power of God's Word. We have noticed the derision he daily faced and the diagnosis he crudely attempted. We must now note carefully the *decision* he reached.

Under the relentless barrage of scorn and mockery, Jeremiah wilted and said to himself, "I will not make mention of him, nor speak any more in his name." That is tantamount to Jeremiah's resignation from the prophetic ministry. The prophet said, "I'll quit the ministry. If I am being ridiculed because of my commitment to preach the Word of the Lord, I'll stop preaching and then the persecution will stop, too. When the Spirit of prophecy comes upon me, I will actively resist Him and refuse to communicate the message given to me."

That was a daring decision to reach! Jeremiah imagined—and how wrong he was—that by resigning he would solve his problem. The grass certainly looked greener over the fence the morning after the night spent in the stocks!

How many of God's servants have come at times to the same decision as Jeremiah came to, so many years ago! But we can all learn from Jeremiah's case.

In deciding to resign his commission as a prophet of the Lord, Jeremiah was not facing the real problem. The real problem lay deeper than his outward circumstances. Rather than face his real problem, Jeremiah decided to throw in the sponge and get out of the ministry.

For Jeremiah that would have been no real solution. By resigning his commission and deserting the field of battle, he would have been perpetuating and compounding his problem to no end!

In deciding to resign, Jeremiah was not looking to the power of the Lord to deliver him and preserve him alive. He had the promise (see 1:19, "I *am* with thee, saith the LORD, to deliver thee"), but he conveniently forgot that Word of the Lord.

How easy in a service to sing, "Standing on the promises of Christ my King"! How difficult in the stocks to sing the same words and really mean them!

This incident from the life of Jeremiah reminds us that rather than running away from what seems to be our Waterloo, we should trust the Lord in the circumstances and let Him turn our defeat into a glorious victory for Himself and His glory.

Are you in hot water? Are you feeling as if you were in the stocks—the object of ridicule and the butt of your foes? Are you right now framing in your mind your letter of resignation? Then stop for a moment and read the account of Jeremiah. Is your thought of resignation really the expression of your defeat at that point where God wants to give you deliverance and continuance?

The Discovery Jeremiah Made

Jeremiah, then, has come to the point of resigning from his commission. But we must now consider the *discovery* that Jeremiah made just at that point in his career. "Then I said, I will not make mention of him, nor speak any more in his name. But *his word* was in mine heart as a burning fire shut up in my bones." There it is, the discovery that Jeremiah made. God gave to His pessimistic prophet a good case of "heart burn"!

As he opposed the word of God's Spirit in his life, Jeremiah discovered that his heart was like an active volcano. The lava of God's Word overflowed all his rebellious thoughts and demanded expression from his lips.

God's Word, then, in the heart of the disobedient minister of God's Word is like a burning fire.

As fire God's Word destroys wilfulness and resistance. It burned into Jeremiah's conscience and consumed his thoughts of rebellion and resignation. It searched out the prophet and burnt up his thoughts of unbelief.

As fire God's Word devours pessimism and gloom. In Jeremiah's heart that fire burnt up the black lumps of melancholy and misery. It brought a vital glow into his sad soul.

As fire God's Word demands expression. Jeremiah had attempted to jam the communication of God's Word, but he found that God's power was such that he could not silence the voice of the Spirit of prophecy. He tried to extinguish its blaze, but found that to pour water upon it was simply to increase its fury.

In the one other place where the symbol of fire is used for God's Word the context indicates that it is the destructive power of God's Word in reference to false teachings that is in view (see Jeremiah 23:29). But the messenger or minister of the Lord will never find God's Word in his mouth as a burning fire destroying the false teachings of men until he has permitted that Word to consume the dross of his rebellion, unbelief, and pessimism.

The Duty Jeremiah Undertook

Our final consideration from this remarkable testimony of Jeremiah is related to the *duty* the prophet undertook. "But *his word*," states Jeremiah, "was in mine heart as a burning fire shut up in my bones, and I was weary with forbearing, and I could not *stay*." We may paraphrase this last statement of Jeremiah in these words: "I became tired of trying to restrain God's Word burning furiously in my heart; in fact, I did not succeed, and I found myself once again preaching the very word which had brought me so much scorn and ridicule."

Give Me That Book!

If the incident recorded in chapter 20 occurred in the reign of Jehoiakim, then we know that Jeremiah continued to minister throughout the reign of Zedekiah, and even after the fall of Jerusalem. We gather, therefore, from his statement in Jeremiah 20:9 that having discovered that he could not oppose God's Word successfully, he resumed his ministry. God's logic was fire, and that fire was so overwhelming that the prophet had to submit to the compulsion of that logic.

For Jeremiah, that resumption of his ministry was both courageous and costly. But the prophet had no other alternative if he were to remain true to his Master.

From that great book for the heart, *A Minister's Obstacles*, by Ralph G. Turnbull, we share the following account:

> It is reported of the late John Robertson of Glasgow, a preacher for forty years, that he was a backslider for a long time. The glow had gone. He decided to resign, and one morning prayed, "O God, Thou didst commission me forty years ago, but I have blundered and failed, and I want to resign this morning."
>
> He broke down as he prayed, and in between his sobs he heard the voice of the Lord saying, "John Robertson, 'tis true I commissioned you forty years ago; 'tis true you have blundered and failed; but, John Robertson, I am not here for you to resign your commission, but to re-sign your commission."
>
> That re-signing was the beginning of greater and new things for the preacher.[1]

So it can be for any preacher or missionary or Christian worker who, defeated and discouraged, is thinking of resigning. The act of resignation will not by any means solve the real problem. The only adequate and abiding solution is for that defeated Christian to turn back to the Lord and lift up the torch of testimony once again in the midst of the world's darkness. If we let God's flaming Word deal with us first, then God Himself will use that same flaming Word to deal with the hearts of others. Our responsibility to the compulsive Word is to receive it without hindrance and relay it without hesitation. Ours be the glorious task!

FOR YOUR FURTHER STUDY

1. How did Amos invoke the law of cause and effect in vindicating his ministry? See Amos 3:3–8.
2. Contrast the two attitudes toward God's Word as found in Jeremiah 15:16 and 20:8.
3. What steps of self-examination should a believer take before resigning from active service for the Lord?

To the Law and to Testimony

Through all my perplexities and distresses, I seldom read any other book, and I as rarely have felt the want of any other. It has been my hourly study.

—**William Wilberforce**

I gratefully receive and rejoice in the light of revelation, which has set me to rest in many things, the manner whereof my poor reason can by no means make out to me.

—**John Locke**

The Bible is equally adapted to the wants and infirmities of every human being. No other book ever addressed itself so authoritatively and so movingly to the judgment and moral sense of mankind.

—**James Kent**

A true love for the great Book will bring us great peace from the great God and be a protection to us. Let us live constantly in the society of the law of the Lord, and it will breed in us a restfulness such as nothing else can.

—**Charles H. Spurgeon**

There is no book like the Bible for excellent learning, wisdom, and use.

—once Chief Justice of England, **Sir Matthew Hale**

When John Jay, the first Chief Justice of the Supreme Court of the United States, was on his deathbed, he was asked if he had any final counsel to leave to his children. His pointed response was, "They have the Book."

—**Will H. Houghton**

If we stray, it is not for want of light; if we persist in obeying our own perverted instincts and impulses, we must not be surprised that we end in the bog of despair . . . . Do not move without consulting the Oracle divine. Let our motto be, "To the law, and to the testimony," and what cannot be confirmed by the spirit of the Book is unworthy to be admitted into our life as an inspiring and directing force.

—**Joseph Parker**

STUDY 15
God's Word Is Consultative

Our Key Scripture—"Thy testimonies also *are* my delight *and* my counsellors"—marginal reading, "men of my counsel" (Psalm 119:24).

Supplementary Scriptures—Exodus 18:19; Joshua 9:4; 1 Kings 3:5, 7, 9; 1 Chronicles 10:13, 14; Psalm 16:7; 73:24; 106:12–15; Proverbs 1:24–31; 3:5, 6; 12:15; 22:20, 21; 27:9; Isaiah 11:2, 3; 28:29; 47:13; Jeremiah 10:23; 42:20; James 1:5–7.

THY testimonies also *are* . . . men of my counsel." The psalmist's vivid symbol for the place and power of God's Word in his life takes us not to a psychiatrist's office but to a king's palace. The Old Testament usage of the concept of counselling justifies us in picturing a king surrounded by a group of devoted counsellors, an inner cabinet of able leaders who act constantly as advisers to his majesty. In times of perplexity and doubt the king asks these men for advice and counsel. They in turn are ever ready to share with their king their insight and wisdom.

This is the picture the psalmist had in mind when he wrote: "Thy testimonies also *are* . . . my counsellors." He is testifying to the fact that in times of need he discovered God's Word to be the source of counsel and direction and guidance. As he meditated upon God's Word, he found the divine testimonies met his need personally and precisely.

Keith L. Brooks thus wrote:

No child of God need be without his board of counsellors, for he has them in the inspired writers of the Word. Though deserted by all his friends, the godly man can meet with his cabinet any time, and get the best advice as to the course to take. These cabinet members will never flatter him, never applaud him in any sin, never discourage him or dissuade him from that which is good. "A man so furnished," wrote Thomas Manton, "is never less alone than when alone." We may instantly summon to our side "holy men of God" whose counsel shall abide forever.[1]

BASIC OUTLINE

As we study the subject of God's counsel, we discover first that counsel is *required*; second, it must be *requested*; third, it will be *received*; and finally, it may be *rejected*.

Required

God's Word presents clearly and convincingly the fact that guidance is *required* by all of us. "O LORD," confessed Jeremiah, "I know that the way of man *is* not in himself: *it is* not in man that walketh to direct his steps" (Jeremiah 10:23).

Our need of guidance in this present world is based upon a number of factors.

First, we must keep in mind at all times our finite and feeble resources. When Solomon succeeded his father David to the throne of Israel, he said to the Lord, "I *am but* a little child: I know not *how* to go out or come in" (1 Kings 3:7), and if Solomon had to describe his personal weakness in such words, how shall we describe ourselves? "A little child" is the epitome of weakness and dependence. "A little child" needs constant supervision, care and direction.

We do well, therefore, constantly to remind ourselves of our own utter and absolute dependence upon God, the source of wisdom and strength. It is when we forget this basic truth that we begin to make decisions and form judgments on our own.

But we need divine counsel also because of our great and grave responsibilities. We are responsible to do all to the glory of God, and this involves many specific and serious responsibilities. We are responsible for our personal life before God. We are responsible for our family life. We are responsible for our part in the fellowship and witness of our local church. We are responsible for our influence upon society. These ever-widening circles of responsibility call for clear-cut and careful decisions.

It was the weight of responsibility felt by Solomon that caused him to ask for wisdom, not for wealth, when God's "blank cheque" was given to him. When God said, "Ask what I shall give thee," Solomon replied, "Give therefore thy servant an understanding heart to judge thy people, that I may discern between good and bad: for who is able to judge this thy so great a people?" (1 Kings 3:5, 9).

We need divine counsel for yet a third reason: We are living in a world that as far as guidance is concerned is faced with various and vocal rivals. This contributes to a vast confusion in the minds of people. Men today are much like the citizens of ancient Babylon to whom God said: "Thou art wearied in the multitude of thy counsels. Let now the astrologers, the stargazers, the monthly prognosticators, stand up, and save thee from *these things* that shall come upon thee" (Isaiah 47:13).

The reference here to occultism and astrology is most remarkable, for at the present time there is a tremendous resurgence of interest in this whole field. And the reason? People are looking for direction, for counsel, for guidance. They are fearful about the future, and are trying desperately to penetrate the curtain that hides the unseen world.

The Scriptures, however, contain many warnings concerning the danger of consulting these occult powers for guidance. In the Old Testament the classic example is King Saul. Concerning him, it is written, "So Saul died for his transgression which he committed against the Lord, *even* against the word of the Lord, which he kept not, and also for asking *counsel* of *one that had* a familiar spirit, to enquire *of it*; And he enquired not of the Lord" (1 Chronicles 10:13, 14).

Occultism represents just one of many rival voices claiming the allegiance of people. Many other "isms" could be listed, such as materialism, modernism, hedonism, humanism, etc. All of them are will-o'-the-wisps that allure men and women from the path of God's will. Accordingly, we desperately need divine guidance lest we make shipwreck of our lives. "The way of a fool," wrote Solomon, "*is* right in his own eyes: but he that hear-keneth unto counsel *is* wise" (Proverbs 12:15).

Requested

We need divine counsel. We have established that fact in the light of various factors. But counsel must be *requested* from the Lord and from His Word if we are to know the wonderful experience of being directed by the Lord.

It is important, however, to grasp the fact that there are certain conditions relating to our request for counsel. We must meet these stipulations if we are to receive God's guidance.

First, we must ask for God's counsel sincerely. We must ask with pure and sincere motives.

In Jeremiah 40–44 we have a most illuminating account of a group of people who were not sincere in their asking of counsel from the Lord through Jeremiah.

After the fall of Jerusalem at the hands of the Babylonians, the remnant left in the land faced various crises. One of these involved the assassination of Gedaliah, the native governor appointed by the Babylonians. Scared that they would lose their lives if the Babylonians undertook reprisals, the remnant asked Jeremiah to seek guidance from the Lord. But the fact was they had already made up their minds as to what they were going to do: they had decided to flee from Judah into Egypt. But they went through the formality of asking guidance from Yahweh (God).

To this remnant Jeremiah said: "Ye dissembled in your hearts, when ye sent me unto the LORD your God, saying, Pray for us unto the Lord our God; and according unto all that the LORD our God shall say, so declare unto us, and we will do *it*" (Jeremiah 42:20). The people had no real intention of doing what the Lord wanted them to do.

Are we ever guilty of this "dissembling"? Are we ever guilty of first making up our minds as to our course of action and then asking the Lord for counsel and guidance? If so, then we have been acting insincerely and hypocritically, and we must repent of our deception.

This means that we must ask for counsel submissively. Probably the best-known verses in the Bible on the subject of divine counsel and guidance are Proverbs 3:5, 6. These verses teach the aspect of submission to His will. "Trust in the LORD with all thine heart; and lean not unto thine own understanding. In all thy ways acknowledge him, and he shall direct thy paths." The next verse, however, should not be lost sight of! "Be not wise in thine own eyes: fear the LORD, and depart from evil."

In Psalm 106 the psalmist tells us why the children of Israel failed in the wilderness. In verses 12–15, after referring to the Red Sea deliverance, he states: "Then believed they his words; they sang his praise. They soon forgat his works; they waited not for his counsel [that is, His plan]: But lusted exceedingly in the wilderness, and tempted God in the desert. And he gave them their request; but sent leanness into their soul."

Israel's sin stemmed from a lack of submission to God, which in turn produced impatience and ingratitude. God had a plan for them, but they could not wait for it to be unveiled. They demanded that their appetites be satisfied. But at what a cost! "Leanness into their soul!"

When we come to God for counsel and guidance, let us come submissively, not self-sufficiently. Let our attitude be one of acceptance, not arrogance.

In seeking God's counsel we must also ask specifically. It is important that we be definite in our requests for guidance. This is illustrated many times in the lives of Bible characters. King David is an excellent example of one who asked for precise directions from the Lord.

On one occasion after the Philistines had invaded his country, David, we are told, "enquired of the LORD, saying, Shall I go up to the Philistines? wilt thou deliver them into mine hand? And the LORD said unto David, Go up: for I will doubtless deliver the Philistines into thine hand" (2 Samuel 5:19). Note the two-fold question of David, and the two-fold answer of the Lord, exactly meeting David's need. David asked, "Shall I go up to the Philistines?" The Lord replied, "Go up." David asked, "Wilt thou deliver them into mine hand?" The Lord replied, "I will doubtless deliver the Philistines into thine hand."

Give Me That Book!

In our requests for guidance we must be as specific as David. We must determine our needs, and then present our requests directly and definitely to the Lord. He loves to answer specifically.

Finally, in asking for God's counsel we must ask steadfastly. We must be firm in faith, believing that God will hear us and answer us. "If any of you lack wisdom, let him ask of God, that giveth to all *men* liberally, and upbraideth not; and it shall be given him. But let him ask in faith, nothing wavering. For he that wavereth is like a wave of the sea driven with the wind and tossed. For let not that man think that he shall receive any thing of the Lord" (James 1:5-7).

These words of James concerning asking for wisdom or for God's counsel, pinpoint the necessity of rocklike faith. We must plead the promises before the throne, assured that God will answer us according to His Word.

Counsel from God, therefore, must be requested, and it must be requested sincerely, submissively, specifically, and steadfastly.

When the armies of Israel were engaged in conquering the land of Canaan, they were faced on one occasion with the necessity of making a decision with reference to a group of people who claimed to be the representatives of a far-off nation. They had all the evidence: old sacks, wine bottles that were old and rent, old shoes, patched garments, and mouldy bread. They asked that the Israelites would enter into a perpetual alliance with them, granting them protection.

But it was all a ruse. Actually they represented a nation that lay in the path of the conquering Israelite army. These people, however, did not want to be exterminated, and thus they cunningly disguised themselves and hoodwinked the leaders of Israel into making an alliance with them.

We might argue that Joshua and his officers should have known better! The inspired writer, however, in explaining why Israel was deceived, simply says, "The men took of their victuals, and asked not *counsel* at the mouth of the Lord" (Joshua 9:14).

Concerning how many compromises of God's people must the words, they "asked not *counsel* at the mouth of the Lord," be invoked! We are all too prone to go by appearances and specious arguments. Concerning the Messiah it is written:

> The spirit of the LORD shall rest upon him, the spirit of wisdom and understanding, the spirit of counsel and might, the spirit of knowledge and of the fear of the LORD; and shall make him of quick understanding in the fear of the Lord: and he shall not judge after the sight of his eyes, neither reprove after the hearing of his ear (Isaiah 11:2, 3).

That is what we need: the Spirit of counsel.

Received

Divine counsel is required by us all. It must be requested from the Lord. And when the conditions are met, counsel will be *received* from the One who is "wonderful in counsel" (Isaiah 28:29). "I will bless the LORD," wrote David, "who hath given me counsel" (Psalm 16:7). So confident was he of divine direction that a psalmist could write: "Thou shalt guide me with thy counsel, and afterward receive me *to* glory" (Psalm 73:24).

The counsel that we receive is readily available. There is no need that can arise in our lives that is not covered in principle by some passage of Scripture. Here is one list, widely used, that illustrates the comprehensive nature of the Bible's counsel. It is entitled, "Help In Time of Need."

1. For comfort in time of sorrow read Romans 8:26–28; 2 Corinthians 1:3–5.
2. For relief in time of suffering read 2 Corinthians 12:8–10; Hebrews 12:3–13.
3. For guidance in time of decision read Proverbs 3:5, 6; James 1:5, 6.
4. For protection in time of danger read Psalm 91; Psalm 121.
5. For courage in time of fear read Ephesians 6:10–18; Hebrews 13:5, 6.
6. For peace in time of turmoil read Isaiah 26:3, 4; Philippians 4:6, 7.
7. For rest in time of weariness read Psalm 23; Matthew 11:28, 29.
8. For strength in time of temptation read 1 Corinthians 10:6–13; James 1:12–16.

9. For warning in time of indifference read Galatians 5:19–21; Hebrews 10:26–31.

10. For forgiveness in time of conviction and confession read Isaiah 1:18; 1 John 1:7–9.[2]

Truly God's Word is filled with counsel and guidance. Edgar A. Guest bore testimony to this fact in his poem:

> And should my soul be torn with grief,
> Upon my shelf I find
> A little volume, torn and thumbed,
> For comfort just designed.
> I take my little Bible down
> And read its pages o'er;
> And when I part from it I find
> I'm stronger than before.[3]

Third, the guidance we receive is fully adequate. While it is true that the Bible is not an encyclopedia of answers to every question that could be asked, it does contain all things necessary for living a godly life.

In the Levitical system part of the High Priest's equipment were the mysterious "Urim and Thummim." In some way they were employed in giving guidance to Israel.

A modernistic young pastor delighted in teasing a godly cobbler about his lack of Bible knowledge. One day he asked him to explain the Urim and Thummim.

The cobbler was not taken off guard, for he immediately answered, "I do not know what they were," and then, pointing to his Bible near at hand, he said, "I find, however, that by usin' and thumbin' that Book, I get all the guidance I need."[4]

That may not be very good exegesis, but it is right and to the point. God used the breastplate of judgment and the Urim and Thummim in the Old Testament economy. It is not necessary for us to know the mechanics of that mystery. But we do have a Book by which we can determine the mind of God on all vital matters of belief and behaviour.

Finally, we notice that the guidance we receive from the Bible is completely authoritative. God is not offering us His opinion in the Bible. He is directing us and commanding us to do His will.

Dr. Harry Ironside used to tell the story of a woman along with her child who was travelling across the prairies in mid-winter. Not knowing the area, she asked the conductor to put her off at her destination. Assured that he would, she relaxed and dozed off.

A businessman had heard her request and, thinking that he knew the district well, decided to help the woman. As the train came to a stop, he woke the woman and told her that she had arrived at her destination. The woman alighted from the train, and the train started off again in the blizzard.

Some time later the conductor appeared in the carriage looking for the woman and her child. Not finding her, he asked the businessman if he had seen her. Of course! He had put her off at her destination some mile back.

The conductor's face turned white. "But that is not her destination," he explained. "That was an unscheduled stop. There is no town or station there."

The train driver reversed the engine, and after searching for some time, the woman was found, but both the mother and her baby had frozen to death on the bare prairies. The businessman's advice had been sincere, but it was wrong. It was not authoritative.[5]

When we accept the counsel of the Scriptures, we are accepting that which is divinely inspired and authoritative. We need have no doubts or hesitations. God has spoken in His Word. We may employ the words of Proverbs 22:20, 21 to indicate this fact. "Have not I written to thee excellent things in counsels and knowledge, That I might make thee know the certainty of the words of truth" (see Luke 1:1–4).

Rejected

The clear teaching of the Bible is, then, that we can receive daily and definite counsel from the Lord. But this counsel may be *rejected.*

Give Me That Book!

We are reminded of a traveller meeting a little old lady standing at a crossroads, throwing her walking stick into the air. After she had done this half a dozen times, he asked what she was doing.

"Well," she explained, "I am trying to get guidance. I throw this stick into the air, and then I will go in the direction in which it falls."

"But why have you thrown it up so often?" was the next question.

"Oh, that is easy," the old woman replied. "So far it has not fallen in the direction in which I wish to go!"[6]

Some of us may be guilty of rejecting the Bible's counsel simply because it does not endorse the plan we have in mind. What a solemn warning is found in Proverbs 1:24–31:

> Because I have called, and ye refused; I have stretched out my hand, and no man regarded; But ye have set at nought all my counsel, and would have none of my reproof: I also will laugh at your calamity; I will mock when your fear cometh; When your fear cometh as desolation, and your destruction cometh as a whirlwind; when distress and anguish cometh upon you.

> Then shall they call upon me, but I will not answer; they shall seek me early, but they shall not find me: For that they hated knowledge, and did not choose the fear of the LORD: They would none of my counsel: they despised all my reproof. Therefore shall they eat of the fruit of their own way, and be filled with their own devices.

Concerning God's Word, the psalmist exclaimed, "Thy testimonies also are . . . the men of my counsel." "Ointment and perfume rejoice the heart," wrote Solomon, "so *doth* the sweetness of a man's friend by hearty counsel" (Proverbs 27:9). Our lives can become fragrant through the precious counsel of God's Word.

> Thou truest friend man ever knew,
> Thy constancy I've tried;
> When all were false, I found thee true,
> My counsellor and guide.

The mines of earth no treasures give
That could this volume buy;
In teaching me the way to live
It taught me how to die.[7]

FOR YOUR FURTHER STUDY

1. What are the qualifications of a good counsellor? Show how the Bible meets each one of these requirements.
2. Draw up your own list of ways in which you have received counsel from the Bible.
3. Explain Proverbs 15:22, relating the "counsellors" to God's testimonies as the psalmist does in Psalm 119:24.

The King's Highway

The commandments of God may be designated a "way" because they describe a course of conduct, a line of duty, and mark the bounds of good and evil, right and wrong.

—**Richard Treffry**

God's laws are ways that lead us to God.

—**Thomas Manton**

Men do not drop into the right way by chance; they must choose it, and continue to choose it, or they will soon wander from it.

—**C.H. Spurgeon**

To Paradise a highway,
The Bible—there it stands!
Its promises unfailing
Nor grievous its commands.
It points men to the Saviour,
The lover of their soul;
Salvation is its watchword,
Eternity its goal.

—**James M. Gray**

The Scriptures teach us the best way of living, the noblest way of suffering, and the most comfortable way of dying.

—**John Flavel**

A careless reader of the Scriptures never made a close walker with God.

—**Author Unknown**

The Lord has given us in the Bible road signs to warn of dangers and to show us the right way. Once having started on the way to Heaven by taking Jesus as Lord and Saviour, you will be guided by His Word and counsel. Pay close attention to the signs in the Book, and you will not only arrive safely but have a most enjoyable trip. Read the warnings in the Bible!

—**M.R. DeHaan**

STUDY 16
God's Word Is Regulative

Our Key Scripture—"Make me to understand the way of thy precepts" (Psalm 119:27).

Supplementary Scriptures—Psalm 119:30, 32, 37; Proverbs 6:23; 15:24; Jeremiah 6:16; Matthew 7:13, 14; Acts 16:17; 18:26; 19:9, 23; 24:14; 2 Peter 2:2, 15, 21. For illustration: Ezra 8:21; Isaiah 35:8; Jeremiah 21:8.

THROUGHOUT Psalm 119 the writer compares God's Word, especially its commandments and counsels, to a way or path for his feet. This, indeed, is one of the central concepts of the psalmist's eulogy of God's Word. The psalmist looks upon the precepts of the Lord as forming a road along which by deliberate consideration and choice the believer progresses in godliness and righteousness. God's Word, then, is really "the King's highway," constructed for God's children.

References to this royal highway are found in various verses of Psalm 119. The first reference is in verse 1:

> Blessed *are* the undefiled in the way,
> who walk in the law of the LORD.

Here the literary parallelism clearly shows that the way trodden by the pure in heart is the law of the Lord. The divine law provides a pathway along which the believer may walk with confidence and calmness.

The same figure underlies the psalmist's earnest prayer in Psalm 119:10 —"O let me not wander from thy commandments." Walking in the way of God's law, the psalmist does not want to deviate from the path of God's Word.

In Psalm 119:14 the symbol appears again: "I have rejoiced in the way of thy testimonies, as *much as* in all riches." To find the road to true wisdom is better than to find the road to riches.

We have the psalmist's prayer in Psalm 119:27—"Make me to understand the way of thy precepts." Reason unaided by divine revelation cannot discover God's highway. The eyes of our understanding must be opened by the Holy Spirit.

A careful check of the entire psalm will reveal that the symbol of the way is used by the psalmist directly or indirectly in verses 1, 10, 14, 27, 30, 32, 33, 35, 37, 59, 101, 102, and 133.

All these references forcibly indicate to us that prominent in the psalmist's mind was the idea that God's Word—His precepts and His promises—forms a highway for His people.

BASIC OUTLINE

Having noticed the psalmist's use of the "highway" symbol, let us now trace some implications of this figure. Four aspects will help us to explore the wealth of teaching found in the figure: first, the *direction* the Bible gives; second, the *decision* the Bible demands; third, the *delight* the Bible gives; and, finally, the *desire* the Bible requires.

Direction

First, then, consider the *direction* the Bible, considered as a path, gives to us. Once we are walking in the way of the Lord, we are delivered from wandering in confusion and frustration. The Bible, with its commandments, cautions, and counsels, gives us direction. We cannot go astray if we but keep on that highway.

Man's basic need is for divine direction. Like the psalmist, each one of us must confess: "I have gone astray like a lost sheep" (Psalm 119:176). Indeed, "all we like sheep have gone astray; we have turned every one to his own way" (Isaiah 53:6). We are as lost as tourists in a foreign country without map or guide, and unable, moreover, to speak the language of the people. States the psalmist: "I *am* a stranger in the earth" (Psalm 119:19).

Speaking of his experience before God's convicting work was begun in his heart, he states, "Before I was afflicted I went astray" (Psalm 119:67).

In the confusion and chaos of our twentieth century, man's basic need for direction has not changed—indeed, it is being more and more confirmed. In his lostness man wanders about, vainly trying a thousand ways to discover peace and rest.

Man's basic delusion is his thought that he can live independent of divine direction. With penetrating insight the psalmist declares in Psalm 119:155, "Salvation *is* far from the wicked: for they seek not thy statutes." That is to say, those who resist God and His Word are doomed to be forever in the labyrinth of their sin simply because they will not seek divine direction. There is a way out, but sinners must humbly seek God's Word.

This basic delusion is evident in every area of personal and national life. Whether it be in the home or the law court or the government, whether it be in literature, or art, or science, man foolishly and fanatically believes he can guide his destiny without divine direction.

Man's basic crime, therefore, is his rejection of divine direction. This was the issue in the Garden of Eden: Would Adam and Eve abide by the divine word, or would they abandon the divine pathway in response to the enticement of the Devil? In Psalm 119:21 the psalmist speaks of those who have rejected the divine word: "Thou hast rebuked the proud *that are* cursed, which do err from thy commandments." And he reveals his own sorrow at the existing condition when he states: "Rivers of water run down mine eyes, because they keep not thy law" (verse 136).

Man's rejection of divine direction is clearly illustrated in Jeremiah 6:16: "Thus saith the LORD, Stand ye in the ways, and see, and ask for the old paths, where *is* the good way, and walk therein, and ye shall find rest for your souls. But they said, We will not walk *therein*."

Man has chosen to walk his own sinful path that leads to destruction, rather than the divine highway provided in the Scriptures. "There is a way which seemeth right unto a man, but the end thereof *are* the ways of death" (Proverbs 14:12).

<u>Decision</u>

Consider now the *decision* God's Word as a highway demands.

It is a momentous moment when an individual, brought to the crossroads of life and confronted with the highway of God's Word, chooses to accept the Bible as God's authoritative message spoken to him in his need. This decision of heart is mentioned by the psalmist: "I have chosen the way of truth" (119:30). Again, in verse 59, he says, "I thought on my ways, and turned my feet unto thy testimonies."

We may speak, therefore, of an initial decision to walk the way of the Word.

The Scriptures make it plain that there must be an individual acceptance of God's Word as the way for our feet. The Saviour Himself faced His hearers with the choice between the narrow way and the broad way: "Enter ye in at the strait gate: for wide *is* the gate, and broad *is* the way, that leadeth to destruction, and many there be which go in thereat: Because strait *is* the gate, and narrow *is* the way, which leadeth unto life, and few there be that find it" (Matthew 7:13, 14).

Has the reader made his decision? Have you with the psalmist deliberately and decisively decided to walk the way of God's law? Have you submitted to God's dominion and direction? Have you brought your life under His control and command? There must be an initial decision that determines our relationship to God and to His Word.

There must be an initial decision, but there must also be for the believer continual decisions to walk in God's way. This aspect is clearly prominent in Psalm 119. The psalmist is thinking primarily of daily decisions that must be made to walk the way of the Word. For him his initial decision had to be followed by repeated decisions as particular issues were raised in his life.

Constantly the believer is faced with issues that demand decision. If the believer is studying God's Word and attempting to apply that Word to his immediate circumstances, he will need to choose to do God's will in preference to his own.

Psalm 119 contains a number of references that indicate that the psalmist had to make his decision to walk in the way of God's commandments in the midst of varying circumstances.

In verse 23 the psalmist writes: "Princes also did sit *and* speak against me: *but* thy servant did meditate in thy statues." In verse 28 he refers to his heaviness of spirit: "My soul melteth for heaviness: strengthen thou me according unto thy word." In verse 51 he refers to the derision of his enemies: "The proud have had me greatly in derision: *yet* have I not declined from thy law." In verse 61 he mentions the fact of his having been robbed: "The bands of the wicked have robbed me: *but* I have not forgotten thy law."

In verse 95 we find that the wicked had plotted to kill him: "The wicked have waited for me to destroy me: *but* I will consider thy testimonies." Again, in verse 110 we read: "The wicked have laid a snare for me: yet I erred not from thy precepts." In verse 157 he states: "Many *are* my persecutors and mine enemies; *yet* do I not decline from thy testimonies." And in verse 161 we read: "Princes have persecuted me without a cause: but my heart standeth in awe of thy word."

Note the psalmist's deliberate decision to walk the way of God's commandments, no matter how hot circumstances might get to be! Slander, heaviness of spirit, derision, robbery, plot to kill, persecution—in the midst of these pressures and problems, the psalmist resolved to follow in the way of God's Word.

What problem are you facing today? What pressures are you bearing? Only that decision which results in your continuing to walk the way of God's Word will honour God and satisfy your own heart.

Delight

Let us now consider the way of God's Word from the standpoint of the *delight* it gives. Throughout the psalm the writer expresses his delight and rejoicing in the path of God's commandments. In verse 14 he exultingly cries out: "I have rejoiced in the way of thy testimonies, as *much as* in all riches" (see also verses 111 and 162). In verse 70 he testifies: "I delight in thy law." And in verse 174 he states: "Thy law *is* my delight" (see also verse 47).

Give Me That Book!

But we ask at this point in our study: Are there any reasons supplied by the psalmist for his delight in the way of the Word? We believe that there are many expressed in Psalm 119, and we select four here for our consideration.

First, the psalmist delighted in the way of the Word because it displays perfection. The perfection of the Word of God is a reflection of the perfection of the God of the Word. Thus the psalmist describes the way of the Word as being:

- Faithful (verse 86)
- True (verse 142)
- Upright (verse 137)
- Good (verse 39)
- Righteous (verse 144)
- Pure (verse 140)

These attributes of the Word are also attributes of Jehovah. And in these attributes—indicating the perfection of the way—the psalmist delighted. Little wonder that he could testify, "I will speak of thy testimonies also before kings, and will not be ashamed" (verse 46), and confess "I have seen an end of all perfection: *but* thy commandment *is* exceeding broad" (verse 96).

Second, the psalmist delighted in the way of God's Word because it brings hope. In verse 49 he prays, "Remember the word unto thy servant, upon which thou hast caused me to hope" (see also verse 116). In verse 81 he confesses: "My soul fainteth for thy salvation: *but* I hope in thy word" (see also verse 114). He recounts in verse 147, "I prevented the dawning of the morning, and cried: I hoped in thy word."

Where is there such good hope as that inspired by the Scriptures? Naturally we are "without hope in the world," but through God's Word, hope is born in our hearts, hope that is centred in the Lord Jesus Christ.

A third reason for the psalmist's delight in the Word of God lies in the fact that it bestows freedom. In verse 45 the writer exclaims: "I will walk at liberty [margin—large]: for I seek thy precepts." Men and women wrongly imagine that subjection to the Word of God is slavery, but here the psalmist states that in actual fact our only true freedom lies in seeking God's precepts. If we would walk at liberty, we must walk in the way of God's law. Life apart from God leads not to a spacious highway, but to an imprisoning cul-de-sac.

Again, the psalmist delighted in God's Word because it offers wonders. God's Word is a scenic highway that thrills the traveller as he makes his way along it. Prays the psalmist: "Open thou mine eyes, that I may behold wondrous things out of thy law" (119:18). Hidden to natural intelligence, these wonders and beauties are clearly seen by God-opened eyes.

Desire

Consider finally the *desire* that God's Word as a highway requires. We remind ourselves again that there is nothing mechanical about travelling on God's highway; we must desire with all our hearts to walk on it moment by moment.

In one sense Psalm 119 is a prayer, and there are various petitions offered by the writer that speak of the desire we must have in relation to God's Word.

We must desire, for example, to be directed by God. Hear the psalmist's earnest desire in verse 5: "O that my ways were directed to keep thy statutes!" Again in verse 33 he prays: "Teach me, O LORD, the way of thy statutes." In verse 35 he prays: "Make me to go in the path of thy commandments." And finally in verse 133 he prays: "Order my steps in thy word."

Each one of these requests reveals the psalmist's intense desire to be in the way of God's Word. If this earnest desire is lacking on our part, we cannot experience the joy and peace that comes through walking on God's highway of holiness. But the psalmist's desire is expressed in other ways. He desires, for example, to be kept from wandering. In verse 10 he pleads: "O let me not wander from thy commandments." He wants above all to walk in the way of God's law.

This wandering, if he gives in to the temptation, may lead on to the path of lying. Accordingly in verse 29 he prays: "Remove from me the way of lying." There is also the danger lest he stray on to the path of covetousness, and with regard to this danger, he prays: "Incline my heart unto thy testimonies, and not to covetousness" (verse 36). He may be led to walk the path of vanity: "Turn away mine eyes from beholding vanity; *and* quicken thou me in thy way" (verse 37). In summary, the psalmist is able to testify: "I have refrained my feet from every evil way, that I might keep thy word" (verse 101).

This steadfastness on the part of the psalmist may be traced to his overwhelming desire to be walking in the way of righteousness. He refuses to be sidetracked. He keeps only within the orbit of God's Word and will.

The psalmist's desire to walk in God's way is expressed, too, in terms of a desire to understand God's Word. Here are some sample petitions from Psalm 119: "Make me to understand the way of thy precepts. Give me understanding, and I shall keep thy law. Give me understanding, that I may learn thy commandments. Through thy precepts I get understanding" (27, 34, 73, 104; see also 98–100, 125, and 169).

Finally, we note that the psalmist's desire is expressed in terms, not merely of wanting to walk in God's way, but to run with zeal and promptness in the way of His commandments. "I will run the way of thy commandments, when thou shalt enlarge my heart" (verse 32).

Because through his own experience the psalmist had discovered that the Lord's way was the right way, he was able to evaluate all other ways. His verdict is given in two verses: "Through thy precepts I get understanding: therefore I hate every false way" (verse 104). "Therefore I esteem all *thy* precepts *concerning* all *things to be* right; *and* I hate every false way" (verse 128).

Is the reader constantly—consciously—cheerfully—walking in the way of God's Word? Are you travelling toward Heaven on the highway of holiness? Are you making progress in your Christian experience by refusing to deviate from the way of God's Word?

Oh, that we might say with the psalmist: "I have inclined mine heart to perform thy statutes alway, *even unto* the end" (119:112), and to pray with him, "Teach me, O LORD, the way of thy statutes; and I shall keep it *unto* the end!" (119:33).

FOR YOUR FURTHER STUDY

1. Draw some spiritual lessons from various signs that we see along our highways; for example, "Yield right of way."
2. What are some of the blessings to be experienced in travelling on God's highway?
3. What would you say to the person who claims that every "holy book" is a way to God?

A Harp of Tuneful Sound

There are no songs to be compared with the songs of Zion.

—**John Milton**

If I would work, the Bible is my tool;
Or play, it is a harp of tuneful sound.
If I am ignorant, it is my school;
If I am sinking, it is solid ground.
If I am cold, the Bible is my fire,
And it gives wings if boldly I aspire.

—**Author Unknown**

The Bible is the window of hope through which we look into eternity.

—**Timothy Dwight**

Oh, this Book is the hive of all sweetness, the armoury of all well-tempered weapons, the tower containing the crown jewels of the universe, the lamp that kindles all other lights, the home of all majesties and splendours, the stepping-stone on which Heaven stoops to kiss the earth with its glories, the marriage ring that unites the celestial and the terrestrial, while all the clustering white-robed multitudes of the sky stand round to rejoice at the nuptials.

This Book is the wreath into which are twisted all garlands, the song into which hath struck all harmonies, the river of light into which hath poured all the great tides of hallelujahs, the firmament in which all suns and moons and stars and constellations and galaxies and immensities and universes and eternities wheel and blaze and triumph.

—**T. DeWitt Talmage**

Concerning the influence of the Bible, **Dr. James M. Gray**, once President of Moody Bible Institute, wrote:

It fills the world with fragrance
Whose sweetness never cloys;
It lifts our eyes to Heaven
It heightens human eyes.

STUDY 17
God's Word Is Festive

Our Key Scripture—"Thy statues have been my songs in the house of my pilgrimage" (Psalm 119:54).

Supplementary Scriptures—Job 35:10; Psalm 19:8; 28:7; 32:7; 33:3; 40:3; 42:8; 69:30; 77:6; 96:1; 98:1; 119:14, 16, 24, 47, 70, 77, 92, 103, 111, 162; 144:9; 149:1; Jeremiah 15:16; Colossians 3:16.

TOO few of God's children look upon the Bible and its message as productive of joy. To many the Bible is a melancholy, not a merry book; it is associated with gloom, not gaiety. It is looked upon as legalistic in spirit, not life-giving. To help remove this prejudice we want to consider God's Word as festive—that is, as essentially joyful and joy-giving.

It is in Psalm 119 that we find the fullest statement of this aspect of God's Word. The writer of this great poem in praise of God's Word had discovered that meditation upon God's law was a delight, not a drudgery. Here is the evidence.

"I will delight myself in thy statutes" (119:16).

"Thy testimonies also *are* my delight" (119:24).

"Make me to go in the path of thy commandments; for therein do I delight" (119:35).

"I will delight myself in thy commandments, which I have loved" (119:47).

"I delight in thy law" (119:70).

"Thy law *is* my delight" (119:77, 174).

"Unless thy law *had been* my delights, I should then have perished in mine affliction" (119:92).

"Trouble and anguish have taken hold on me: *yet* thy commandments *are* my delights" (119:143).

The key word in all these texts is *delight*. The psalmist found his supreme joy in God's Word. Indeed, he employs various figures to set forth his delight in the law of God.

The psalmist's joy in God's Word was like the joy of the soldier in battle who finds great plunder: "I rejoice at thy word, as one that findeth great spoil" (119:162).

His joy was greater than the one who has much wealth: "The law of thy mouth *is* better unto me than thousands of gold and silver" (119:72; cf. 14).

His joy was like that of someone eating a sweet morsel with relish: "How sweet are thy words unto my taste! *yea, sweeter* than honey to my mouth" (119:103). This, too, was the experience of Ezekiel the Prophet when he was given his message. Concerning the scroll handed to him in his vision (see Ezekiel 2:9–3:3), Ezekiel states: "Then did I eat *it*; and it was in my mouth as honey for sweetness" (3:3; see Revelation 10:10).

Finally, we note that the psalmist's joy in God's Word was like the joy of one who has just received a great inheritance: "Thy testimonies have I taken as an heritage for ever: for they *are* the rejoicing of my heart" (119:111).

In its May 1, 1972 issue, *Newsweek* recalls the discovery of the tomb of King Tutankhamen in 1922 by Howard Carter. Here is *Newsweek's* account of how the tomb with its priceless treasures was found:

> Carter was digging in the mysterious Valley of the Kings, located not far from Thebes. The Pharaohs had themselves buried in this sacred ground, surrounded with treasures and totems to see them through their voyages into the afterworld. The ground had been scoured by both researchers and thieves.

But Carter was convinced that Tutankhamen's tomb was still there, despite the skepticism of his colleagues. One of his last attempts was in a plot of land that had already turned up the tomb of Rameses VI. Carter went beneath that earlier find and came upon a stairway leading deep down into the ground.

With mounting excitement, Carter's men picked and chipped patiently away, until they reached the very door of the tomb itself. Lady Evelyn (daughter of Carter's patron, the late Lord Carnarvon) was there with her father on the day Carter finally opened a section of the door and peered in by the light of a candle. At first he was speechless. "Then my father asked if he could see anything," says Lady Evelyn. "He replied: " 'Yes, wonderful things' "!¹

Has not this been the experience of many of us with regard to the Bible? We approached it as a tomb, full of the dead bones of history, but found it to be filled with treasure. Well do we pray with the writer of Psalm 119:18: "Open thou mine eyes, that I may behold wondrous things out of thy law," and if necessary we should be prepared to pray with the little girl, "open my eyes a little wider."

BASIC OUTLINE

With this as a background we are ready to examine how the Bible is the source of delight and joy and pleasure to the believer. The Word of God is the source of pleasure for us because of what it *proclaims*, and because of what it *predicts*, and because of what it *provides*.

What the Bible Proclaims

First, the Bible is the source of delight and pleasure because of what it *proclaims*. The Bible contains history, law, poetry, prophecy, and letters. Each of these strands holds its own element of delight. But supremely the Bible delights the believer because it is a revelation of God's heart and mind.

The Bible reveals the nature and character of God Himself. Here we learn that the Lord God is "merciful and gracious, longsuffering, and abundant in goodness and truth, Keeping mercy for thousands, forgiving iniquity and transgression and sin, and that will by no means clear *the guilty*"

(Exodus 34:6, 7). Where in all the writings of mankind is there a revelation of God as full, as clear, as inspiring as that?

The Bible also reveals "the inside story" of mankind. It presents man as a creation of God. It makes clear his dignity—and his depravity; his potential—and his predicament; his greatness—and his guilt. It is only in the Bible that a balanced picture of man is maintained.

The Bible proclaims, too, God's great plan for fallen man. It is the story of how God devises means that His banished be not expelled from Him (see 2 Samuel 14:14). From the Bible we learn how God sent His only begotten Son into the world to die for those who were His enemies that they in turn might receive life, light, and liberty. "Other books have poems," wrote Dr. D.J. Burrell, "but no other sings the song of salvation and gives the troubled soul a peace that floweth like a river."[2]

In its proclamation of these great and glorious truths the Bible utters them clearly. While the Bible indeed speaks of sublime mysteries, its basic message is not communicated in terms incomprehensible to the mass of people. It employs no special philosophical terminology or intellectual jargon. "In the beginning God created the heavens and the earth" is the first sentence of the Bible, and the simplicity and clarity of that sentence marks its most profound revelation.

In spite of this essential clarity, how often people set the Bible aside with the plea that it is too difficult to read! If we would only come to the Scriptures with a prayer in our heart that God would teach us, how much light would break upon its pages! John G. Whittier wrote:

> We search the world for truth; we cull
> The good, the true, the beautiful
> From graven stone and written scroll,
> From all old flower-fields of the soul;
> And, weary seekers of the best,
> We come back laden from our quest
> To find that all the sages said
> Is in the Book our mothers read.[3]

But the Bible proclaims its truths and revelations confidently. There is no doubt, no speculation, no hesitation in the minds of the writers. Indeed, it has often been pointed out that the Bible presents no systematic arguments for the existence of God. There is no system of apologetics in the Word of God. "In the beginning God" is the assumption of every one of its writers.

In approaching the Bible, then, we must approach it with the same confidence. We must approach it with sympathy for its message. If we come with hatred and hostility, we will find only passages to feed the flames of criticism in our hearts. Scotland's bard, Sir Walter Scott, warned readers against coming to the Bible in order to scorn its message.

> Within this ample volume lies
> The mystery of mysteries.
> Happiest they of the human race
> To whom God has granted grace
> To read, to fear, to hope, to pray,
> To lift the latch and force the way.
> And better had they ne'er been born
> Who read to doubt, or read to scorn.[4]

Finally, we note that in the proclamation of its great truth the Bible speaks consistently. Here is one of the abiding miracles of the Scriptures. Written over a period of many centuries, penned by many human authors, arising from vastly differing circumstances, the Bible is homogeneous in its teachings about God, man, sin, and salvation.

This remarkable fact testifies to the divine inspiration of the Book. Turn where you will, and the Bible speaks with one voice. God is holy and righteous; man is sinful and rebellious; salvation has been provided and published; Heaven is real, and hell is a grim reality. It is true that each writer makes his own distinct contribution to the full-orbed presentation of these doctrines in the Bible, but there is never any confusion, contradiction, or conflict among its writers.

"This Book," wrote W.P. White, "is a harp with a thousand strings. Play on one to the exclusion of its relationship to the others, and you will develop discord. Play on all of them, keeping them in their places in the divine scale and you will hear heavenly music all the time."[5]

The consistency and harmony of Scriptures caused John Dryden to ask:

Whence but from Heaven could man unskilled in arts,
In several ages born, in several parts,
Weave such agreeing truths? Or how, or why
Should all conspire to cheat us with a lie?
Unasked their pains, ungrateful their advice,
Starving their gain and martyrdom their price.
Then for the style, majestic and divine,
It speaks no less of God in every line—
Commanding words whose force is still the same
As the first fiat that produced their frame.
All faiths beside, they did by arms ascend,
Or sense indulged has made mankind their friend.
This doctrine only doth our lust oppose,
Unfed by nature's soil on which it grows.[6]

What the Bible Predicts

The Bible is the believer's source of delight because of what it proclaims. But the Bible also delights the Christian because of what it *predicts*.

Unfortunately the predictive element in Scripture has been watered down; indeed, some have even ruled it out. The inspired prophecies of godly men moved by the Holy Spirit (2 Peter 1:21) have been characterized as brilliant guesses or hypotheses. Some have even dared to say that what appears as prophecy was actually written after the events took place.

But if our heart is in tune with the Author of the Bible we recognize the predictive portions of Scripture for what they are—dramatic unveilings of future events.

What are some of these events?

Central to the Bible's portrait of the future is the second coming of our Lord Jesus Christ. We do not deal here with the various systems of prophetic interpretation that have been elaborated in order to harmonize the multiple details of the word of prophecy. Rather, we wish simply to stress the glorious fact, announced by Christ, affirmed by angels, and authenticated by apostles that "this same Jesus, which is taken up from you into heaven, shall so come in like manner as ye have seen him go into heaven" (Acts 1:11). That means that He shall return personally, bodily, visibly, and suddenly.

Our response to this revelation of Christ's second coming should be delight, not debate; adoration, not argument; the result of our study should be light, not heat; greater fervency rather than greater feuding.

When John heard the risen Lord proclaim in solemn words, "Surely I come quickly," John's response was: "Amen. Even so, come, Lord Jesus" (Revelation 22:20). There is the normal and normative attitude of the true believer to the fact of Christ's imminent coming. He longs to see his Lord and to be in His presence.

The second coming of Christ, however, is not an isolated event; it is an integral part of a greater whole—the plan of God for the heavens and the earth. "I saw," wrote John, "a new heaven and a new earth: for the first heaven and the first earth were passed away" (Revelation 21:1). Peter, too, speaks of that event. "Nevertheless we, according to his promise, look for new heavens and a new earth, wherein dwelleth righteousness" (2 Peter 3:13).

From scores of prophetic passages of God's Word we could fill in the details of the Bible's vast panorama of the future. Such portions of God's Word are there to remind us that human history is progressing toward a goal. History, according to the Bible, is not cyclic or evolutionary, but progressive—each era and epoch unfolding the plan of God for mankind.

Here, then, is the Christian answer to all the plans and proposals of man for the creation of a Utopia wherein there will be peace and justice and harmony among men. The Bible is insistent that man cannot by himself usher in any such age. Only the man Christ Jesus has been appointed by God to undertake such a plan.

By its revelation of the glorious future that awaits all God's children, the Bible delights and charms and captivates its readers. This is why Dr. T. DeWitt Talmage could write in his oratorical style: "Where is the youth with music in his soul who is not stirred by Jacob's lament, or Nathan's dirge, or Habakkuk's ode, or Paul's march of the resurrection, or John's anthem of the ten-thousand-times-ten-thousand doxology of elders on their faces, answering to the trumpet blast of the archangel?"[7]

What the Bible Provides

This leads us finally to consider what the Bible *provides*. The Word of God is our source of delight because of what it proclaims and because of what it predicts and consequently because of what it provides.

There is only one problem in seeking to determine what the Word of God provides, and that is: Where shall we conclude our investigation? It is like asking what the sun does for our earth, or what does oxygen do for an individual, or what does water do for a fish. Once we begin to examine and explore this aspect of our subject, we find it difficult to find the end of the chain of consequences that is brought into being through the Bible. One aspect leads to another, ad infinitum.

We begin, then, by remarking that the Bible provides and produces life. We have seen this in an earlier study, but we mention it here again because this aspect is fundamental to any other aspect we could list. "Thy word," declared the psalmist in Psalm 119, "hath quickened"—that is, has brought life to—"me" (verse 50). Earlier he had prayed for this: "Quicken thou me according to thy word" (119:25).

The Bible, then, is not primarily designed to provide learning, but life. We have the Bible primarily to bring us into touch with the life-giving God, not to construct elaborate systems of theology (important as these undoubtedly may be). The Bible is a bridge over which we cross to meet God; it is the table around which we reason together in order to receive cleansing and forgiveness (see Isaiah 1:18).

But the Bible provides not only life, but strength. Amid trials and temptations, believers need to be strengthened. Jeremiah the Prophet testifies that through his delight in God's Word he was strengthened amid persecution. "Thy words were found, and I did eat them; and thy word was unto me the joy and rejoicing of mine heart" (Jeremiah 15:16). An unknown poet has written:

> We've travelled together, my Bible and I,
> When life had grown weary, and death e'en was nigh;
> But all through the darkness of mist or of wrong
> I found there a solace, a prayer, and a song.[8]

The Bible produces life and strength. It also produces hope. Indeed, this is one of its most beneficial and blessed virtues. The Bible produces hope both in this life and for the next. We refuse to accept the notion that the Bible acts simply as a drug. Religion, formal and lifeless, may indeed be the opiate of the people, but the Bible received into the heart, rather than deadening man's aspirations and ambitions, actually quickens them into life, and motivates the individual to seek the highest. This is the testimony of history wherever the Bible has been given its rightful place in the heads and hearts of people. "I long," wrote Erasmus, "that the husbandman should sing portions of the Scriptures to himself as he follows the plough, and that the weaver should hum them to the tune of his shuttle, that the traveller should beguile with these stories the tedium of his journey."[9]

It is with regard to man's destiny that the Bible speaks with that authority that brings hope and comfort. W.A. Rice reminds us concerning Sir Walter Scott's request for the Bible to be read during his final illness:

> During his final illness, he asked his son-in-law, Mr. J.G. Lockhart, to read to him out of the Book, and when Mr. Lockhart inquired, "What book?" he replied: "There is only one Book—the Bible. In the whole world it is called 'The Book.' All other books are mere leaves, fragments. The Bible is the only complete and perfect Book. Its light sheds brightness over the grave and into eternity. It is the only Book."
>
> Mr. Lockhart added: "I chose the fourteenth chapter of John's Gospel." He listened with mild devotion and said, when I had done, "Well, this is great comfort."[10]

But how different and depressing is the voice of unbelief! Concerning death Colonel Robert Ingersoll wrote:

> It may be best in the happiest moments of the voyage, when eager winds are kissing every sail, to dash against the

unseen rock, and in an instant hear the billows roar above the sunken ship. For whether in mid-sea or among the breakers of the farther shore, a wreck must mark the end of each and all. Every life will, at its close, become a tragedy as sad and deep and dark as can be woven of the warp and woof of mystery and death.[11]

Life, strength, hope—and we could keep adding to the list, for the Word of God is productive of manifold blessings in the hearts of its readers. It sets up a chain reaction in the believer which is never-ending. We conclude by quoting a verse from the pen of Charles Wesley, whose hymns were written because of the Word of God delighting his heart.

> When quiet in my room I sit,
> Thy Book be my companion still;
> My joy Thy sayings to repeat,
> Talk o'er the records of Thy will,
> And search the oracles divine,
> Till every heartfelt word is mine.[12]

FOR YOUR FURTHER STUDY

1. Why do many Christians find no delight in God's Word?
2. Which aspects of the Bible delight your own heart?
3. We referred to the Bible producing life, strength, and hope. Can you now add to this list?

The Best in the World

The Bible is stamped with specialty of origin, and an immeasurable distance separates it from all competitors.

—**Wm. E. Gladstone**

We account the Scriptures of God to be the most sublime philosophy. I find more sure marks of authority in the Bible than in any secular history whatever.

—**Sir Isaac Newton**

A single line in the Bible has consoled me more than all the books I ever read besides.

—**Kant**

There is a Book worth all other books which were ever printed.

—**John Milton**

The Bible is the best Book in the world.

—**John Adams**

Concerning his New Testament, Coleridge once said: "I have only one Book, and that is the best.

I put the Scriptures above all the sayings of the Fathers, angels, men, and devils. Here I stand.

—**Martin Luther**

I read all kinds of books, including sacred books, but the Bible stands alone because it reads me.

—**J.W. von Goethe**

Holding up his Greek Testament, the German scholar Ewald said to Dean Stanley, "In this little Book is contained all the wisdom of the world."

The Bible will take care of itself if the church will distribute it and get it read.

—**Robert E. Speer**

STUDY 18
God's Word Is Competitive

Our Key Scripture — "Finally, brethren, pray for us, that the word of the Lord may have *free* course, and be glorified, even as *it is* with you: And that we may be delivered from unreasonable and wicked men: for all *men* have not faith" (2 Thessalonians 3:1, 2).

Supplementary Scriptures—1 Samuel 5:1–4; Job 32:8; Psalm 147:15; Jeremiah 30:13; Acts 17:2–4; 19:18–20; Colossians 1:5, 6; 2 Timothy 2:9; 3:15–17.

GOD'S Word competitive? And does 2 Thessalonians 3:1 really have something to say about such an aspect of God's Word?

To answer these questions, some would reword Paul's message to the Thessalonian believers to read as follows—

"Finally, brethren, pray for us that the word of the Lord may spread [margin: run] rapidly and be glorified, just as it did also with you."[1]

Still others would say—

"Finally, my fellow Christians, pray for us that the Lord's Word will run well and win glory as it did among you."[2]

And yet another words it —

"Furthermore, brothers, do pray for us, that the word of the Lord may run its course and be glorified as it was among you."[3]

The key to the meaning of Paul's appeal lies in two Greek words, translated in the *Authorized Version* as "may have free course" and "be glorified." "In the former of those terms," writes Dr. S.T. Bloomfield, "there is the same metaphor (taken from a race course) as in Psalm 147:15, which passage was probably in the mind of the Apostle" (*The Greek Testament with English Notes*). The second term may also be related to an athlete who excels in the race and is glorified by having the laurels placed on his brow amid the applause of the watching crowd.

What, then, is Paul appealing to the Christians at Thessalonica to do? He is beseeching them to pray that the Word of the Lord might run its course well and win glory like a triumphant athlete in the Grecian games.

This gives direction for all believers as they pray for the Word of the Lord. For Paul that Word was the Gospel message which he had been commissioned to preach. For us the Word of the Lord is still the Gospel message, but in written form in the inspired Bible, and as Christians we are to pray that this Word may be swift and successful in its mission.

BASIC OUTLINE

We are convinced that as Christians we should be praying for the *circulation*, the *communication*, and the *conquest* of the Scriptures.

Circulation

With regard to the Word of God we should pray that it may excel in its *circulation*. "Wherever God's Word is circulated," wrote Bishop Simpson, "it stirs the hearts of people. It is God speaking to man."[4]

But we should be more specific in the matter of prayer for the circulation of God's Word.

We should pray that *Christians will have a clear understanding of the objectives of Bible circulation*. We are not to spread God's Word as if it were some kind of a magic charm or talisman—as if there is something miraculous or momentous in the number of Bibles published and propagated.

We have used the word circulation for this aspect of our subject. We could easily have used the word dissemination. This word may help us to understand more clearly the objectives of Bible circulation. The verb disseminate comes from two Latin words meaning "in every direction" and "seed"—that is, to scatter as seed in all directions.

Thus when we circulate God's Word we are to remember that we are circulating seed. Mark 4:3–8 records the well-known parable of the sower and the seed. In giving His own interpretation of the details of the parable, the Lord Jesus said: "The sower soweth the word" (4:14). Here is our basis for identifying God's Word as seed, and when we circulate the Bible we are to keep in mind that we are sowing that which contains life, and when received into the heart will ultimately bring forth a harvest.

But the other part of the verb "disseminate" reminds us that God's Word is for all people. We are to sow it in all directions. Writing to the Colossian Christians, Paul was able to describe the word of the truth of the Gospel as being at that time "in all the world; and bringeth forth fruit"(Colossians 1:5, 6).

Most of us have heard of Brother Andrew, known popularly as "God's Smuggler." He has reminded us earnestly and emphatically that God's Word must be circulated, even in those countries which we have come to label as "closed doors." Christians in the West must undertake to make Bibles available to our fellow Christians in Russia, the Eastern European countries, in China, and wherever the Bible has been banned.

Further, with regard to the circulation of the Bible, we should pray that *Christians may make use of all opportunities for spreading the Scriptures.* Thank God for all the agencies engaged in distributing the Bible, but the task must not be left to organizations alone. Individuals and churches must become involved in spreading the Scriptures and in sowing the seed. With Bibles to suit every eye and every purse the Christian should engage in a personal campaign to share the Word of God.

Christians may help directly in the propagation of the Bible by investing in the work of translation, publication, and distribution of the Scriptures. Various societies are continuously engaged in these phases of sowing the seed. Christians may not be able to go overseas personally, but most certainly through their wise and faithful stewardship they can help in the production and promotion of the Bible.

Finally, with regard to the circulation of God's Word we should pray that *Christians may triumph over all obstacles that stand in the way of disseminating the Scriptures.*

Give Me That Book!

This is precisely what Paul asked for in his request of 2 Thessalonians 3:1, 2. "Pray for us," he appealed, "that the word of the Lord may have *free* course, and be glorified, even as *it is* with you: And that we may be delivered from unreasonable and wicked men." In presenting this request Paul is asking not so much for himself personally as for himself in his official capacity as a herald of the good news of Christ. He recognized that the progress of the Gospel could be hindered through the attacks and assaults of men upon himself.

King Jehoiakim of Judah, as recorded in Jeremiah 36, attempted to take God's Word out of circulation by burning Jeremiah's scroll, which contained messages from the Lord. Callously and coldly he cut the scroll into pieces and arrogantly burned each piece. But Jehoiakim could not triumph over God's Word. A second scroll was prepared, to which were added more messages in condemnation of the king. Jeremiah triumphed over his adversary; God's Word triumphed over the word of the king.

Throughout the centuries this same divine Word has been banned, blasted, buried, and burned. Yet, in spite of the hostility of men, the Bible survives and miraculously continues to spread. Holding up a copy of the Bible, Ingersoll defiantly boasted: "In fifteen years I'll have this Book in the morgue."[5] But Ingersoll is now in the grave, and the Bible lives on. Isaac Taylor was certainly right when he affirmed: "This deathless Book has survived three great dangers: the negligence of its friends, the false systems built upon it, and the warfare of those who have hated it."[6]

Dr. Samuel M. Zwemer drew attention to the Bible's ability to triumph over its foes by quoting the inscription found on the monument to the Huguenots in Paris:

> Hammer away, ye hostile hands.
> Your hammers break; God's anvil stands.[7]

This is how John Clifford has expressed the same truth:

> I paused last eve beside the blacksmith's door,
> And heard the anvil ring, the vesper's chime,
> And looking in, I saw upon the floor
> Old hammers, worn with beating years of time.

222

"How many anvils have you had?" said I,
"To wear and batter all these hammers so?"
"Just one," he answered. Then, with twinkling eye:
"The anvil wears the hammers out, you know."

And so, I thought, the anvil of God's Word
For ages skeptics' blows have beat upon,
But, though the noise of falling blows was heard,
The anvil is unchanged; the hammers gone.[8]

Its Communication

It is not enough, however, to pray that the Word of God may be glorified in its circulation. Paul's request indicates that we should pray, too, that the Word of the Lord may run well and be glorified in the matter of *its communication.* This is suggested in our basic text by Paul's words: "Finally, brethren, pray for us, that the word of the Lord may have *free* course, and be glorified, even as *it is* with you." In the phrase, "even as *it is* with you," Paul recalls how the Word of the Lord was communicated to and received by the Thessalonian believers.

We are not in the dark as to how the Word of the Lord was communicated to the Thessalonians by Paul. In Acts 17 we have the record of the coming of the Gospel to Thessalonica. In the city there was a synagogue of the Jews—

> And Paul, as his manner was, went in unto them, and three sabbath days reasoned with them out of the scriptures, Opening and alleging, that Christ must needs have suffered, and risen again from the dead; and that this Jesus, whom I preach unto you, is Christ. And some of them believed, and consorted with Paul and Silas; and of the devout Greeks a great multitude, and of the chief women not a few. (2–4)

Paul communicated the Word of the Lord as a supernatural Book. To Paul the Old Testament was divinely inspired and prophetic in nature, being fulfilled in the Lord Jesus.

In 1 Thessalonians 2:13 we have remarkable proof that Paul's listeners received his message as a supernatural one. "For this cause also thank we

God without ceasing, because, when ye received the word of God which ye heard of us, ye received *it* not *as* the word of men, but, as it is in truth, the word of God, which effectually worketh also in you that believe." Note the contrast drawn by Paul: "the word of men" — natural, finite, ineffective; "the word of God"—supernatural, infinite, powerful.

Second, Paul communicated the Word of the Lord as a superior Book and message. In 1 Corinthians 1 and 2 he demonstrates the superiority of the message of the Gospel to the philosophies of the world's wise men. To Paul "the foolishness of God is wiser than men; and the weakness of God is stronger than men." The Bible is often ridiculed both as a foolish and as a feeble Book, but history demonstrates that it is stronger than the strong books and wiser than the wise books of humanity.

Paul also communicated the Word of the Lord as a saving Book. The Old Testament Scriptures spoke to the hearts of men and women and pointed them to the Lord Jesus Christ. Concerning these same Old Testament Scriptures Paul wrote to Timothy: "From a child thou hast known the holy scriptures, which are able to make thee wise unto salvation through faith which is in Christ Jesus" (2 Timothy 3:15).

According to *Telenotes* of the Alberta Government Telephones, "Talking books make a lot of sense. Sounds odd? Not really. Because talking books are making life happier for blind Albertans. What exactly are talking books? They're books read onto tape cassettes."[9] In a different way the Bible is a "talking Book." In it we hear the voice of God. Depending upon the attitude of the reader, it speaks words of comfort or condemnation, mercy or judgment, despair or hope.

Finally, we notice that Paul communicated the word of God as a sufficient Book. It is true that the Bible does not contain an answer to every question that could be asked about every subject. It is not a supernatural computer. What the Bible teaches about itself, however, is that its contents are sufficient to enlighten us with regard to life's basic issues. "All Scripture," states Paul, "*is* given by inspiration of God, and *is* profitable for doctrine, for reproof, for correction, for instruction in righteousness" (2 Timothy 3:16). The sufficiency of the Scriptures enables "the man of God" to be "perfect, throughly furnished unto all good works" (3:17).

As Christians, then, we must pray fervently and frequently, not only for the circulation of the Bible, but for its communication. As the late Dr. A.W. Tozer has written: "It is not how many Bibles are sold that counts, nor even how many people read them; what matters is how many actually believe what they read and surrender themselves in faith to live by the truth. Short of this, the Bible can have no real value for any of us."[10]

Its Conquest

On the basis of Paul's request in 2 Thessalonians 3:1, 2 we have suggested that Christians should pray for the circulation of the Scriptures as well as the communication of the Scriptures. But we should pray also for the *conquest* of the Bible over all its competitors and rivals. The Bible, of course, is not the only book that seeks the allegiance of men's hearts. There are many other books in the race.

There are books that compete with the Bible in its statement of man's origins. There are books, indeed, that are diametrically opposed to the Bible's presentation of man's creation by God as recorded in the opening chapters of Genesis.

The essential distinction between the Bible and all other books is that the Bible claims to be a divine revelation. When the Bible, therefore, speaks about the origin of the universe and the origin of man, it is giving us information that could not be secured in any other way.

It is important to note, however, that the Bible presents its teaching concerning the origin of man in a moral framework. People would not be opposed to the Bible's claim that God made man if that claim did not involve man in a direct relationship to God and if that claim did not insist that man has certain responsibilities to God as the moral Governor of the universe. It is because the Bible exposes the sin and rebellion of man that is ridiculed, reviled, and rejected by men.

In 2 Thessalonians 3:2 Paul makes mention of man's innate opposition to the Word of the Lord. He asks prayer that "we may be delivered from unreasonable and wicked men: for all *men* have not faith." The Word of the Lord has faced this kind of opposition ever since the days of Paul, and that opposition has not always come from rebels and rogues; often it has come from priests, philosophers, and scientists!

Give Me That Book!

There is a second class of books competing with the Bible. There are books that compete and conflict with the Bible in its solution of man's problems. The Bible announces a remedy for man's sickness; there are other books that offer remedies as well. But concerning these books we must say: "Thou hast no healing medicines" (Jeremiah 30:13). The productions and publications of ungodly men are like the words of Job's friends, concerning whom the patriarch said: "Ye *are* forgers of lies, ye *are* all physicians of no value" (Job 13:4).

According to Dick Hillis, "In the vast mainland of China, the sayings of Chairman Mao Tse-Tung are holy writ to nearly 800 million people."[11] *The Little Red Book* is in the hands and minds of China's millions.

In one of his writings, "Where Do Correct Ideas Come From?" Chairman Mao affirms: "Where do correct ideas come from? Do they drop from the skies? No. Are they innate in the minds? No. They come from social practice, and from it alone."[12]

But what saith the Scriptures? Was not Elihu right when he stated: "*There is* a spirit in man: and the inspiration of the Almighty giveth them understanding" (Job 32:8)? According to the Bible, man owes his intelligence, rationality, and progress to the creative activity of God Himself. Progress in society is not the result of an evolutionary advance in social practice.

There is, then, a great gulf fixed between the Bible and the writings of natural man. The Bible proclaims that man needs deliverance from sin and the new birth of the Spirit. It proposes a radical solution to man's problems. It treats man as being in a desperate plight, from which only the power of God can deliver him.

We would refer to a third class of books. There are books that compete with the Bible in its survey of man's destiny. There is a great increase today in the number of books on astrology and divination. Man is both curious and concerned about the future. He tries to pull aside the curtain that covers the future. Concerning these books, we may paraphrase the words of Isaiah in his condemnation of the idols of his day: "Shew the things that are to come hereafter, that we may know ye *are* [divine books]: yea, do good, or do evil, that we may be dismayed, and behold *it* together" (cf. Isaiah 41:23).

Wherever the Bible is accepted and trusted, it triumphs over such books. After the victory of the Gospel in Ephesus, we read that "many that believed came, and confessed, and shewed their deeds. Many of them also which used curious arts, brought their books together, and burned them before all *men*: and they counted the price of them, and found *it* fifty thousand *pieces* of silver" (Acts 19:18, 19). What a bonfire that was! But note especially the next sentence: "So mightily grew the word of God and prevailed" (19:20). In that situation the Word of the Lord ran swiftly and was glorified.

An Old Testament illustration demonstrates how the Bible is triumphant over all its foes. In 1 Samuel 5 we learn that when the Ark of the Lord was placed in the Temple of Dagon, the idol of Dagon fell to the ground, its head and its hands mysteriously cut off. When the Bible is made supreme, all other books which are false in their contents are exposed and condemned. This blessed "Ark of the Lord" is triumphant over all forms of evil and error.

In the light of Paul's prayer request (2 Thessalonians 3:1, 2) we should not be content to pray, "Lord, bless thy word." We should be more specific. We should pray for its circulation; we should pray for its communication; and, above all, we should pray for its conquest over the hearts of men. Pray earnestly that the Word of the Lord may run the race and win the crown! "Scatter the Bible without stint," wrote C.H. Spurgeon. "Spread the Scriptures till they are as universal as the light; as all-pervading as the air; as all-refreshing as the dew!"[13]

FOR YOUR FURTHER STUDY

1. Is it sufficient to circulate the Bible? If not, why not?
2. When we affirm concerning the Bible that it is sufficient, in what ways are we to understand the claim?
3. Draw up a list of contrasts between the Word of God and the writings of men.

In God's Furnace

God is the Refiner, the Purifier. He tries, proves, and establishes those who yield to His moulding. It is a slow process; not hurried. He sits down to His work, He takes plenty of time. He is even willing to wait years with His subject to perfect it into the ideal image. It depends upon content. Some individuals take a long time to learn a single lesson, and the Refiner is perfectly willing to wait until that lesson is learned. Others He will get through with at once, if they are willing to take a quicker process—through the hotter fire.

—**Marie Taylor**

No vessel of gold is moulded without fire. Shrink not from the flame of divine love. If you would be moulded, you must be melted.

—**Author Unknown**

Lord, shall we grumble when Thy flames do scourge us?
Our sins breathe fire; Thy fire returns to purge us.
Lord, what an alchemist art Thou, whose skill
Transmutes to perfect good from perfect ill.

—**Francis Quarles**

Fire must separate the dross from the gold in normal refining processes. But after undergoing the fire, the gold is pure gold, though it may be less in volume than before the fiery refining process.

—**A.E. Wilder Smith**

In Palestine the refiner sat before his crucible, fixing his eyes on the metal, taking care that the heat was not too great, and letting the metal stay in the crucible only so long as was necessary for all the dross to be consumed. The indication of this was the reflection of the refiner's own image in the glowing mass.

—**Author Unknown**

Other books were given for our information; the Bible was given for our transformation.

—**Author Unknown**

The refiner is never far from the mouth of the furnace when his gold is in the fire, and the Son of God is always walking in the flames when His holy children are cast into them.

—**Charles H. Spurgeon**

STUDY 19
God's Word Is Transformative

Our Key Scripture—"[God] sent a man before them, *even* Joseph, *who* was sold for a servant: Whose feet they hurt with fetters: he was laid in iron: Until the time that his word came: the word of the LORD tried [Hebrew: refined] him. The king sent and loosed him; *even* the ruler of the people, and let him go free. He made him lord of his house, and ruler of all his substance" (Psalm 105:17–21).

Supplementary Scriptures—Job 23:10; Psalm 66:10; Proverbs 17:3; Isaiah 48:10; Daniel 12:10; Zechariah 13:9; Malachi 3:3; 1 Peter 1:7.

HIDDEN by the *Authorized Version* of Psalm 105:19, but clearly indicated by the original Hebrew word, is an aspect of the power of God's Word that can provide both instruction and inspiration to the believer in the midst of his trials.

In his inspired commentary on Joseph's experiences the psalmist notes that during the time he was in prison, "the word of the LORD refined him." Surely "the word of the LORD" here refers to the prophecies and promises given to him regarding his ultimate triumph and supremacy. But for a time, Joseph had to languish in prison, forgotten alike by baker and butler.

Joseph's prison experience, however, did not prove worthless, for during that time he was transformed by the power of God's Word. "The word of the LORD refined him," and he came forth from that prison "as gold" (cf., Job 23:10). God's Word consumed the dross of vain desires and ambitions, and produced the gold of meekness, patience, and godliness in his life.

BASIC OUTLINE

With the psalmist's inspired commentary before us, we have a key to unlock the mystery of Joseph's life in its diverse circumstances. With the refining symbolism in mind, consider three aspects of Joseph's life: first, Joseph *at home*, needing to be refined; second, Joseph *in prison*, being refined; third, Joseph *in the palace*, refined and on display.

At Home

Our first picture of this young man is Joseph *at home*, needing to be refined. This is found in Genesis 37:1–14. Inasmuch as this passage is familiar to students of the Bible, let us summarize what is told to us.

We note first the distinction that was conferred upon Joseph. "Now Israel loved Joseph more than all his children, because he *was* the son of his old age: and he made him a coat of *many* colours" (37:3). Without being dogmatic we suggest that this demonstration of paternal favouritism was unwise. Israel's motive was to favour Joseph above all his other sons, and this resulted in hostility and enmity in the family. Thus we read: "When his brethren saw that their father loved him more than all his brethren, they hated him, and could not speak peaceably unto him" (37:4).

Did Joseph come through this experience of favouritism completely unscathed? Did his father's discrimination between him and his brothers not leave in his mind, although perhaps never expressed, a feeling of superiority? Did there come into his life a spirit of pride? It is difficult to imagine that Israel's gesture toward his son promoted meekness and lowliness of spirit.

This leads us to consider the dreams that were communicated to Joseph. Joseph had two dreams in which his supremacy over his parents and brothers was symbolized. It is our conviction that these dreams were divinely originated. We feel, however, that Joseph did not have to divulge his dreams to his brothers. In doing so he created more tension and hostility between himself and them. Perhaps it was necessary for Joseph to tell only his father (note the different reaction of his father as compared to his brothers in Genesis 37:11).

Did Israel's favouritism, then manifested toward Joseph, actually contribute to Joseph's rehearsal of his dreams? Did he glory in his dreams and use them to put his brothers further into the shade?

There is one more aspect of the story of Joseph at home that will help us to grasp what was going on. We refer to the duty that was committed to Joseph. In Genesis 37:12–14 we read that Israel sent Joseph to his brothers as they were watching their flocks at some distance from their home. Does this mean that Joseph had been given exemption from ordinary labour in the fields? Had Israel arranged for Joseph to be at home while his other sons toiled hard and long, caring for the flocks of sheep? Joseph's assignment, at least, suggests that this was so.

Such exemption was not good for the young man. It simply added fuel to the fire of his brothers' hatred.

The evidence of Genesis 37:1–14, then, is to the effect that, although providentially marked out as God's man for great service, Joseph needed to be refined. He needed to be purified from any spirit of pride that may have crept into his life because of his father's favouritism. He needed to be cleansed from any feeling of superiority that his dreams may have produced. He needed to be set free from any attitude of smugness that may have entered his life through his inactivity and lack of hard work.

In the same way the man who is going to serve God today must undergo the refining work of God's Spirit through the Word of God. The dross of sin, not in general, but specifically, must be removed: the sins of ambition, pride, self-sufficiency, arrogance, etc.

In Prison

The second major scene in this story is that of Joseph *in prison*. Again, the story is well-known, and we need but sketch in the outlines.

When Joseph, after leaving home, made contact with his brothers, "they conspired against him to slay him." Through Reuben's intervention this dastardly deed was not perpetrated, and Joseph was eventually sold, instead, to a company of Ishmeelite traders on their way to Egypt.

In Egypt Joseph was purchased by Potiphar, an officer in Pharaoh's army. In Potiphar's home Joseph prospered—for a while. Through the false accusations of Potiphar's wife, Joseph eventually found himself thrown into prison.

While in prison, he was instrumental in interpreting the dreams of two fellow prisoners. Both promised, upon their own release, to intercede for Joseph. It was two years, however, before one of them, the chief butler, remembered his promise and brought Joseph to the attention of Pharaoh who, at the time, was in desperate need of an interpreter of a dream that had deeply disturbed him.

But what about Joseph in prison? What was going on in his own spiritual experience?

Genesis 39:21–23 tells us the following:

> But the Lord was with Joseph, and shewed him mercy, and gave him favour in the sight of the keeper of the prison. And the keeper of the prison committed to Joseph's hand all the prisoners that *were* in the prison; and whatsoever they did there, he was the doer *of it*. The keeper of the prison looked not to any thing *that was* under his hand; because the Lord was with him, and *that* which he did, the Lord made *it* to prosper.

That is a description of Joseph's outward condition: promotion and prosperity. We are indebted, however, to the writer of Psalm 105 for an inspired insight into Joseph's inner spiritual condition during the time of his imprisonment.

Concerning Joseph, the psalmist writes: God "sent a man before him, *even* Joseph, *who* was sold for a servant: Whose feet they hurt with fetters: he was laid in iron: Until the time that his word came: the word of the Lord tried [refined] him" (vs. 17–19).

What was going on in Joseph's heart while he was in prison? God's Word was refining him. His cell was his crucible, and in that cell the dross of vanity and pride and self-sufficiency was removed. He was humbled in order that he might be exalted. He suffered before he reigned. And in that time of suffering the dross of his life was extracted, and he came forth as pure gold.

There is a most interesting verse in Isaiah 1. The Lord, speaking concerning Jerusalem, states: "I will...purely purge away thy dross, and take away all thy tin" (v. 25). Back in 1642 Bishop Bedell, Anglican minister, together with a large group of fellow Protestants, was imprisoned during the Irish rebellion. He preached on this very text, Isaiah 1:25, to his fellow prisoners.

This was the verse that Bishop Bedell had chosen as his life's motto. And here is the reason why he chose it. The word *tin* in Hebrew is *bedel*. The good Bishop liked to quote the verse: "I will purely purge thy dross and take away all thy [bedel] tin!" He had come to loathe his sin, and desired to be purified.[1]

George Whitefield, one of England's greatest evangelists, is often quoted as having written:

> I remember some years ago I went into a glasshouse; and standing very attentive, I saw several masses of burning glass, of various forms. The workman took a piece of glass and put it into one furnace, then he put it into a second, and then into a third. I said to him: "Why do you put this through so many fires?"
>
> He answered, "Oh, sir, the first was not hot enough, nor the second, and, therefore, we put it into a third, and that will make it transparent."
>
> Thus we must be tried and exercised with many fires, until our dross is purged away, and we are made fit for the Master's use.[2]

We are accustomed to thinking that this purifying work is accomplished by trials. This, indeed, is a truth of Scripture (see 1 Peter 1:7). But we must not forget that God employs His Word, too, as an instrument in the refining process. God's Word, hidden in the heart, can burn up the dross of selfish desire and sinful thought and purify the child of God. Indeed, unless we are responding to the Word of the Lord in our hearts, outward trial will accomplish nothing as far as spiritual progress and purification are concerned. It is trial interpreted by God's Word that alone proves beneficial to us.

In times of trial, therefore, we should be in the Scriptures, searching them, studying them, applying them, more than ever. The Word of God should dwell in us richly, and there will be a rich result in our lives.

Was not Henry Ward Beecher right when he wrote:

> The steel that has suffered most is the best steel. It has been in the furnace, on the anvil, in the jaws of the vice. It has felt the teeth of the rasp and has been ground by emery. It has been heated and hammered and filed until it does not know itself. Misfortunes are God's best blessings, moulding influences, which give shapeliness and edge and durability and power.[3]

In the Palace

Our third picture of Joseph, then, is Joseph *in the palace*. His prison experience did not last forever. "Until the time that his word came: the word of the Lord tried him. The king sent and loosed him; *even* the ruler of the people, and let him go free. He made him lord of his house, and ruler of all his substance."

This, of course, is a condensed version of the story of Joseph. The longer account is found in Genesis 41 (see also chapters 42–50).

After his term in prison Joseph was summarily brought into Pharaoh's presence to interpret the king's dream. The Spirit of the Lord enabled him to give the true interpretation of the dream. Pharaoh was delighted and said to his servants, "Can we find *such a one* as this *is*, a man in whom the Spirit of God *is*?" (Genesis 41:38).

To Joseph, Pharaoh said: "Forasmuch as God hath shewed thee all this, *there* is none so discreet and wise as thou *art*: Thou shalt be over my house, and according unto thy word shall all my people be ruled: only in the throne will I be greater than thou" (41:39, 40). Imagine it! From prison to palace in one leap! Formerly a "jailbird," now the second ruler in the nation! What a true success story!

Because the Word of the Lord refined Joseph while he was in prison, he was prepared for his exaltation.

To Joseph was committed great authority. It is to be doubted, however, that without his prison experience, Joseph would have been ready to wield that power righteously. Unrefined, he might well have misused the power given to him.

To Joseph was given opportunity for service. He became the saviour of Egypt and wisely administrated the affairs of Pharaoh. Eventually, as we know, he became the saviour of his own family, including the brothers who had wronged him. We may well imagine that during his prison experience Joseph thought about his brothers and their cruel treatment of him, but through the refining process of God's Word, all bitterness and hatred against them were removed from his heart.

Is it not significant that when Pharaoh exalted Joseph to the position of second ruler, he put a gold chain about his neck (Genesis 41:42)? To Pharaoh the gold chain meant that he was conferring authority upon Joseph. But we may take that gold chain to signify that Joseph had graduated from his class in prison, and that he himself had come forth from the furnace as pure gold.

With Joseph's story before us, various verses of God's Word take on fresh meaning:

The Lord "shall sit *as* a refiner and purifier of silver" (Malachi 3:3).

"Thou, O God, hast proved us: thou hast tried us, as silver is tried" (Psalm 66:10).

"He knoweth the way that I take: *when* he hath tried me, I shall come forth as gold" (Job 23:10).

God subjects each one of His children to the refining process. His Word burns up the dross and purifies the gold.

Ezekiel the Prophet was sent with an exceedingly tragic word concerning the people of Israel. We find the message in Ezekiel 22:18, "Son of man, the house of Israel is to me become dross: all they *are* brass, and tin, and iron, and lead, in the midst of the furnace; they are *even* the dross of silver." Israel, in other words, was nothing but slag; the nation produced no silver.

Surely that is the greatest tragedy that can befall a life—to contribute nothing eternal or enduring to God's praise and glory.

To conclude our study, then, perhaps some definite counsels will be helpful, keeping the example of Joseph in mind. First, don't forget God's Word. During his two-year term in jail Joseph did not lose sight of that which God had promised. The promise of the Lord is clear: "They that wait upon the LORD [that is, who patiently wait for the fulfillment of His Word] shall renew *their* strength; they shall mount up with wings as eagles [Joseph 'flew' out of prison!]; they shall run, and not be weary; *and* they shall walk, and not faint" (Isaiah 40:31).

Failure in the life of service often arises from forgetfulness of God's promises.

In spite of appearances we must believe that which God has spoken. We walk by faith, not by sight.

Don't pray for the heat to be turned down or turned off. The separation of dross from gold requires a certain degree of heat. God knows just how much heat is necessary to remove the dross from your life.

Joy Ridderhof related some of the trials through which by God's grace she has come. At one time, when the heat was turned on high, she found herself praying, "Lord, don't turn the heat off; just work out Thy will for me." God took her at her word, and brought her through a very great time of testing. But she has come forth as pure gold.[4]

Finally, don't run away from the circumstances. Joseph couldn't! He was in prison, and there was no way he could escape. In his cell Joseph accepted his circumstances, and when God's time came he was ready, refined, and reflecting God's glory.

"The word of the LORD tried [refined] him"—that is the psalmist's commentary on the life of Joseph. God's Word is still used by the Holy Spirit in the process of refining God's children. Let us make sure that we respond to whatever God says to us in His Word.

FOR YOUR FURTHER STUDY

1. What is it in our lives that is equivalent to the dross that must be removed in order for the gold to be purified?
2. What precious truth is suggested by the verb *sit* in Malachi 3:3?
3. What according to Malachi 3:3 is the purpose of the refining process in the life of the believer?

Before the Judge

If we allowed the Word of God to criticize us a little more, we would criticize it a great deal less.

—**W.H. Griffith Thomas**

It is the recipients, and not the Word, which need to be criticized and corrected.

—**Clark H. Pinnock**

The Holy Scriptures are the rule of our faith and life; therefore, also, the judge of theological controversies.

—**Gerhard**

The Word will turn the inside of a sinner out, and let him see all that is in his heart.

—**Matthew Henry**

Mark Twain once observed that he was not troubled by the portions of the Bible which he could not understand, but by those which he did understand.

We must expect to have our most secret thoughts, relations, and purposes questioned, criticized, and measured by the Word of God. No court of inquiry was ever presided over by a more exact inquisitor than this.

—**F.B. Meyer**

Let us come to that Word and allow it to search and cut and penetrate and criticize everything in us that is contrary to the mind of God.

—**George Henderson**

God's Word is a perfect instrument for exposing and judging the most secret emotions of the heart and nature. To the believer this is exceedingly precious, for he rejoices in that which infallibly exposes the deepest emotions of his being.

—**George Williams**

Men do not reject the Bible because it contradicts itself, but because it contradicts them.

—**Unknown**

It is not men's thoughts about the Bible that judge it; it is the Bible which judges men and their thoughts.

—**Robert E. Speer**

STUDY 20
God's Word Is Discriminative

Our Key Scripture—"The word of God *is* . . . a discerner of the thoughts and intents of the heart. Neither is there any creature that is not manifest in his sight: but all things *are* naked and opened unto the eyes of him with whom we have to do" (Hebrews 4:12, 13).

Supplementary Scriptures—1 Samuel 16:7; Psalm 44:21; 139:1–6; Jeremiah 11:20; 17:9, 10; 20:12; Matthew 9:4; 12:25; 22:18; Luke 6:8; John 1:47; 2:24, 25; Revelation 1:14; 2:18.

IN the light of the fact that there are so many critics of God's inspired Word, it is highly significant that, in the one context where the word *critic* appears in Scripture, it refers to the amazing power of that Book as the Spirit's voice to trace and try the thoughts of men. God's Word is, par excellence, the critic of mankind.

In the first part of Hebrews 4:12 the writer compares God's Word to a sword. He states: "The word of God *is* quick, and powerful, and sharper than any twoedged sword, piercing even to the dividing asunder of soul and spirit, and of the joints and marrow. " This presentation of God's Word as a sword seems to have suggested a second figure, and he adds, "The word of God *is* . . . a discerner of the thoughts and intents of the heart."

The word used here and translated as *discerner* is *kritikos* (from which, of course, comes our English word critic) and means basically, "fit for judging, skilled for judging."[1] In relationship to the Bible, what is stressed by this unusual figure is the power of God's Word to pierce and probe the conscience of man as the Holy Spirit uses His Word in the preaching of the

Gospel. Try as he will a man cannot keep that Word from gaining entrance into his heart and there shattering all his fond delusions and exposing all his fatal deceptions.

BASIC OUTLINE

Let us see, first, how this amazing power of God's Word as critic of the heart is *explained* by other passages of Scripture; then let us see how it is *exemplified* in the ministry of the Lord Jesus; and, finally, let us determine how this power may be *employed* by us in our ministry today.

Explained

Consider, first, how this power of God's Word is *explained* by other passages of Scripture. When God's Word is spoken or read or studied, what power does it actually have in the heart?

Our first answer to that question surely must be that God's Word has power to search out and to speak to the hidden thoughts of the heart. God's Word is "a discerner of the thoughts and intents of the heart." It penetrates the mask which so often hides the true thoughts of individuals. It pierces the shield which otherwise is impenetrable. It is equipped to search out and to sift the thoughts of men.

Wherever, then, the Word of God is preached in the power of the Holy Spirit, it sits in judgment on the heart. It tries all the arguments and alibis of the soul, and exposes whatever is false and perverse. Each man's heart becomes a courtroom, and the Word of God becomes the *kritikos* [critic] of the soul.

This power of the Scriptures is directly related to the Author of the Scriptures. He is the eternal, omniscient Judge. He, the living Word, has equipped the written Word to become the critic of the heart. It is as He employs the Word that the heart is searched out.

"O LORD, thou hast searched me, and known me." So stated the psalmist, and it is only when we read and study the written Word that we begin to realize how fully He has searched us and known us. There is no secret of the heart that is hidden from Him. In the Word and through the Word every hidden thought stands revealed as in the sunlight.

God's Word Is Discriminative

God's Word considered as a critic not only ferrets out the hidden thoughts of the heart, but it sits in judgment on haughty thoughts as well. In a great passage where he discusses the wisdom of God as revealed in the Gospel message, Paul clearly shows that God has condemned the wisdom of man by the "word of the cross" (see 1 Corinthians 1:17–31). The Word of God as a skillful critic explodes the balloon of man's pride, and brings him tumbling down to the ground in misery and shame.

Hidden thoughts, haughty thoughts, and we must add now, hostile thoughts. As the supreme critic of the heart God's Word is able, not only to reveal hidden thoughts, but it is able also to overthrow hostile thoughts and schemes of the heart. Surely this is what Paul teaches in 2 Corinthians 10:3–5—"Though we walk in the flesh, we do not war after the flesh: (For the weapons of our warfare *are* not carnal, but mighty through God to the pulling down of strong holds;) Casting down imaginations, and every high thing that exalteth itself against the knowledge of God, and bringing into captivity every thought to the obedience of Christ."

What power! God's Word does not cease from its work until it has tried the heart, sentenced it, and brought it back under the dominion and authority of Christ. It looks upon the heart as being in revolt against Christ's authority, and its aim is to defeat and disarm rebellious men.

As we consider this wonderful power of God's Word, we are reminded of the woman who had just been given the Bible in her own language.

"Do you enjoy reading the Bible?" she was asked.

"Sir, I am not reading the Bible; the Bible is reading me."

This is the power of God's Word to act as a critic and judge of the heart.

W.B. Knight tells of a colporteur in Ceylon. He entered a village and there sold a copy of the Book of Proverbs to a notoriously dishonest man who took bribes and bore false witness in the courts.

The next day the man returned the book to the colporteur and said, "Take back this Book. It speaks against me, and reproves everyone who is in the wrong path. Take it, and give me back my money!"[2]

Give Me That Book!

Once, when Dr. John Chamberlain had read to the people of an Indian city the first chapter of the Epistle to the Romans, an intelligent Brahman said to him, "Sir, that chapter was written by one of your missionaries about us Hindus. It describes us exactly."[3] And yet Paul's words were penned hundreds of years before the era of modern missions to India! Such is the power of God's Word to sit in judgment on the heart of the sinner.

A learned Chinese student was once employed to translate the New Testament into his own language. At first he worked stolidly, but after a few weeks he came to the missionary greatly agitated.

"What a wonderful Book this is," he said.

"And why is that?" questioned his employer.

"Because," the translator replied, "it tells me so exactly about myself. It knows all that is in me. The One who wrote this Book must be the One who made me."[4]

That is sound reasoning, and reflects again the power of God's Word as *kritikos* [critic].

A missionary gave a Bible to a nonChristian Chinese man. Soon it was returned with the explanation: "Every time I read it, it kicks me."[5] That is another way of saying that the Bible criticizes and condemns the sinful thoughts of men.

Before we discuss another aspect of our subject, let us pause to set out these points again in order, and to interrogate ourselves in their light.

1. God's Word as a critic searches out the hidden thoughts of the heart. Am I trying to hide something from that all-searching Word?
2. God's Word as a critic judges the haughty thoughts of the hearts of men. Am I harbouring thoughts of pride and arrogance?
3. God's Word as a critic passes sentence upon the hostile thoughts of the heart and brands them for what they really are: treason against the King. Am I in present rebellion against God's will?

Exemplified

It is most helpful to compare the discriminative power of the written Word with the discriminative power of the living Word, the Lord Jesus

Christ. Concerning the Lord Jesus it is written, "He knew all *men*, And needed not that any should testify of man: for He knew what was in man" (John 2:24, 25). Here the power of God's Word to discern the thoughts and motives of the heart is *exemplified* in Him, who is the living Word of God.

Let us take four examples of the Lord Jesus as Critic of the hearts of men, and trace the parallels between the living Word and the written Word.

In Matthew 9:4 we read: "Jesus knowing their thoughts said, Wherefore think ye evil in your hearts?"

In Matthew 12:25 we read: "Jesus knew their thoughts, and said unto them, Every kingdom divided against itself is brought to desolation."

In Matthew 22:18 we read: "Jesus perceived their wickedness, and said, Why tempt ye me, *ye* hypocrites?"

In Luke 6:8 we read: "He knew their thoughts, and said to the man which had the withered hand, Rise up, and stand forth in the midst."

A careful study of the complete context in the case of each of these four quotations will reveal a general pattern: First, there is an attitude adopted toward the Lord Jesus. That attitude of heart is variously described. In one place it is described as an evil attitude; again, in another passage it is described as a wicked attitude; in the parallel account of Mark it is described as an attitude of hypocrisy (compare Mark 12:15 with Matthew 22:18). These attitudes are still prevalent with regard to the Lord Jesus.

Not only is there an attitude in each passage; there is an analysis. The Lord Jesus analyzed the hearts of His hearers. Isaiah wrote of the Messiah: "He shall not judge after the sight of his eyes, neither reprove after the hearing of his ears" (Isaiah 11:3). Indeed, as we read the four passages consecutively, we can only say in the words of our key Scripture: "The word of God"—even the Lord Jesus— ..."*is* a discerner of the thoughts and intents of the heart. Neither is there any creature that is not manifest in his sight: but all things *are* naked and opened unto the eyes of him with whom we have to do."

Finally, we note that with regard to each of these passages there is an admonition from the lips of the Lord Jesus. Having analyzed the thoughts of the hearts of His hearers, the Lord Jesus proceeded to rebuke them for their evil or wickedness or hypocrisy, or whatever was lurking within.

With the example of the Lord Jesus before us, we can now relate these aspects to the written Word of God.

As an individual reads the Bible, he may do so with various attitudes of heart. The attitude may be that of ridicule or unbelief or agnosticism or pride or opposition. But as he reads he discovers that the Book itself is beginning to make an analysis of him so that every secret thought and intent are exposed in its pages. And if he continues to read, he discovers that the written Word rebukes him and admonishes him with regard to his sin and unbelief.

Once, a tourist visited a Florence art gallery and looking around perfunctorily said: "Are these your masterpieces? I certainly don't see much in them."

"Sir," said the guide, "these pictures are not on trial; it is the tourists who are on trial."[6]

When a man comes to the marvellous picture gallery of God's Word, let him remind himself that it is not the Bible that is on trial but the individual himself. It is the Bible that is the critic of the heart, not the heart that is the critic of the Bible.

Employed

Let us now indicate some of the practical uses of God's Word considered as a skillful critic. The discriminative power of God's Word may be *employed* by us in various ways.

First, for our defence of the Bible we have in the discriminative power of God's Word a tremendous argument for its divine inspiration.

There is a familiar argument proposed first by John Wesley that is well worth repeating. Wrote Wesley:

> The Bible must have been written by God, or by good men, or by bad men, or by angels, or by devils. Bad men or devils would not write it because of the condemnation of sin and pronouncement of fearful judgment upon the sinner.

Good men or angels would not deceive men by lying as to its authority and claiming that God was the writer. Therefore, the Bible must have been written, as it claims to have been written, by God, who by His Spirit inspired men to record His words, using the human instrument to communicate it to man.[7]

Let those opposed to the Bible feel the force of that argument. In the Bible the sins and subterfuges of the heart are laid bare. By the Bible the sinner is criticized and condemned. He is warned of his doom in Hell and is told there is no hope apart from his accepting a divinely provided salvation. Is there not here a powerful argument for the inspiration of the Scriptures?

An anonymous writer summarizes this argument well. He writes:

> If I had a lock of very complicated construction, and there was only one key that would unlock it, I should feel very sure that key was made by the one who understood the construction of that lock.
>
> So when I find that, notwithstanding all the windings and mysteries of iniquity in the human heart, the Bible, and the Bible only, is adapted to it throughout, and is able to penetrate its most secret recesses, I am constrained to believe that the Bible was made by Him who alone "knowest the hearts of the children of men."[8]

But we must keep in mind the discriminative power of God's Word, not only in our defence of the Scriptures, but also in our declaration of the Scriptures. We must keep in mind that the Holy Spirit employs the Word to be the critic of the heart. The Word becomes His voice as it is preached and taught.

F.W. Boreham tells the story of Edwin Rushworth, who had been a skeptic for many years. One day he resolved to read for an hour a day the book he had so long derided.

"Wife," he said, as he looked up from his first perusal, "if this book is right, we are all wrong!"

He continued his reading for another week. "Wife," he exclaimed, "if this book is right, we are lost!"

He went on reading with more avidity than ever. "Wife," he said earnestly a few nights later, "if this book is right, we may be saved." The book had done its work, and Rushworth and his wife were gloriously saved.[9]

Finally, with regard to our devotion to the Bible we must keep in mind its power to discriminate and reprove. In our devotion to the Bible we should be willing to listen to its voice of correction. "All scripture," states Paul, is both "given by inspiration of God, and *is* profitable for doctrine, for reproof, for correction, for instruction in righteousness" (2 Timothy 3:16). Many who publish abroad their allegiance to the inspiration of the Bible are not as willing to expose themselves to the inquisition of the Bible. John Burton wrote:

> Holy Bible, Book divine, precious treasure, thou art mine;
> Mine to chide me when I rove, mine to show a Saviour's love;
> Mine thou art to guide my feet, mine to judge, condemn, acquit:[10]

A commercial traveller, who was also a Gideon, made it a practice to read his pocket Bible while on his railroad trips. Once he was asked by an unbelieving fellow traveller why he spent so much time reading a book which everybody criticized.

"My main object," replied the Christian, "is not to criticize the Bible, but to let it criticize me."[11]

Some of us may be like the maid referred to by G.F. Allee.

The maid's mistress demanded of her, "Jane, have you been meddling with the barometer again?"

"Yes, ma'am," confessed the maid. "You see, tonight's to be my night off, and as I had promised to go out with my regular friend, I set it to 'fine.' "[12]

We are not to correct the Bible, but to allow it to correct us. We dare not tamper with God's "weather warnings," or seek to modify the predictions of His Word.

G.F. Allee also tells of a New York businessman who had a fine collection of etchings and one of them, "The Leaning Tower of Pisa," hung on the wall behind his desk. Morning after morning he noticed that it was hanging crooked, despite the fact that every morning one of his first acts was to set it straight. Finally he spoke to the maid about it. Was she the one who caused it to hang crooked each morning?

"Yes, I am," she quickly replied. "The only way I can make the tower hang straight is to turn the frame like that."[13]

Let us beware of twisting the Scriptures in order to make them please us. Let us, rather, accept the verdict that they pronounce upon us that we have all sinned and that in that condition we all come short of the glory of God. It is we who are out of plumb, not the Bible.

FOR YOUR FURTHER STUDY

1. How did Paul discover God's Word to be a critic of the thoughts and intents of his heart (see Romans 7:7–10)?
2. How would you apply Proverbs 27:6 to the Word of God: "Faithful are the wounds of a friend"?
3. If God's Word as critic may be considered faithful, what other attributes can you suggest are equally descriptive of the Bible?

No Other Standard

God is always with His plumbline trying our lives. What is His plumbline? The grand old Book! By this, too, we ought all to be trying ourselves.

—David Davies

The Scripture revelation of the will of God must be the plumbline of our actions, and the guiding star of our lives. Every question, great or small, must be settled in the light of the Word of God, and every circumstance of our lives finds its interpretation there.

—Sister Eva of Friedenshort

Has John Bunyan announced some fearless exposition of truth? Hark how he disarms opposition and challenges scrutiny! Give me a hearing: take me to the Bible, and let me find in thy heart no favour if thou find me to swerve from the standard.

—W.M. Punshon

There are ten thousand plumblines in use, but only one is true and exact.

—T. DeWitt Talmage

God's Word is the only Rule of righteousness, the Standard by which all our motives and actions are to be measured, the Rule by which they are to be regulated.

—A.W. Pink

If the Scriptures are not reliable, we have absolutely no ultimate standard by which to determine the truth or falsity of any religious thesis.

—D.J. Burrell

Someone has divided people into three classes, according to their attitude to the Bible: 1) Those who neglect it altogether; 2) Those who try to put it right; 3) Those who wish it to put them right.

The Bible, and the Bible alone, is the ultimate standard of reference.

—Matthew Simpson

STUDY 21
God's Word Is Constructive

Our Key Scripture—"Behold, the Lord stood upon a wall *made* by a plumbline, with a plumbline in his hand. And the Lord said unto me, Amos, what seest thou? And I said, A plumbline. Then said the Lord, Behold, I will set a plumbline in the midst of my people Israel: I will not again pass by them any more" (Amos 7:7, 8).

Supplementary Scriptures—Psalm 11:7; 45:7; 48:10; 72:2; 96:13; 119:172; Hebrews 5:13; 1 John 3:7, 10.

A little boy watched his father using a spirit level to see if his work was true and straight.

"What's the use of being so careful, father?" he asked. "It looks very good."

"Guessing won't do in carpenter work, son," replied his father, sighting along the edge of a board and shaving it the least bit. "You have to be exactly right. Folks guess at too many things. God doesn't like that way of living."

"But there aren't any spirit levels for living by!" laughed the boy, watching his father's face.

"Yes, there are," said his father earnestly. "You'll find them in the Bible. Try all your actions by that. Make them true and straight, and no guesswork about them. In that way you will please God."[1]

The father was right. There is a spirit level, a plumbline, by which we may test all our convictions and conduct, and that plumbline is God's Word.

BASIC OUTLINE

In this study we want to help you first to *understand* the plumbline of God's written Word, and then to *use* that plumbline daily.

Understanding the Plumbline

In order to profit fully from this study we must have a *clear understanding* of a plumbline, first, as a tool or instrument employed by builders, and second, as a type of illustration of one quality of God's Word.

A plumb or plummet, by dictionary definition, is a small weight used to see if a wall is vertical. Hence, a plumbline is the line with the plumb or plummet at one end, used to test the straightness of a wall. T. DeWitt Talmage, that great preacher-orator, explained the use of the plumbline in these words:

> Bricklayers and stonemasons and carpenters in the building of walls used an instrument made of a cord, at the end of which a lump of lead is fastened. They drop it over the side of the wall, and, as the plummet naturally seeks the center of gravity in the earth, the workman discovers where the wall recedes and where it bulges out, and just what is the perpendicular.[2]

In one of his children's books, Hugh T. Kerr described a plumbline he had seen on his travels:

> The plumbline was attached to an old, old wall in the city of Verona in Italy. The wall is part of the old theater which is as old as the story of the Gospel. The theater is built like a college stadium. It is built like the Coliseum in Rome, the model of all our stadiums and bowls where football and baseball are played. This theater, or as it is called, amphitheater, has forty-five rows of seats rising one above the other. It is open to the sky and is in such good condition that it is still used for concerts and plays....
>
> One of the walls nearby, but apart from the theater, looks as if it might fall at any time. I was quite timid about going near it, although it has been like this for hundreds of years. When I got close I found a wire hanging from the topmost

stone of the wall and on the end near the ground a heavy ball of lead. It was a plummet, and it hangs there day and night so that at any time those in charge may know if the wall has moved and become unsafe. The plumbline tests the safety of the wall every minute.[3]

In summary, then, a plumbline has a two-fold purpose: positively, it reveals what is straight and true and perpendicular; negatively, and conversely, it exposes that which is crooked and askew and deformed. No mason really looks upon the purpose of his plumbline as destructive, but as constructive, enabling him to build a wall that is both safe and to his credit as a workman.

With the picture of the plumbline in our minds we can now seek to understand its use as a type or illustration of spiritual truth. It is Amos the Prophet who was given a vision of Jehovah standing upon a wall that had originally been constructed with the use of a plumbline and had passed the Master Mason's test for straightness. But years have passed by, and that Master Mason has returned to test the condition of the wall. As the plumbline is fixed to the wall, the prophet sees that there has been decay and deterioration in the fabric. The wall is no longer "plumb." It will have to be demolished as constituting a menace.

The details of the vision granted to Amos seem to be quite clear as to their meaning. The wall is Israel. At the beginning Israel as a nation had been built according to the plumbline—which here must symbolize God's righteousness as expressed in His law (see Isaiah 28:17). But Israel has backslidden, and now God has come to examine His people and to expose their moral and spiritual deviation from His standards of righteousness. Israel must, therefore, be removed—that is, be taken into exile as a punishment for their crimes.

In the light of our suggested interpretation of Amos' vision, we would identify the plumbline as God's moral law and, therefore, by extension of the basic concept, God's Word. It is not our idea of righteousness as constructed by reason or by conscience that forms the divine plumbline; rather, it is His revelation of that righteousness given to us in His Word.

Give Me That Book!

The following quotation is to our mind a classic statement on the place of the Bible in the life of the Christian and of the Church. We commend it to our readers. It comes from a sermon given by Rev. William Souper at the Mundesley Bible conference in England during the year 1914:

> The Bible is the norm, the regulative source for all conceptions and statements of Christian doctrine, whether they be creedal or theological. The Bible is the abiding source from which all conceptions and statements of Christian truth are to be drawn; it is supreme and regulative of all.
>
> If further light and truth are vouchsafed unto men by the Holy Spirit, then that light and truth are to be tested by the biblical teaching; nothing that is contradictory or inconsistent with the teaching of Scripture is to be admitted or received by Christians as Christian truth. For myself I have this to say: I do not find that any additional spiritual revelation of truth has been granted to men since the writings of the New Testament: fresh life and light have broken forth from time to time from the Scriptures; but no new additional truth of revelation has come from men.
>
> Of course, this may be denied, very probably will be denied; but I await the proof that any new revelation of spiritual realities has come from man since the close of the New Testament canon. That the truths therein stated have been unfolded and seen in fresh light I most willingly grant, and I testify further that this is precisely what the Holy Spirit does for men in relation to the Holy Scriptures. As He inspired the writers at the first, so He gives to the reverent and loving student of Scripture the spirit of knowledge and interpretation in what He first gave as revelation to the original writers.
>
> In a word then, the Bible is the norm, the standard and source of all Christian teaching, whatever form that teaching may take: that is the place of the Bible.[4]

Master that statement, for it embodies the whole idea of what is symbolized by the plumbline.

Using the Plumbline

Having sought to understand the plumbline and its symbolism, we must now give attention to the *use* of the plumbline. If we are to become workmen needing not to be ashamed (see 2 Timothy 2:15), we must learn how to use the plumbline of God's Word.

First, we must use God's plumbline correctly. According to the Apostle Paul we must learn how to rightly divide the Word of truth. Much harm has been done by zealous people who have misapplied God's Word and twisted the divine plumbline to support their own prejudices or preconceptions. Peter wrote concerning those, "unlearned and unstable," who wrest the Scriptures to their own destruction. When we read some attempts to interpret God's Word, we are reminded of the sign seen hanging outside a black-smith's shop: "All kinds of fancy twistings and turnings wrought here"!

Basic to the correct use of God's Word is a holy fear of offending God through manipulation of His truth. We should be able to say with Paul: "We are not as many, which corrupt [deal deceitfully with] the word of God; but as of sincerity, but as of God, in the sight of God speak we in Christ" (2 Corinthians 2:17), and "have renounced the hidden things of dishonesty, not walking in craftiness, nor handling the word of God deceit-fully; but by manifestation of the truth commending ourselves to every man's conscience in the sight of God" (2 Corinthians 4:2).

We must use God's plumbline confidently. We must believe that it is inspired, infallible, and inerrant. We must believe that it will not lead us astray, that it will not register error. We must be absolutely convinced that it is divine and therefore dependable.

H.P. Barker wrote about a man who, wandering in the woods, was overtaken by night. Feeling certain that he was going in the right direction, he neglected his compass. At last he consulted it. It showed he was going west, although he believed he was going east. Disgusted, he was about to throw away his compass, but he thought: "It has never deceived me yet: I'll trust it now." He did so, turned around, followed its guidance and came out right.[5]

Give Me That Book!

Let us who have God's Word in our hands, trust it in our hearts. Let us never throw it away in order to follow the voice of reason or conscience or tradition. The Bible has never failed us yet. Let's trust it implicitly.

Let us use God's Word as a plumbline continually. We cannot afford to build any part of our lives without reference to its guidance.

The late Dr. M.R. DeHaan used the following illustration to show the necessity of constant reference to the Bible as our standard:

> The Bible is God's clock, which is the perfect expression of His will. But man, too, has a clock. This is his conscience. It convicts him of right or wrong. Every man must follow his own conscience, but it is not a reliable guide unless checked constantly and adjusted completely to the Word of God. As watches differ in time, so consciences differ on many matters. Your conscience must be your guide, but your conscience must be regulated by God's perfect revelation, the Word of God.
>
> Before going to catch a train or plane, I always "check the time," so I will not be late. So, too, to begin this day without checking with the Word of God may result in tragedy. Follow your conscience, but be sure it is "on time" by consulting God's "chronometer"—the Bible. Sit down, brother! Don't go until you have made the check.[6]

Let Dr. David J. Burrell expand on the place of God's Word in the life of the Christian:

> The prime object of prayer is to arrive at that which the perverted and unaided conscience cannot give, to wit, a clear expression of the divine will. We are bound to do right, not merely what we believe to be right. We are bound to live as God in His Word enjoins us to live. It is not enough to say that our lives are adjusted to the requirements of conscience; they must be adjusted to the divine law as an enlightened conscience enables us to see it.
>
> And this enlightenment is through the divine Word; precisely as a skipper corrects his compass by taking an

observation of the stars. This Word, therefore, is ultimate, inasmuch as it is the medium through which God speaks to those who are cordially disposed to hear and obey Him.[7]

J. Reid Howatt tells us that since Italy is a land of volcanoes and earthquakes, builders in that country have taken pains to show that their original work was upright and true.

The builders of the cathedral in Florence chose a very ingenious way of proving the perfection of their work:

> High up, in the center of that beautiful building, is a lofty dome, like that of St. Paul's, with stained windows all round. On the casement of one of these windows is a small iron ring, and it is by this that the uprightness of the tower is tested every year. For, on a certain day in June, at a certain hour, the sun shines through that ring, and its light falls on a brass plate let into the marble floor far beneath.
>
> So long as the sunbeam falls on a spot there, on that day and at that moment, it proves that the building is as erect as on the day it was finished; if it had tilted ever so little to the one side or the other, that long ray of light would have proved it, for then it could not have fallen exactly on the right spot.[8]

Oh, that day by day—not merely one day in the year—the rays of the Sun of righteousness may prove that we, like Zacharias and Elisabeth, are "righteous before God, walking in all the commandments and ordinances of the Lord blameless" (Luke 1:6).

Closely related to the preceding point is the thought that we must use God's plumbline consistently. By that we mean we must relate God's Word and its standard of righteousness to matters both of creed and conduct, of belief and behaviour.

It will not do for us to say that the Bible is regulative for us in matters of creed only. It is true that it is from the Bible that we must draw all our conceptions of God, and it is by the Bible that all our teachings about God must be tested. But we must see that the Bible also applies to our conduct, our pattern of living.

This is illustrated by the method employed by Paul in his epistles. Generally his letters begin with a statement of doctrine—for example, in Colossians 1 and 2 it is the doctrine of Christ—His superiority and sufficiency. This is followed, however, by various practical applications and appeals—in Colossians it is chapters 3 and 4. C.H. Spurgeon once commented about Colossians 3 that it begins in heaven and ends in the kitchen![9]

God's plumbline, the Bible, is for our personal lives, our families, our work, our churches, our schools, in short, for our entire life here on earth. There are principles set forth in God's Word that affect every aspect and area of our lives. Let us use the plumbline consistently.

In learning how to use God's plumbline we must see to it that we employ it constructively. We have already observed that a plumbline is not an end in itself; it is a means to an end, and that end, of course, is construction that is "right" and "true."

Commenting on the word correction in 2 Timothy 3:16 ("All scripture is ... profitable for doctrine, for reproof, for correction, for instruction in righteousness:"), A.W. Pink states:

> The Greek word occurs nowhere else in the New Testament, but signifies "setting right." The reproving is but a means to an end: it is showing us what is wrong that it may be put right. Everything about us, both within and without, needs correcting, for the Fall has put man all out of joint with God and holiness. Our thoughts on everything are wrong and need readjusting. Our affections are all disorderly and need regulating. Our character is utterly unlike Christ's and has to be conformed to His image. Our conduct is wayward and demands squaring with the rule of righteousness.
>
> God has given to us His Word that under its guidance we may regulate our beliefs, renovate our hearts, and reform our lives. Hence it answers but a poor end to read a chapter once or twice a day for the sake of decency, without any definite intention of complying with the mind of God as revealed therein. Since He has given us the Scriptures "for correction," we should ever approach them with a sincere purpose of bringing

into harmony with them everything that is disorderly within us and irregular without us.[10]

It is only as we use the plumbline in this way that we will avoid being "unskilful in the word of righteousness" (Hebrews 5:13; see Psalm 119:123, "the word of thy righteousness").

In using God's Word as a plumbline, we must employ it charitably, especially in our relationships with others. Perhaps the word plumbline suggests a cold, mechanical operation that lacks any real concern or compassion for those whom we are examining with regard to their faith in God and His Word. There can be no doubt that some fundamentalists have used God's plumbline in this way—more interested in their finds than in their responsibilities for those whose lives are out of plumb.

Paul's words to Timothy should govern our use of the divine plumbline: "The servant of the Lord must not strive; but be gentle unto *all* men, apt to teach, patient, In meekness instructing those that oppose themselves" (2 Timothy 2:24, 25).

But having said that, we hasten to add that we must use God's plumbline courageously. For Amos to leave the southern kingdom of Judah and to become a "foreign missionary" to Israel in the north, which at the time was filled with idolatry and immorality, took backbone. Indeed, the prophet faced persecution at the hands of the religious leaders of the north. But Amos did not shrink back from holding God's plumbline alongside the northern kingdom and exposing the sins of that nation.

We are living in days that require the constant use of God's plumbline. Our motto must be: "To the law and to the testimony: if they speak not according to his word, *it is* because *there* is no light in them" (Isaiah 8:20). Concerning every matter of faith we must ask with Paul: "What saith the scripture?" (Romans 4:3). We must say with Martin Luther as he spoke at the Diet of Worms: "My conscience is captive to the Word of God."[11]

FOR YOUR FURTHER STUDY

1. Why cannot we accept either reason or tradition or conscience as our plumbline?

2. Show how the title, "the word of righteousness" (Hebrews 5:13), means that God's Word is both characterized by righteousness and contributes to righteousness.

3. What areas of your own life need to be tested by God's plumbline?

At Home in Our Heart

Do I wish to advance in knowledge and in power? Do I long to be consistent, holy, fearless? I must spend time in the company of the Word of God, and His commandments must be ever with me. When I come to them each day expectantly and lovingly, they emancipate from sin, and raise me into the likeness of Christ.

—as quoted by E. Matheson

Let us now stop and ask ourselves, What has my mind been occupied with today? What has it been running after? Could you say, "The word of Christ has dwelt in me richly"? Now, perhaps, we have been occupied with politics, perhaps with the town talk, or with something of our own. Has the word of our own heart, the work of our own mind, filled up the greater part of our day? That is not Christ.

—J.N. Darby

May the Word of God dwell in you richly! And may the Spirit of truth prepare your heart to seek the law of the Lord, and go with you into the holiest of all, in the temple of truth, and light up the otherwise dark dwelling-place of God; and then give you a heart to do it, and to teach the Word to others!

—G.F. Pentecost

The heart of man, in its natural condition, may be compared to a wilderness; but when renewed by divine grace, to the garden of the Lord, and to a vine of His own right-hand planting. God Himself is the great Husbandman, who cultivates the heart of man, and makes it bring forth the fruits of holiness. The means which He adopts to exchange the thorns and briars of sin for the fir trees and myrtles of grace, and to render the heart prosperous and happy, is His Holy Word, which He has declared shall not return to Him void, but shall accomplish that which He pleases, and make the desert to rejoice and to blossom as the rose.

This word, being the seed which is to produce the fruit of immortality, it is desirable to have it richly sown in the hearts of all those who hope to be, when life shall terminate, transplanted into the eternal paradise above.

—W. Nicholson

Used effectively, the Word of God brings victory to the child of God. As a matter of fact, lodged in the heart of the believer, in itself it becomes a power for holiness.

—William Culbertson

STUDY 22
God's Word Is Formative

Our Key Scripture—"Let the word of Christ dwell in you richly" (Colossians 3:16).

Supplementary Scriptures—Deuteronomy 6:6; 11:18; 32:46; Psalm 37:31; 119:11; Isaiah 51:7; Ezekiel 40:4; Luke 2:19, 51.

A poor woman living in a dreadful slum area of a large British city was given a beautiful white flower in a pot to take home with her. It was an expression of the love of the Christian workers in the mission near her home.

When she got home, the woman placed the flower on the table. As she looked at the dirty table, she said to herself, "I must clean the table. The flower doesn't look right on a dirty table."

She proceeded to wash the table.

Then she looked at the floor. It had not been swept or scrubbed for many days. "I must clean the floor," the woman resolved.

The floor was cleaned.

Then the woman glanced at the once-white curtains. They were soiled and unattractive. Taking them down, she washed them and hung them out to dry.

Soon, other parts of her kitchen and home were being cleaned up—all because of the beauty and influence of a flower being placed in her home.[1]

This, in illustration, is what will happen in our lives if we obey the apostolic exhortation to let the word of Christ dwell in us richly. With that pure and powerful word in our hearts, it will soon indicate all that needs to be cleaned up. It will bring about a complete heart-cleaning.

BASIC OUTLINE

Paul's command invites us to consider four aspects of the indwelling Word: first, the *meaning* of its indwelling; second, the *miracle* of its indwelling; third, the *method* of its indwelling; and, fourth, the *measure* of its indwelling.

Meaning

"Let the word of Christ dwell in you richly." What is the *meaning* of this indwelling? Our answer to this question will depend in large measure upon our understanding the words, "the word of Christ." The words may have two possible meanings.

First, "the word" may be teaching about Christ—that is, Christ may be the subject of the teaching. Thus we may amplify the *Authorized Version* translation in this way: "Let the teaching that has Christ as its content dwell in you richly."

But we may also understand "the word of Christ" to refer to the teaching that comes from Christ—that is, Christ may be the source of the teaching. Again we may paraphrase: "Let the teaching which came from Christ's lips dwell in you richly." Elsewhere Paul writes: "If any man teach otherwise, and consent not to wholesome words, *even* the words of our Lord Jesus Christ, and to the doctrine which is according to godliness; ... He is proud" (1 Timothy 6:3, 4). The words of the teachings of the Lord Jesus were circulated in the early Church.

It may not be necessary for us to choose between these alternative understandings of Paul's words. The teachings about Christ are ultimately derived from the teachings of Christ.

Nor do we need to limit the scope of Paul's words to the teachings of the Lord Jesus which are now recorded for us in the Gospels. In their widest meaning his words include all the Scriptures. This claim may be substantiated by the following passages: "The testimony of Jesus is the spirit of prophecy" (Revelation 19:10)—that is, the purpose of the prophetic word is to bear witness to Jesus; "Search the scriptures; for in them ye think ye have eternal life: and they are they which testify of me" (John 5:39); Peter refers to the Spirit of Christ who was in the prophets, "when [He] testified beforehand the sufferings of Christ, and the glory that should follow" (1 Peter 1:11).

What, then, does it mean to let this word of Christ dwell in us richly? The English word "dwell" is a good translation of the Greek verb. The word of Christ is to have its home in our hearts.

This will involve the following:

First, we must recognize the Scriptures as being the word of Christ.

In the light of the Scriptures already quoted we are to acknowledge the whole Bible as in a very definite sense the word of Messiah. He is both the source (cf. 1 Peter 1:10, 11) and the subject (cf. John 5:39) of the Bible.

In his excellent book, *The Wonder of the Word*, Gwynn M. Day writes:

> There is a remarkable copy of the Bible in the library of Baker University, Baldwin, Kansas. When the book is tightly closed, the gold edges of the leaves do not appear unusual, but when they are slightly parted a beautiful picture of Christ and His disciples is ingeniously displayed on the edges of gold. Beneath the scene are the words: "It is I Myself; handle Me and see."
>
> This offer of empirical proof which Christ made to His confused friends following the resurrection, He still makes today. The person who will accept that challenge and "handle" the Word of Life with his mind, heart, and soul will always find that it is imbued with the living Spirit of God. He will meet Christ in its pages! When that happens there is no need for further proof.[2]

Elsewhere in the book Gwynn Day affirms:

> In truth, Christ and the Word are inseparably one. He permeates it from beginning to end: It bears His image, records

His words, expresses His mind, pulsates with His Spirit, reveals His presence, works His will, proclaims His name.[3]

James Burns tells us that Rossini was once presented with a watch by the King of France—of which he was justly proud. Several years after, showing it to a friend, he was told that though he had possessed it for so long he did not know its real value.

"Impossible," said Rossini. Whereupon the friend, taking the watch, touched a secret spring, at which an inner case flew open disclosing a beautiful miniature painting of Rossini himself.[4]

There are people who have owned and read a Bible for years. To them it is precious, but tragically they have never discovered the full value of the Scriptures. Only let the Holy Spirit touch a secret spring and the Bible will open to disclose, not the reader's own picture, but the picture of Christ in all His glory and beauty. Have you made that discovery?

In coming to God's Word, then, as the Word of Christ, we do well to pray with Mary A. Lathbury:

> Oh, send Thy Spirit, Lord,
> Now unto me,
> That He may touch my eyes,
> And make me see.
>
> Show me the truth concealed
> Within Thy Word,
> And in Thy Book revealed
> I see the Lord.[5]

In one of his books Dr. A.B. Simpson emphasized that we must recognize that the Bible points us to Christ:

> I once saw a picture of the Constitution of the United States, very skillfully engraved in copperplate, so that when you looked at it closely, it was nothing more than a piece of writing, but when you looked at it from a distance, it was the face of George Washington. The face shone out in the shading

of the letters at a little distance, and I saw the person, not the words or the ideas.

Then I thought: "That is the way to look at the Scriptures and understand the thought of God; to see in them the face of love shining through and through; not ideas, not doctrines, but Jesus Himself as the Life and Source and sustaining Presence of all our life."[6]

Annie Johnson Flint expressed the truth well in her poem thus:

> God's Book is a portrait, limned and coloured
> In the utmost skill of the painter's art;
> The Spirit of God is the Master Artist,
> The Son of God takes the sitter's part.
> Prophecy, history, type, and symbol
> Blend and mingle in sweet accord
> As background, foreground, and middle distance
> For the Perfect Form of the Living Word.[7]

But recognizing the Scriptures as the Word of Christ is not sufficient; we must also receive them into our hearts as the Word of Christ. That is really the point of Paul's exhortation: "Let the word of Christ dwell"—take up its abode—"in you." That Word is to be the occupant of our heart. It is to be more than a periodic visitor; it must become a permanent resident.

Maude Frazer Jackson caught this point penetratingly in her poem, "Does It Matter What I Say?" Here is the first verse:

> What if I say—
> "The Bible is God's Holy Word,
> Complete, inspired, without a flaw"—
> But let its pages stay
> Unread from day to day,
> And fail to learn there from God's law;
> What if I go not there to seek
> The truth of which I glibly speak,
> For guidance on this earthly way—
> Does it matter what I say?[8]

Give Me That Book!

It is instructive to discover that in 2 Timothy 1:14 Paul employs the same word as in Colossians 3:16. Paul refers to the Holy Spirit "who dwells in us." Linking both references together, we may say that the indwelling Spirit employs the indwelling Scriptures to accomplish His work in our lives.

Miracle

This leads us to consider the *miracle* of the indwelling Word of Christ. When we permit that Word to make its home in our hearts, the Holy Spirit employs it to change us. This is why we affirm that God's Word is formative. "Some books," it is said, "are informative, but the Bible is transformative."

Let that Word dwell in your heart, and it will form your ideals. It will set before you God's pattern for living. It will disclose God's standards for every area of life. It will exhort you to "live soberly, righteously, and godly, in this present world" (Titus 2:12).

Let that Word dwell in your heart, and it will form your interests. It speaks with authority. It commands: "Seek ye first the kingdom of God, and his righteousness; and all these things shall be added unto you" (Matthew 6:33).

Let a man be governed by the Word of Christ, and his priorities will then be sorted out. He will begin to live for the things of God rather than the things of man; he will give himself to the pursuit of the things of eternity rather than the things of time; his horizon will widen out to include the things of the spiritual world, rather than only the things of the material world.

Finally, let that Word take up its permanent abode in you, and it will form your influence. Influence is not something that can be artificially manufactured. What is in the heart of man will ultimately be reflected in his total influence upon others. It is only the person in whose heart the Word of God is resident and president who has an influence that points people to Christ.

If that Word is dwelling in the heart, then no outward circumstances can destroy your influence for God. As an unknown poet stated:

> Like the vase in which roses
> Have once been distilled,

266

You may break, you may shatter
The vase if you will.
But the scent of the roses
Will cling to it still.[9]

Even when shattered and broken, the life that is governed by the Word of Christ will still be fragrant.

Ian Macpherson illustrates the power of Christ in the following words:

Henry Drummond tells the now well-known story of a woman whose son went up to the university. When visiting him in his room, she was shocked to find the walls covered with obscene pictures. Being a wise parent, she did not protest against the pictures nor show her feeling about them in any way.

Instead, she bought a picture of Christ and asked him to put that up in his room. He did. When next his mother called to see him, she was secretly delighted to discover that what she had expected to happen had in fact taken place. The picture of Christ had made impossible the display of all the others. Only the pure features of Jesus were to be seen on the wall.[10]

According to Paul, we are to hang up on the walls of the rooms of the heart the Word of Christ. We are to let that Word influence us toward holiness and godliness. If we have eyes to see, the face of Christ will be revealed in His Word.

"Why are you so determined to be a sailor?" a puzzled mother asked her teenage son.

The boy didn't answer for a minute, and then he said: "This may sound silly to you, but I've always liked that big picture of the sea above the mantel in the living room, and for years I've dreamed of being a sailor."[11]

That is the influence one painting had in the life of a boy; let us be sure we are being influenced by the Word of Christ.

<u>Method</u>

Consider now the *method* of this indwelling. How are we to permit the Word of Christ to dwell in us richly?

On this point an Old Testament passage is most enlightening. We refer to Deuteronomy 6:4–9.

> Hear, O Israel: The Lord our God *is* one Lord: And thou shalt love the Lord thy God with all thine heart, and with all thy soul, and with all thy might. And these words, which I command thee this day, shall be in thine heart: And thou shalt teach them diligently unto thy children, and shalt talk of them when thou sittest in thine house, and when thou walkest by the way, and when thou liest down, and when thou risest up. And thou shalt bind them for a sign upon thine hand, and they shall be as frontlets between thine eyes. And thou shalt write them upon the posts of thy house, and on thy gates.

There is an adequate scriptural answer to the question: How shall we let the Word of Christ dwell in us richly? We may summarize the teaching of this passage in this way: We are to let the Word of God dwell in our hearts and in our homes.

First, the Word of God is to dwell in our hearts. By reading, study, and meditation, the Word of Christ is to fill our minds and hearts. This will require patience and persistence as day by day we open God's Word and open our hearts to receive that Word. It is as we allow that Word to change our lives that Christ's image is seen in us.

Mr. Moody tells of a visit to Prang's chromo establishment in Boston. Mr. Prang showed him a stone, on which was laid the colour for making on a sheet of paper the first impression toward producing the portrait of a distinguished public man: but he could see only the faintest possible line of tinting. The next stone that the paper was submitted to, deepened the colour a little, but still no trace of the man's face was visible. Again and again, the sheet passed over successive stones, until at last the outlines of a man's face were dimly discerned.

Finally, after some twenty impressions, from as many different stones, were taken upon the paper, the portrait of the distinguished man stood forth so perfectly that it seemed only to lack the power of speech to make it living.[12]

The image of Christ is only reproduced on the paper of our lives as there is repeated contact with the Word of Christ, and for that we must allow that Word to dwell in our hearts.

But we must permit the Word of Christ also to dwell in our homes. Moses instructed the people—and parents—of Israel that there had to be formal and informal teaching of God's Word in their homes.

"Thou shalt teach them diligently"—that involves the formal instruction of God's Word in our homes. There are many ways in which Christian parents can undertake to give formal instruction in the Scriptures to their children. There are many aids available for such education. The important thing is that such instruction actually be carried out.

"Thou...shalt talk of them when thou sittest in thine house, and when thou walkest by the way, and when thou liest down, and when thou risest up"—that involves informal instruction. The Word of God is to be made the subject of conversation in our homes. This is to be done, not in any legalistic or mechanical way, but spontaneously and gladly.

To remind the people of Israel of their responsibilities, the Lord required them to associate His Word with their total lives: "Thou shalt bind them for a sign upon thine hand, and they shall be as frontlets between thine eyes. And thou shalt write them upon the posts of thy house, and on thy gates."

Unfortunately these outward reminders lost their significance, and God's people later came to prize the letter of the law rather than its spirit. They obeyed God's Word with regard to these external symbols, but did not obey that Word in their hearts.

Christian homes do well to have pictures and symbols that remind the members of the family of their responsibilities to God. We remember reading that the father of Dr. G. Campbell Morgan once visited the home of his sons. After having been taken on a tour of the house, Mr. Morgan expressed himself as being disappointed.

"And why?" was the response of his son.

"Because there is no way in which I can tell that this is a Christian home. You have no pictures or texts on the walls to show that your home is Christian."[13]

The rebuke was accepted, and soon there appeared various texts and pictures on the walls of the rooms, indicating to all that the home was a Christian home.

Measure

We have considered the meaning, the miracle, and the method of this indwelling of God's Word. Finally, we call attention to the *measure* of its indwelling. "Let the word of Christ dwell in you richly." The adverb indicates the measure.

The Latin translation of our key Scripture is most interesting: *Sermo Christi inhabitet in vobis copiose.* Readers will recognize that some of our English words are anticipated by the Latin—indeed, shaped by the Latin. We call attention to the word *copiose*—from which, of course, we get our word copiously. We are to let the Word of Christ dwell in us copiously, abundantly, plentifully.

This means we are not to restrict the influence and inspiration of God's Word to just one room of our heart. The Word of Christ is to enter and occupy each room.

There is always a danger in compartmentalizing our lives. We classify all our activities, and then attempt to isolate the influence of God's Word to so-called "spiritual" aspects. The New Testament would teach us that God's Word is to permeate our lives fully.

George F. Pentecost wrote:

> Read the Bible widely, "Eat, O friends; drink, yea, drink abundantly, O beloved!" (Song of Solomon 5:1) should be our motto in coming to the Word of God. The Bible furnishes spiritual food for the soul; yea, the best intellectual food for the

270

soulful man. Why, if most Christians took no more breakfast, especially if that were their only meal for the day, than they take of Bible, they would not have strength to go through their ordinary daily duties! If they did not feed the body better than they do the soul with the food God has given for it, they would be starvelings, walking skeletons.

Indeed, if we could see the leanness of many souls, aye, Christians' souls—the sight would arouse the pity, if not the contempt, even of the world. Do not snatch a few verses now and then; but read chapters, many chapters, or even a whole book at a sitting. How many of you ever did this, even on the Lord's Day? How many of you ever read the Book of Genesis, or John's Gospel, or the Acts, or an Epistle, through, at one sitting? And yet I know Christians who will sit for half a day at a time reading history, or a biography, or a novel: many even read far into the night. You would enjoy no book if you read it as some of you read the Bible—a scrap here and a scrap there, and occasionally a chapter or two.[14]

"Read the Bible widely"—that is one way to fulfill Paul's command to let the Word of Christ dwell in us richly. Let that Word, once read, be assimilated into the spiritual system in order to derive health and strength from the Bible's vitamins. Let it be applied to every need of the heart, and let it be authoritative with regard to every decision.

FOR YOUR FURTHER STUDY

1. According to Peter (1 Peter 1:10, 11), how was Christ predicted in the Old Testament?
2. What is the relationship between the indwelling of the Spirit and the indwelling of the Scriptures? (Compare Colossians 3:16 with Ephesians 5:18, 19.)
3. What must you now undertake to do in your own life in order to obey the directive of Colossians 3:16?

The Bible Our Treasure

One of the marvels of the Bible is its singular fullness. It is not a book of goldleaf beaten thin as most books are, but its sentences are nuggets of unalloyed truth.

—**C.H. Spurgeon**

Here are my choicest treasures hid.

—**Isaac Watts**

One gem from the ocean is worth all the pebbles of earthly streams.

—**R.M. McCheyne**

Of the Bible we may say in words first penned in description of the land of Havilah, "The gold of that land is good."

This precious Book I'd rather own
Than all the gold and gems
That e'er in monarchs' coffers shone,
Or on their diadems.
And were the seas one chrysolite,
This earth one golden ball,
And diamonds all the stars of night,
This Book were worth them all.

Ah, no, the soul ne'er found relief
In glittering hoards of wealth;
Gems dazzle not the eye of grief,
Gold cannot purchase health.
But here a blessed balm appears
To heal the deepest woe,
And those who read this Book in tears
Their tears shall cease to flow.

—**Unknown**

No man is poor or desolate who has this treasure for his own.

—**Henry Van Dyke**

I never knew all there was in the Bible until I spent those years in jail. I was constantly finding new treasures.

—**John Bunyan**

STUDY 23
God's Word Is Remunerative

Our Key Scripture—"The law of thy mouth *is* better unto me than thousands of gold and silver" (Psalm 119:72).

Supplementary Scriptures—Psalm 12:6; 19:9–11; 119:127, 162; Proverbs 2:1–6; 3:13–15; 16:16; 20:15; 2 Timothy 3:16.

ARCHIBALD Naismith, for over forty years a Christian teacher in India, tells us that when his family returned once to Great Britain on holiday, one of his sons, a lad about six or seven years, attended school in that country for the first time.

One day the lad came home and reported that he had to write a short essay on the subject, "My Greatest Treasure." His parents wondered which of his treasured possessions he would choose to write about.

When the lad finally showed his parents his completed composition, they were thrilled to find that his first sentence was, "My greatest treasure is my Holy Bible."[1]

The little lad's testimony should be the testimony, too, of every Christian. Each believer should be able to say, "I love thy commandments above gold; yea, above find gold" (Psalm 119:127).

BASIC OUTLINE

When God's Word is described as a priceless treasure, at least three aspects of what should be our attitude toward the Scriptures are stressed. The word treasure suggests: 1) something of the *value* that we must establish with regard to the Bible's contents; 2) something of the *vigour* we must expend with regard to its study; and 3) something of the *vigilance* we must exercise with regard to its preservation, protection, and propagation.

Value

Consider first the *value* we must establish with regard to the Bible's contents.

Concerning the judgments of the Lord, the psalmist said: "More to be desired *are they* than gold, yea, than much fine gold . . . in keeping of them *there* is great reward" (Psalm 19:10, 11).

Here, then, is an evaluation of the Bible and its message—the Bible is far more valuable to us than any amount of gold or silver. Its preciousness far surpasses earth's stores of gold, silver, and precious stones. "All the books that ever were written," wrote Charles Simeon, "are of no value when compared with the sacred volume."[2]

Concerning the value of the Bible, hymn writers have expressed themselves in glowing terms.

William W. How wrote in description of the Bible:

> It is the golden casket,
> Where gems of truth are stored;
> It is the Heaven-drawn picture
> Of Christ, the living Word.[3]

Edwin Hodder described God's Word in these glowing terms:

> Thy Word is like a deep, deep mine,
> And jewels rich and rare
> Are hidden in its mighty depths
> For every searcher there.[4]

Anne Steele saw the Bible as the source of endless spiritual wealth:

> Here may wretched sons of want
> Exhaustless riches find;
> Riches, above what earth can grant,
> And lasting as the minds.[5]

Isaac Watts identified the Bible as the pearl of greatest price:

This is the field where hidden lies
The pearl of price unknown;
That merchant is divinely wise
Who makes the pearl his own.[6]

Julia Sterling gave her testimony in the words:

Each line has a treasure,
Each promise a pearl.[7]

And John Burton wrote concerning the Book:

Holy Bible, Book divine,
Precious treasure, thou art mine.[8]

Dr. Thomas Guthrie, faithful preacher in Scotland, told of a famous philosopher who had devoted his life to the pursuit of science and knowledge and who had made a name for himself in the world of scholarship.

But as an old man God saved him. Following his conversion he, who had read deeply in science, began to spend time with his Bible. To others he declared that if he had his life to live over again he would spend it in the study of the Word of God.

States Guthrie:

He felt like a miner, who, after toiling long and to little purpose in search of gold, with one stroke of his pickaxe lays open a vein of the precious metal and becomes rich at once— the owner of a vein that grows the richer the deeper the mine is driven. Such a treasure the Bible offers to those whose eyes God has opened to see its wonders of grace and glory. It is inexhaustible.[9]

But not all see the Bible as a treasure to be prized above everything else.

A wealthy gentleman living in London in the last century on one of his birthdays invited his servants into the drawing room to receive presents.

"Which will you have?" he asked, addressing the hostler, "this Bible or a five-pound note?"

Give Me That Book!

"I would take the Bible, sir, but I cannot read; so I think the money will do me more good," replied the hostler.

"And you—which will you have?" he asked the gardener. "My poor wife is so ill that I sadly need the money," responded the gardener with a bow.

"Mary, can you read?" asked the rich man, turning to his cook. "Will you have the Bible?"

"I can read, sir, but I never get time to look into a book, and the money will buy a fine dress."

Next was the chambermaid, but she, too, had a reason why she needed the money.

Finally came the errand boy.

"My lad," asked his kind benefactor, "will you take these five pounds, and replace your shabby clothes with a new suit?"

"Thank you, sir, but my dear mother used to read to me that the Law of the Lord was better than thousands of gold and silver. I will have the good Book, if you please."

"God bless you, my boy! And may your choice prove riches and honour and long life to you."

As the lad received the Bible and unclasped its covers, a bright gold coin rolled to the floor. Quickly turning its pages, he found them thickly interleaved with bank notes, while the other servants, discovering the mistake of their covetousness, hastily departed in chagrin.[10]

In contrast to the young lad is the young man who heard with disgust that his wealthy uncle had left a Bible to him in his will. The will read thus: "To my nephew I leave a copy of God's priceless Word, which I trust he will use daily and find within its pages real treasure."

The beneficiary threw the Bible into an old trunk in the attic of his home, disgusted and disappointed with his share in his uncle's bequest. Years passed by, and one day, pressed beyond measure, he turned to the Bible for comfort. Between its pages he found bills worth hundreds of dollars. But beyond the material wealth, he found also the exceeding riches of Bible truth, for the Scriptures led him to trust Christ.[11]

A Christian once entered a house in Germany, and found conditions there very wretched—no fire, no furniture, no food. Everything bore the appearance of utter poverty. But, glancing around, he saw in a neglected corner, a copy of the Bible, and when he went away, he said to the poor people, "There is a treasure in this house that would make you all rich."

After he had gone, the people began to search the house for what they thought must be a jewel or a pot of gold, and finding nothing, they began to dig up the floor itself, in hopes of discovering the hidden store of wealth. All, however, was in vain.

One day after that, the mother lifted up the old Bible, and found written on the flyleaf of it the words, "Thy testimonies are better to me than thousands of gold and silver."

"Ah!" she said to herself, "can this be the treasure the stranger spoke of?" So she told the others of her discovery, and together they began to read the Bible, received Christ, and became changed in character. The Bible had proved itself to be priceless treasure to them.[12]

An English nobleman, we are told, once presented a well-known actress with a lovely copy of the Bible and, at the same, time told her there was a treasure hidden within its pages, which she might find and possess. She supposed he referred to the plan of salvation, which she knew was the theme of the entire Bible; accordingly, she laid the Bible aside.

Years later she died in poverty. Her possessions were sold at an auction to pay her debts. The man who purchased her Bible discovered a 500-pound note tucked away between two of its pages. Ignoring the Bible and its message, the actress had denied herself great wealth.[13]

How many people have Bibles in their homes, who are oblivious of its wealth. We must learn how to evaluate the Bible, and say with the psalmist, "I love thy commandments above gold; yea, above fine gold."

<u>Vigour</u>

We have seen how the word treasure suggests to us something of the value that we must establish with regard to the Bible's contents. Now let's think of the *vigour* we must expend with regard to its study. The Bible does not yield its treasure to the indolent or indifferent. We are to:

> Search the Scripture's precious store
> As the miner digs for ore.[14]

Louis Albert Banks tells us how in 1901 a prospector discovered a great gold mine in Arizona:

> In the bottom of a gulch, he ran across a rock about the size of a man's head. He knew at a glance that it was a live rock. He was wildly excited. He abandoned all else and began a search for the ledge or outcropping from which the chunk in the gulch had been detached. He crawled up and down the barren, scorched hillside many times. He crept over wide areas on his hands and knees, looking, scrutinizing, and gazing all about him. He turned over hundreds of bits of oxidized rocks there. He chipped away pieces of outcroppings and he pulled up dried sage-brush and peered into the holes left by the roots.
>
> In his feverish restlessness he forgot all about hunger, and he paid little attention to the sun's burning heat which beat upon his back. When noon came he was no nearer finding the spot from which the float-rock had been displaced. He slid down the hillside and climbed up the opposite side of the gulch, all the time scrutinizing everything about him with the nicety of a bird examining a flower. Not a thing anywhere to indicate whence the float had come.
>
> But with the patience of prospectors he stuck to the search. He went all over the hillside and found nothing. He retraced his steps and went down into the gulch to resurvey the topography of the locality. He gazed up and down, before and back. Suddenly, he saw in the late afternoon's sunlight a protruding mass of rocks a half-mile farther up the gulch that resembled in color the float he had come across early in the morning. He

hastened up the gulch and climbed over boulders and through sage-brush. He knew he was at last going to his golden find.

Just at sunset he reached the outcropping—a sharp, rugged, reddish-brown boulder jutting from out a steep area of yellow, sterile soil. He drew himself up to it and excitedly knocked off a chunk. It was identical with the float of early morning. The golden specks were everywhere abundant where oxidation had not dulled the precious metallic deposits....[15]

Evangelist J.E. Wolfe, writing in 1889, stated:

What a golden mine of truth is the precious Word of God! What inexhaustible stores of wealth lie enfolded within its bosom! Blessed thought, too, that it contains no dross, quartz, or earth, from which it must needs be separated. The Book, from the beginning to the ending, is composed of multitudinous nuggets of the purest gold. And yet it requires patient, prayerful digging in order to obtain the treasure. For near a score of years I have been digging in this mine, and have found it a most pleasurable and profitable task.[16]

Dr. J. Todd gave his testimony in these words:

Some look upon the Bible as a garden of spices, in which you may walk, and at your leisure pluck the flowers and gather the fruits of the Eden of God. But this does not accord with my experience. I have found it more like a mine, in which you must dig and labour, the wealth of which is not to be obtained without labour—a mine rich in gold and precious things, but it must be wrought day and night in order to produce them.[17]

Another writer adds his observation:

Not infrequently, the most precious things are the most difficult to attain. Iron and coal and gold do not lie on the surface of the ground; they have to be sought for carefully, and with great trouble. So with the Bible. Some of its highest truths by no means lie on the surface. They are there most certainly, and they are to be found; but they need patient investigation and humble, prayerful thought in order that they may be discovered.[18]

Sir Walter Scott affirmed that—

> The most learned, acute, and diligent student cannot in the longest life obtain an entire knowledge of this one volume. The more deeply he works the mine, the richer and more abundant he finds the ore; new light continually beams from this source of heavenly knowledge, to direct conduct and to illustrate the work of God and the ways of men; and he will at last leave the world confessing that the more he studied the Scriptures, the fuller conviction he had of his own ignorance, and of their inestimable value.[19]

J.J.S. Perowne stressed the necessity of diligent search in these words: "Of all the books in the world, the Bible is one which will not yield up its riches and its sweetness except to the diligent and faithful and earnest student."[20]

In searching the Scriptures for its precious truths we must not skim over the surface of the Bible. We must sink a shaft into a chapter or a verse and dig for the Bible's riches. As Dr. George F. Pentecost wrote:

> There is "hid treasure" in the Bible, lying deep beneath the surface, unseen and unpossessed by the careless and superficial reader. Such a reader may find enough of this heavenly gold even on the surface to keep him from spiritual pauperism; but if he does not dig for hid treasure, he will never become opulent in the truth. I wish, therefore, to excite in you spiritual cupidity for the hidden treasure of God's Word—hidden, not in the sense that there is anything beyond the understanding of the unlearned; not because God does not wish you to know and have the best things; but hidden because you are careless and indolent, because you do not read your Bible with the same attention and interest that you give to textbooks used in pursuit of human learning.[21]

Some years ago a Christian businessman found pleasure in visiting fellow Christians in their homes for a time of fellowship in spiritual things.

One day, being in a mining area, he called on a Christian friend who was a miner. It was late in the afternoon, and the miner, having returned from the pit, had bathed and changed his clothes, and was now poring over his well-worn Bible.

"Well, Jamie, where are you gleaning today?" asked his visitor.

"In Romans 8," was Jamie's reply.

A few weeks later the businessman again called at the miner's cottage and found him, as usual, studying his Bible, and still at Romans 8.

"Why, Jamie, you were digging into that chapter when I came to see you some weeks ago," he said.

"Aye, sir," was the miner's reply, "I'm sinking a shaft here."[22]

Concerning her sister, Frances Ridley Havergal, Maria V.G. Havergal wrote: "She read her Bible at her study table by seven o'clock in the winter; sometimes, on bitterly cold mornings, I begged that she would read with her feet comfortably to the fire, and received the reply, 'But then, Marie, I can't rule my lines neatly; just see what a find I've got!' "[23]

Evangelist D.L. Moody claimed:

> We must study the Bible thoroughly, and hunt it through, as it were, for some great truth.
>
> If a friend were to see me searching about a building, and were to come up and say, "Moody, what are you looking for? Have you lost something?" and I should say, "No, I haven't lost anything; I'm not looking for anything in particular," I fancy he would just let me go on by myself and think me very foolish. But if I were to say, "Yes, I have lost a dollar," why, I might expect him to help me find it.
>
> Read the Bible as if you were looking for something of value. It is a good deal better to take a single chapter and spend a month on it than to read the Bible at random for a month.[24]

Give Me That Book!

Wrote A.T. Pierson:

> All who, for themselves, will prayerfully search...will find the reward of the explorer who, from new paths of investigation and discovery, brings new trophies; or of the miner who digs up new nuggets of gold or gems. Here are to be found ever new truths, precious stones of beauty and radiance surpassing the gold of Ophir, the precious onyx and the sapphire.[25]

R.E. Neighbour gave his testimony in a simple rhyme:

> I mined deep down within God's Word
> Where riches all abound;
> God helped me, and my heart rejoiced,
> His gems of gold I found.[26]

Again, in our study of the Scriptures we should not neglect familiar passages. In Europe we have seen beautiful antique desks. These desks are fitted with many drawers, but, unknown to the casual viewer, the craftsmen have included secret drawers in a variety of places. Touch a secret spring, and lo, another drawer for concealing riches, opens to view.

The Bible is like that. Even in its most familiar passages there are "secret drawers," where the Spirit has placed valuable treasures. It is for us to search and to study to avail ourselves of these treasures.

In the "green room" at Dresden, where for centuries the Saxon princes gathered their gems and treasures, there used to be a silver egg, a present to one of the Saxon queens. When a secret spring was touched, the egg opened and revealed a golden yolk. Within this yolk was hid a chicken, which also opened to disclose a splendid golden crown, studded with jewels. Another secret spring being touched revealed in the centre of the crown a magnificent diamond ring.

Even so, the treasures of the Bible are not all discovered at first glance, but, when laid open, are found to contain still more treasures waiting to be possessed.[27]

Finally, in studying the Bible for its treasures, we should not neglect passages which appear to us at first sight to be devoid of riches. In the words of Chrysostom:

> As in mines of gold, anyone who is skilled in such matters could not bear to overlook even the slightest vein, inasmuch as it is capable of yielding great riches; so in like manner in the divine Scriptures, we cannot pass over one jot or one tittle without loss; but it is necessary throughout to investigate all things. For all these things are spoken by the Holy Spirit; nor is there in them anything which is superfluous.[28]

And Matthew Simpson exhorted seminary students in these words:

> Let me caution you against underrating any portion of the Holy Scriptures. The Psalms are beautiful, the Gospels and Epistles are rich and instructive, but they are only parts of the Word of God. Never allow yourself to speak or think disparingly of the Old Testament. It is as much the Word of God as the New. It would not have been revealed, but that God saw it was necessary for our humanity. Its necessity is not merely historical, prophetical, or explanatory; but there are rich veins of truth cropping up amid its local histories, and even its darkest narratives, like the veins of gold and silver amid the rugged quartz of the mountains, that will amply repay and enrich the devoted searcher.[29]

Let J.H. Vincent remind us of the depths of God's Word:

> There are depths below depths in this deep volume. The superficial student who climbs to its summits may find flowers and fruits on the surface. Here is a soil whence may come to him still richer and worthier products. Underneath that soil are layers of rocks and veins of precious mineral, and here and there glittering gems of rare value. Deeper still there are caverns dark as night to the worldling, but rich with untold brilliancy to the spiritually enlightened, and underneath all are the firm foundations of doctrine, concerning the infinite God,

His character, His essential being, His will, His history, His providence, His holy and everlasting purposes.[30]

J. Edwards encourages us in this way:

"The prospector does not find the nuggets of gold by scraping the surface. It is by earnest and prayerful study of the Bible that we discover truths we may call our own."[31]

In his book, *Sesame and Lilies*, John Ruskin, English art critic, says concerning the reading of a good book:

When you come to a good book, you must ask yourself, "Am I inclined to work as an Australian miner would? Are my pickaxes and shovels in good order, and am I in good trim myself, my sleeves well up to the elbow and my breath good?" And, keeping up the figure a little longer, even at cost of tiresomeness, for it is a thoroughly useful one, the metal you are in search of being the author's mind or meaning, his words are the rock, which you have to crush and smelt in order to get at it. And your pickaxes are your own care, wit, and learning; your smelting furnace is your own thoughtful soul.[32]

If John Ruskin wrote that way concerning the reading of a good book, what shall we do about the reading of the best Book? Only let us remember, "The words of the LORD *are* pure words: *as* silver tried in a furnace of earth, purified seven times" (Psalm 12:6), and that it is the Holy Spirit who helps us to understand the meaning of God's Word. "The Bible," wrote Amos R. Wells, "yields its gold only to the pick and shovel of earnest thought."[33]

As we consider the Bible gold mine, may we pray with Edwin Hodder:

Oh, may I love Thy precious Word,
May I explore the mine.[34]

Vigilance
We have indicated and illustrated the value that we must establish with regard to the Bible's contents; we have suggested the vigour we must expend with regard to the Bible's study; now let's consider the *vigilance*

we must exercise with regard to the Bible's preservation, protection, and propagation.

We have read of crooks who have taken gold coins and bored out the precious metal, leaving only the shell. Then they filled up the shell with a vastly inferior metal and recirculated the coins as if they were of the same original value.

In a similar way there are theologians and teachers who take the gold coins of Scripture language, extract the real meaning from the Bible's words, and then circulate them among God's people. But what is given out is only the shell of biblical teaching; the real meaning and value have been removed.

Some speak and write, for example, of the inspiration of the Bible. What they mean is merely that the Bible inspires men and women as they read its pages; most certainly they do not believe that the Bible is the product of the Holy Spirit's work.

Others attempt to remove the Bible by suppressing it. There are public libraries, for example, where no Bible can be found!

Some years ago a missionary in Italy offered a Bible to a stonemason who was building a wall. He did not want the Bible, but upon the missionary's insistence finally accepted it. When the lady left, the man removed a stone from the wall and placed the Bible into the space. He then continued building the wall around it, laughing to think how he had fooled her.

Not many years after, there was an earthquake which caused many buildings and walls to fall. One dangerous wall was standing, and workmen were sent to demolish it. "Perhaps there is a treasure there," one worker said as he moved part of the stones. Imagine the workman's surprise when he found a "treasure" indeed, the Bible which had been hidden there years before.[35]

The foundations of our society are crumbling; the walls of civilization are breaking down; it may be that in the midst of our present crisis, men and women will rediscover the Bible, which previous generations have hidden because they did not want to face God's truth.

Give Me That Book!

Centuries ago, in spite of perils and persecutions, the Waldenses of Europe sought various methods by which to disseminate their faith in God. Some of them assumed the guise of gem merchants in order to gain access to people's homes. After the Waldensian had shown his wares and had perhaps made a few sales, he would say, "If you promise not to betray me to the clergy and to the civil authorities, I will show you another diamond—one that is far more precious and lustrous than the others I have shown you. Its radiant light is able to banish the darkness of your hearts and illumine the path that leads to the heart of God."

Then, taking a bundle from the folds of his garment and unwrapping it, he would produce a Bible and seek to lead his hearers into a saving knowledge of its mighty truths.[36]

Surely our study of God's Word as treasure should lead us to say with Sir H.W. Baker:

> Who can tell the pleasure,
> Who recount the treasure
> By Thy Word imparted
> To the simple-hearted?[37]

FOR YOUR FURTHER STUDY

1. Why do some people see no value in the Bible?
2. Why may we take the Berean Jews, mentioned in Acts 17:11, as a pattern for ourselves in the study of God's Word?
3. Discuss ways in which we as Christians may defend the purity and demonstrate the preciousness of God's Word.

Our Noble Inheritance

It is my confident hope that my subjects may never cease to cherish their noble inheritance in the English Bible, which is the first of national treasures. Its spiritual significance is the most valuable thing the world affords.

—King George V

I have made a covenant with my God that He send me neither visions, dreams, nor even angels. I am well satisfied with the gift of the Holy Scriptures, which give me abundant instruction and all that I need to know both for this life and for that which is to come.

—Martin Luther

I entered the world's great library doors;
I crossed their acres of polished floors;
I searched and searched their stacks and nooks,
But I settled at last on the Book of books:
The Bible.

—Author Unknown

My love for the Holy Bible and its sacred truth is stronger at ninety than it was at nineteen.

—Fanny Crosby

Asked how often he had read the Bible through, George Mueller replied: "Well, as you ask me, I may say that I have read it through sixty-six times, and I am now going through it for the sixty-seventh time, and it gets more interesting and sweeter every time I read it."

The books of men have their day, and then grow obsolete. God's Word is like Himself, "the same yesterday, today, and for ever." Time passes over it, but it ages not. Its power is as fresh as if God spake it but yesterday.

—R. Payne Smith

What would you take for your Bible if you couldn't buy another?

STUDY 24
God's Word Is Compensative

Our Key Scripture—"Thy testimonies have I taken as an heritage for ever: for they *are* the rejoicing of my heart" (Psalm 119:111).

Supplementary Scriptures—Deuteronomy 33:4; 1 Kings 21:1–16; Psalm 16:5, 6; Proverbs 13:22; 1 Peter 1:4.

HAVE you ever said to yourself, "Oh, if only someone would remember me in his will, that would solve all my financial problems"? It is true, is it not, that many people go through life looking for a legacy and hoping that by this means they will get rich?

In this study we offer no formula for getting legacies, but we do offer an example of one who had found a heritage vastly superior to any earthly inheritance and who was daily enjoying his legacy. We refer to the psalmist who, in Psalm 119:111, gives us his personal testimony: "Thy testimonies have I taken as an heritage for ever." What a marvellous decision! May each one of us follow in his footsteps.

BASIC OUTLINE

God's Word is the believer's heritage. But what should we do with this legacy? We suggest that we should *prize* it, *possess* it, and *preserve* it for succeeding generations.

<u>Prize It!</u>

As our heritage we should *prize* the Bible. This attitude, we believe, is absolutely vital for the Christian.

A Christian wrote:

Give Me That Book!

> I wonder, if some of us realize what a legacy and inheritance the Bible really is—God's Word to us.... It comes to us, in the stress and strain of our life today, like music from a far country. It is like cooling waters in a hot and thirsty land. It is like a still, small voice that speaks to a troubled soul in the night and says, "Be strong and of good courage."[1]

Because Christians in the past have prized the Word of God, they have refused to surrender it to persecutors or to critics.

For us to prize the Bible today will involve decision. This is illustrated for us in the psalmist's words: "Thy testimonies have I taken as an heritage for ever." That indicates consideration and decision. God's testimonies had so blessed the psalmist that he made a covenant to prize and preserve God's Word as his legacy forever.

M.J. Smith challenges us in this way:

> Cling to the Bible, though all else be taken;
> Lose not its precepts so precious and pure.
> Souls that are sleeping its tidings awaken,
> Life from the dead in its promises sure.
>
> Cling to the Bible—this jewel and treasure
> Brings life eternal, and saves fallen man.
> Surely its value no mortal can measure;
> Seek for its blessing, O soul, while you can.[2]

But for us to prize the Bible will involve more than decision. There will have to be determination as well. Our claim to God's Word will not go unchallenged. Various pressures will be brought to bear on us appealing to us to surrender our heritage.

The Old Testament records the noble example of Naboth. Naboth, a godly Israelite, owned a fertile vineyard, which was situated close to the palace of Ahab, King of Samaria. With covetous eyes Ahab asked Naboth to sell the vineyard to him. To the king's request, Naboth replied: "The LORD forbid it me, that I should give the inheritance of my fathers unto thee" (1 Kings 21:3).

That is how the Christian should reply to all those who try to make us surrender our heritage of God's Word. To the arrogant appeals of liberal theology, to the blatant appeals of agnosticism, to the subtle appeals of neo-orthodoxy, we must respond emphatically: "The LORD forbid it me, that I should give the inheritance of my fathers unto thee."

For Naboth his decision and determination brought upon him the hatred of Ahab and his wife Jezebel. Jezebel arranged for Naboth to be falsely accused of blasphemy against God and the king and to be stoned to death. Naboth's stand, therefore, brought opposition and resulted in his martyrdom.

Let us be like Naboth, then, prepared, if necessary, to seal our testimony with our lifeblood. As W.M. Whittemore wrote:

> We won't give up the Bible,
> For pleasure or for pain;
> We'll buy the truth and sell it not
> For all that we might gain.
> Though man should try to take our prize
> By guile, or cruel might,
> We'd suffer all that man could do,
> And God defend the right.[3]

If we are to prize the Bible, there must be decision and determination. But there must be defence as well. We must be prepared to defend the Bible as our inheritance.

Second Samuel 23 gives us a list of David's mighty warriors and their feats. Concerning Shammah it is written: "The Philistines were gathered together into a troop, where was a piece of ground full of lentiles: and the people fled from the Philistines. But he stood in the midst of the ground, and defended it, and slew the Philistines: and the LORD wrought a great victory" (23:11, 12).

Doubtless that piece of ground was Shammah's inheritance, and he was prepared to fight for it against the invaders.

Charles H. Spurgeon is sometimes quoted as having said, "Defend the Bible? There is no more need to defend the Bible than there is to defend a lion. Just let the lion out of its cage."[4] But Mr. Spurgeon was not thereby teaching that we should not be prepared to stand by the Bible (as witness his own valiant attempts to stem the tide of theological modernism in the Baptist Union of England). His words must not be used to support a policy of indifference and apathy. Like Shammah we must stand our ground; as we do so, the Lord will work a great victory. Great vision will be rewarded with great victory:

> Guard the Bible well;
> All its foes repel ....
> Guard what God revealed,
> As our sun and shield.
> Never, never yield
> His holy Word.[5]

Possess It!

We must prize God's Word as our heritage. But more than that: We must *possess* it. Wrote Goethe: "What thou hast by inheritance from thy fathers, that thou must acquire if it is to be thine own."[6] There are many who profess to prize the Bible as their inheritance, who do not make it their aim to possess it individually and increasingly for themselves. They profess to have a spiritual gold mine, but live like paupers.

We cannot read Psalm 119 without realizing that the writer was a man who possessed his possessions. He had taken the testimonies of God as his inheritance, and he made it his daily practice to possess something more of his legacy.

When Israel was brought out of Egyptian bondage, they were promised possession of "a land of hills and valleys, *and* drinketh water of the rain of heaven" (Deuteronomy 11:11), "a good land and a large, unto a land flowing with milk and honey" (Exodus 3:8). But the people of Israel had to take possession of that land by their own action and trust in God's promise. Thus Joshua was instructed "to go in to possess the land, which the LORD your God giveth you to possess it" (Joshua 1:11).

The Bible, too, is a land fertile and fruitful, a land "flowing with milk and honey." The Bible is potentially the inheritance of each believer, but it must be possessed practically and personally by us.

How, then, shall we possess our possessions? In three ways:

First, we may possess our inheritance, the Bible, through acquaintance with its parts. There is no substitute for a familiarity with the hills and the valleys, the rivers and the lakes, the flowers and the fruits of the great Bible "land." And, moreover, there is no way to become acquainted with the contents of the Bible except through daily and diligent reading of its pages.

We stress diligent reading of the Bible because it is perilously easy to read a page of the Bible and later not be able to recall anything of what we read.

D.L. Moody used to illustrate this point in this way:

> At one time I read so many chapters of the Bible a day that if I did not get through my usual quantity, I thought I was getting cold and backsliding. But, mind you, if a man had asked me two hours after as to what I had read, I could not tell him; I had forgotten it nearly all.

> When I was a boy, I hoed corn on a farm; and I used to hoe it so badly in order to get over so much ground, that at night I had to put down a stick in the ground so as to know the next morning where I had left off. That was somewhat in the same fashion as running through so many chapters every day.[7]

We possess our inheritance through acquaintance with its parts. But we may also possess the Bible through appropriation of its promises.

A godly Christian once possessed a Bible in which on various pages she had written "T. and P." When asked what she meant by the words, she replied: "Tried and Proven. Next to every promise of God I have put 'T. and P,' that is my own personal witness to the truthfulness of God's Word."

That is how to appropriate the promises of God! Peter teaches us that to us are given "exceeding great and precious promises: that by these ye might be partakers of the divine nature" (2 Peter 1:4). But those promises must be appropriated by faith. We must not stagger at the promises of God through unbelief, but, rather, be strong in faith, giving glory to God (see Romans 4:20).

Give Me That Book!

Years ago, Henry G. Weston wrote: "There is nothing in the Bible that benefits you unless it is transmuted into life, unless it becomes a part of yourself, just like your food. Unless you assimilate it and it becomes body, bone, and muscle, it does you no good."[8] "A man owns as much of the Bible," writes another, "as he obeys."[9]

Finally, we suggest that we may possess our possessions, the Holy Scriptures, through application of its principles. There are, according to Hebrews 5:12–6:1, both elementary and advanced principles in the Word of God. All believers are exhorted to advance beyond the "childhood" principles to the "adulthood" principles.

Here is what the writer of Hebrews says:

> When for the time ye ought to be teachers, ye have need that one teach you again which *be* the first principles of the oracles of God; and are become such as have need of milk, and not of strong meat. For every one that useth milk *is* unskilful in the word of righteousness: for he is a babe. But strong meat belongeth to them that are of full age, *even* those who by reason of use have their senses exercised to discern both good and evil. Therefore leaving the principles of the doctrine of Christ, let us go on unto perfection.

Fellow Christian, are you possessing your possessions? Are you making the Bible your own? By reading, by study, by memorization, by sharing are you making the Scriptures your personal inheritance? Concerning Israel, it is written that they "shall possess their possessions"—the land of Palestine: the mount . . . the plain . . . the fields . . . the cities (see Obadiah 17–21). There is no reason why God's people today should not possess the Scriptures in their entirety—from cover to cover.

> The Word in the Book is gold in the mine;
> The Word in the heart is purse-carried coin.[10]

G.B.F. Hallock wrote:

> I would that every student of the Bible would take the motto which Bengel took for his guidance in study: "Apply thyself wholly to the Scriptures, and the Scriptures wholly to

thyself." Some are applying themselves wholly to the Scriptures with microscopic intensity of search and research, but they neglect the other half.[11]

Another has written:

> He reads and hears God's Word well who seeks to realize it in his life. More knowledge of God's Word will be gained by a single effort to live one of its commands than by a year of reading with no effort to keep the Word of God. Trusting a promise will enable one to know its sweetness far better than to commit it to memory.[12]

Preserve It!

With regard to their wonderful inheritance, the Bible, Christians should prize it and possess it. But they should also be concerned to *preserve* it for succeeding generations. The Bible is not a legacy to be selfishly enjoyed by one generation and sinfully kept from following generations. The Bible must be transmitted in its power and purity to our descendants.

We must preserve the Bible in our churches. We must make sure that the Word of God is central to the fellowship and ministry of God's people. Let each local church test itself in this regard. Let them ask themselves the following questions:

Is the Word of God kept central in our services? Does our pastor preach the Word of God in its fullness? Are decisions of the board and the congregation made on the basis of God's Word and its principles?

The Word of God must be preserved in our Sunday schools. Historically, the Sunday school came into existence in order that the Word of God be taught to children. Are our Sunday schools doing this today? Is the Bible central in the curriculum, or is it just quoted here and there to give the materials a flavour of Scripture?

The Bible must be preserved in our Bible colleges and seminaries. Writing in a brochure printed for the newly founded Biblical School of Theology, Dr. Allan A. MacRae argues that Christian young people should not study at a college or seminary where some of the faculty believe in the inspiration of God's Word and others deny the authority and trustworthiness of Scripture. Dr. MacRae states:

> If the seminary faculty has some men who believe the Bible to be true and dependable in its entirety, but also others who believe and teach that the Bible is full of errors, contradictions and paradoxes, the student is sailing on an uncharted sea. He is not there to hear the eternal truths of God and learn them, nor is he there to hear falsehood and reject it. He will hear a mixture of truth and falsehood, and he will find himself totally unequipped to separate the true from the false. It might almost be said that the more truth is presented, the more dangerous is the mixture, because the helpless student is all the more apt to be taken in by what is false.
>
> A student who attended such a theological seminary described his experience thus: "I would sit in class and for a time everything the professor said would sound absolutely right to me. It would seem entirely in line with the Word of God and thoroughly reasonable. Step by step his logic would proceed, each point seeming to flow naturally out of what had just been said.
>
> Then suddenly I would realize that what he was saying was in direct opposition to the Word of God, although it had seemed to follow logically from everything he had said before. Immediately I had to stop and think: "Now, where am I?" I would go back and try to remember what was said between. It was usually very difficult and sometimes even impossible to find the place where he had slipped the track and stepped off the path of Bible belief to the path of Bible denial.[13]

The Word of God must be preserved in our missionary and evangelistic agencies. Nothing must be allowed to usurp the Bible in the ministry of such organizations. A picture once appeared in a Canadian newspaper showing a hand holding out a loaf. The hand was labelled "The Church." The loaf was marked: "Christ." Underneath the picture appeared the caption, "She has nothing else to offer."[14]

That, indeed, is the emphasis of the Bible itself. The church's function is to offer the Bread of Life to men and women famishing and seeking relief in many ways that bring no satisfaction, spending their money "for that which is not bread" (Isaiah 55:2).

The Word of God must be preserved, too, in our homes. Tragically, the observance of family worship or family devotions is disappearing from our Christian homes. Paul was able to say to Timothy, "From a child thou hast known the holy scriptures, which are able to make thee wise unto salvation through faith which is in Christ Jesus" (2 Timothy 3:15), and that instruction was received initially in his home (see 2 Timothy 1:5). Christian parents need not be at a loss to know how to conduct family worship. There are various helps, geared to children of all ages, available in Christian bookstores. But there must be a firm resolve that nothing will permit the family to dispense with the daily time of worship and prayer.

All of this means that the Bible must be preserved by each individual Christian. The task of preserving our spiritual inheritance is not the task of the state; it is the duty of Christians. We look in the wrong place if we expect political power to guarantee the transmission of our spiritual heritage to future generations. We have this responsibility, and no one else.

Let us remind ourselves constantly of the psalmist's testimony, which forms our Key Scripture: "Thy testimonies have I taken as an heritage for ever." Let us make the same decision and find the same delight in God's Word.

Walter B. Knight tells us that during World War II a minister visited a poor woman in hospital in Surrey, England. The woman's home had been destroyed by bombs, and she had lost all her possessions.

Reflecting upon her situation, the woman said to the minister: "I've lost everything now—husband, home, and earthly possessions."

There was a pause. Then the woman spoke up again: "I've lied," she exclaimed. "I have the Lord and His Word to begin my new home with. These are treasures beyond compare!"[15]

That Christian had found God's Word to be her abiding inheritance.

Give Me That Book!

Let Charles Gulston bring our series of studies to a close by his challenging words:

> The Bible is the heritage of every nation, which has rendered it into its own tongue. It is more. It is the heritage of every man who strives to obey its precepts, and who in simple trust and with a thankful spirit, accepts what it freely offers. "Thy testimonies," declares the Psalmist, "have I taken as an heritage for ever." There is none greater.[16]

FOR YOUR FURTHER STUDY

1. What things may subtly take the place of God's Word in our lives?
2. List the ways in which you personally are making God's Word your daily possession.
3. Review the place God's Word has in your home, your church, and any Bible college or seminary in which you may have an interest.

APPENDIX 1
The Symbols in Prose

While this review of materials dealing with the symbols of Scripture does not claim to be exhaustive, we have indicated some of the main sources for those who wish to do further study.

Jabez Burns, *500 Sketches and Skeletons of Sermons* (Kregel, 1968), pp. 594–601. Included are food, medicine, light, fire, hammer, rain, and snow.

Sidney Collet, *The Scripture of Truth* (London: S.W. Partridge, 1905), pp. 64–74. Included are critic, lamp or light, mirror, laver, food, gold, fire, hammer, sword, seed, sun, rain and snow, the Word of God.

Norman B. Harrison, *His Things of Power* (The Bible Inst. Colp. Ass'n, 1935), pp. 11–15. Mr. Harrison classified the symbols under three main headings: The Bible as a Rectifier, as an Accomplisher, and as a Satisfier.

Benjamin Keach, *Preaching from the Types and Metaphors of the Bible* (Grand Rapids: Kregel, 1972), pp. 526–598. Symbols studied include: light, kisses of Christ's mouth (!), a net, gold, milk, meat, honey, fire, sword, hammer, leaven, a mirror, seed, rain, dew, and treasure.

F.E. Marsh, *Similes of the Christian Life* (Wheeler, 1886), pp. 125–127; *The Spiritual Life* (Des Moines: The Boone Pub. Co., 1958), pp. 44–54. Marsh examines the symbols of seed, mould, judge, food, plan.

Mark Guy Pearse, *Thoughts on Holiness* (London: Paternoster Row, n.d.), pp. 105–110. Symbols are food, seed, water.

Give Me That Book!

Charles H. Spurgeon, *The Metropolitan Pulpit* (Pasadena, Texas: Pilgrim, various dates). See sermons 980, 1079, 1208, 1372, 1607, 1652, 1848, 2010, 2201, 2278, 2410, 2460, 2498, and 2577. There are sermons on fire, hammer, mirror, food, rain and snow, treasure, sword, songs, and runner.

W.H. Griffith Thomas, *Life Abiding and Abounding* (Chicago: The Bible Inst. Colp. Ass'n, n.d.), pp. 28–31. Symbols are mirror, water, and food.

R.E.O. White, *Sermon Suggestions in Outline II* (Grand Rapids: Eerdmans, 1966), pp. 77–80. Symbols studied are: rain, seed, mirror, lamp, and sword.

APPENDIX 2
The Symbols in Poetry

Christian poets have written some of their finest tributes to the Word of God.

We have included thirty-nine of these poems covering a period of well over four hundred years. Writers include George Herbert, Isaac Watts, John Newton, Horatius Bonar, James M. Gray, and Gwynn McLendon Day. We have documented these selections as completely as possible, indicating the author's complete poetic works when such was available.

These poems may be used for meditation or memorization. Preachers may want to make selections from them in a series on the symbols of Scripture.

THE BOOK OF GOD!

The Book of God! And is there then a book
Which on its front that awful title bears?
Who hold it, what high duty must be theirs,
And what high privilege, therein to look,
To read, mark, learn, digest! But in this nook
Of earth pent up, and blinded by earth's cares,
Its hopes and joys, if man the treasure dares
To scorn, such scorn shall the great Author brook!
How longed the holy men and prophets old
God's truth to see! How blest, whom He hath willed
To see His truth in His own book enrolled!
Pure is the Book of God, with sweetness filled;
More pure than massive, unadulterated gold,
More sweet than honey from the rock distilled.

Yes, 'tis a mine of precious jewelry,
The Book of God; a well of streams divine!
But who would wish the riches of that mine
To make his own; his thirst to satisfy
From that pure well; must ear, eye, soul, apply;
On precept precept scan, and line on line;
Search, ponder, sift, compare, divine, combine,
For truths that oft beneath the surface lie.
Yes; there are things which he who runs may read,
Nor few there are, which yield a harder part,
To mark, discern, and know. With cautious heed,
'Tis God's command, survey thy safety's chart;
Lest arduous things, distorted, death-ward lead
The mind unlearned, and the unstable heart.

—**Bishop Richard Mant**[1]

THE HOLY SCRIPTURES

Part 1

O Book! infinite sweetness! Let my heart
Suck every letter, and a honey gain,
Precious for any grief in any part;
To clear the breast, to mollify all pain.

Thou art all health, health thriving, till it make
A full eternity: thou art a mass
Of strange delights, where we may wish and take.
Ladies, look here; this is the thankful glass,

That mends the looker's eyes: this is the well
That washes what it shows. Who can endear
Thy praise too much? thou art Heaven's Lieger here,
Working against the states of death and hell.

Thou art joy's handsel: heaven lies flat in thee,
Subject to every mounter's bended knee.

Part 2

Oh that I knew how all thy lights combine,
And the configurations of their glory!
Seeing not only how each verse doth shine,
But all the constellations of the story.

This verse marks that, and both do make a motion
Unto a third, that ten leaves off doth lie:
Then as dispersed herbs do watch a potion,
These three make up some Christian's destiny.

Such are thy secrets, which my life makes good,
And comments on thee: for in every thing
Thy words do find me out, and parallels bring,
And in another make me understood.

Stars are poor books, and oftentimes do miss:
This book of stars lights to eternal bliss.

—**George Herbert**[2]

THE BIBLE

The Bible? That's the Book. The Book indeed,
The Book of Books;
On which who looks,
As he should do, aright, shall never need
Wish for a better light
To guide him in the night:

Or, when he hungry is, for better food
To feed upon,
Than this alone,
If he bring stomach and digestion good:
And if he be amiss,
This the best physic is.

The true Panchreston 'tis for every sore
And sickness, which
The poor, and rich
With equal ease may come by. Yea, 'tis more,
An antidote, as well
As remedy 'gainst Hell.

'Tis Heaven in perspective, and the bliss
Of glory here,
If any where,
By saints on earth anticipated is,
Whilst faith to every word
A being doth afford.

It is the looking-glass of souls, wherein
All men may see,
Whether they be
Still, as by nature they're, deform'd with sin;
Or in a better case,
As new adorn'd with grace.

Give Me That Book!

'Tis the great magazine of spiritual arms,
Wherein doth lie
The artillery
Of Heaven, ready charged against all harms,
That might come by the blows
Of our infernal foes.

God's cabinet of reveal'd counsel 'tis:
Where weal and woe
Are order'd so,
That every man may know which shall be his;
Unless his own mistake
False application make.

It is the index to eternity.
He cannot miss
Of endless bliss,
That takes this chart to steer his voyage by.
Nor can he be mistook,
That speaketh by this Book.

Book, to which no Book can be compared
For excellence;
Pre-eminence
Is proper to it, and cannot be shared.
Divinity alone
Belongs to it, or none.

It is the Book of God. What if I should
Say, God of Books?
Let him that looks
Angry at that expression, as too bold,
His thought sin silence smother,
Till he find such another.

—**Christopher Harvey**[3]

ON READING THE BIBLE

If thou art merry, here are airs;
If melancholy, here are prayers;
If studious, here are those things writ
Which may deserve thy ablest wit;
If hungry, here is food divine;
If thirsty, nectar, heavenly wine.

Read, then; but, first, thyself prepare
To read with zeal and mark with care;
And when thou read'st what here is writ,
Let thy best practice second it:
So twice each precept read shall be,
First in the book, and next in thee.

—**Peter Heylyn**[4]

BREAD THAT STRENGTHENETH MAN'S HEART
(John 6:35)

Man, earthy of the earth, an-hungered feeds
On earth's dark poison tree —
Wild gourds, and deadly roots, and bitter weeds;
And as his food is he.
And hungry souls there are, that find and eat
God's manna day by day —
And glad they are, their life is fresh and sweet,
For as their food they are.

—**Gerhardt Ter Steegen**[5]

GOD'S WRITTEN WORD

Laden with guilt and full of fears,
I fly to Thee, my Lord,
And not a glimpse of hope appears
But in Thy written Word.

The volume of my Father's grace
Does all my griefs assuage;
Here I behold my Saviour's face
Almost in every page.

This is the field where hidden lies
The pearl of price unknown,
That merchant is divinely wise
Who makes the pearl his own.

Here consecrated water flows,
To quench my thirst of sin,
Here the fair tree of knowledge grows,
No danger dwells therein.

This is the judge that ends the strife,
Where wit and reason fail,
My guide to everlasting life
Through all this gloomy vale.

Oh may Thy counsels, mighty God,
My roving feet command,
Nor I forsake the happy road
That leads to Thy right hand.

—Isaac Watts[6]

OUR HERITAGE

Lord, I have made Thy word my choice,
My lasting heritage;
There shall my noblest powers rejoice,
My warmest thoughts engage.

I'll read the histories of Thy love,
And keep Thy laws in sight,
While through the promises I rove
With ever fresh delight.

'Tis a broad land of wealth unknown,
Where springs of life arise;
Seeds of immortal bliss are sown,
And hidden glory lies.

The best relief that mourners have;
It makes our sorrows blest;
Our fairest hope beyond the grave,
And our eternal rest.

— **Isaac Watts**[7]

THE GUIDE OF YOUTH

How shall the young secure their hearts,
And guard their lives from sin?
Thy Word the choicest rules imparts
To keep the conscience clean.

When once it enters to the mind,
It spreads such light abroad,
The meanest souls instruction find,
And raise their thoughts to God.

'Tis like the sun, a heavenly light,
That guides us all the day;
And through the dangers of the night,
A lamp to lead our way.

The men that keep Thy law with care,
And meditate Thy word,
Grow wiser than their teachers are,
And better know the Lord.

Thy precepts make me truly wise;
I hate the sinner's road;
I hate mine own vain thoughts that rise
But love Thy law, my God.

Thy Word is everlasting truth;
How pure is every page!
That holy Book shall guide our youth,
And well support our age.

—**Isaac Watts**[8]

THE BIBLE, THE LIGHT OF THE WORLD

A glory gilds the sacred page,
Majestic, like the sun:
It gives a light to every age;
It gives, but borrows none.

The hand that gave it still supplies
The gracious light and heat;
Its truths upon the nations rise;
They rise, but never set.

Let everlasting thanks be Thine
For such a bright display,
As makes a world of darkness shine
With beams of heavenly day.

My soul rejoices to pursue
The steps of Him I love,
Till glory breaks upon my view
In brighter worlds above!

—**William Cowper**[9]

THE WORD MORE PRECIOUS THAN GOLD

Precious Bible! what a treasure
Does the Word of God afford!
All I want for life or pleasure,
Food and Med'cine, Shield and Sword:
Let the world account me poor,
Having this, I need no more.

Food to which the world's a stranger
Here my hungry soul enjoys;
Of excess there is no danger,
Though it fills, it never cloys:
On a dying Christ I feed,
He is meat and drink indeed!

When my faith is faint and sickly,
Or when Satan wounds my mind,
Cordials to revive me quickly,
Healing med'cines here I find:
To the promises I flee,
Each affords a remedy.

In the hour of dark temptation,
Satan cannot make me yield;
For the Word of consolation
Is to me a mighty shield:
While the Scripture truths are sure,
From his malice I'm secure.

Vain his threats to overcome me,
When I take the Spirit's sword;
Then with ease I drive him from me,
Satan trembles at the Word:
'Tis a sword for conquest made,
Keen the edge, and strong the blade.

Shall I envy, then, the miser,
Doting on his golden store?
Sure, I am or should be wiser,
I am rich, 'tis he is poor:
Jesus gives me, in His Word,
Food and Med'cine, Shield and Sword.

—**John Newton**[10]

314

GOD'S WORD IN OUR HEARTS

O God! by whom the seed is given;
By whom the harvest blest;
Whose Word, like manna shower'd from Heaven,
Is planted in our breast;

Preserve it from the passing feet,
And plunderers of the air;
The sultry sun's intenser heat,
And weeds of worldly care!

Though buried deep or thinly strewn,
Do Thou Thy grace supply;
The hope in earthly furrows sown
Shall ripen in the sky!

—Reginald Heber[11]

LIKE SEED INTO THE GROUND

Almighty God: Thy Word is cast
Like seed into the ground;
Now let the dew of heaven descend,
And righteous fruits abound.

Let not the foe of Christ and man
This holy seed remove;
But give it root in every heart
To bring forth fruits of love.

Let not the world's deceitful cares
The rising plant destroy,
But may it yield a hundred-fold
The fruits of peace and joy.

Let not Thy Word so kindly sent
To raise us to Thy throne,
Return to Thee, and sadly tell
That we reject Thy Son.

Oft as the precious seed is sown,
Thy quickening grace bestow;
That all, whose souls the truth receive,
Its saving power may know.

—Cawood[12]

SYMBOLS OF HOLY SCRIPTURE

Thy Word, O God, is named — *Light*:
 It bends o'er us like starry night;
 Thou Book of God, all darkness flies
 When unto Thee I lift my eyes;
 Brighter my path grows and more bright;
Great Book of God, 'tis well-nam'd Light.

Thy Word, O God, is named — *Life*:
 O precious name untouch'd of strife:
 It comes as with a mystic breath
 To wake the soul out of its death,
 With every gracious meaning rife;
Great Book of God, 'tis well-name'd — Life.

Thy Word, O God, is named — *Bread*:
 By which our life is nurtured:
 More sweet than angel's food that fell
 Upon Thine ancient Israel;
 As day by day, Lord, I am fed:
Great Book of God, 'tis well-nam'd Bread.

Thy Word, O God, is named — *Sword*:
 A name of awe, yet in accord;
 For even as by flashing blade
 Way to life's citadel is made;
 So pierces me, O God, Thy Word:
Great Book of God, 'tis well-nam'd — Sword.

O Book of God! O god of books!
 Whoe'er into thy pages looks,
 If brain and heart the Spirit touch,
 Will thy divineness sure avouch:
 O God, Thou in Thy Word hast spoken!
Of Light, Life, Bread, and Sword, the token.

      —Alexander B. Grosart[13]

THE GUIDING LAMP

"Thy word *is* a lamp unto my feet and a light unto my path"
(Psalm 119:105).

Sometimes I know not what to do,
Whether to give up, or pursue;
When darkness and when dangers meet,
Thy Word, a lamp unto my feet.

I look around, and none is near,
To whom I may confide my fear;
Ah! then I see the Mercy-seat —
Thy Word, a lamp unto my feet.

When flesh, or world, or devil would win
My steps to tread the paths of sin;
O God, to Thee I make retreat —
Thy Word, a lamp unto my feet.

When I am languid, weary, slow,
And my "first love" has lost its glow;
Give grace, more grace, I Thee entreat —
Thy Word, a lamp unto my feet.

Alas! dear Lord, how may I tell
How vainly conscience clangs her bell;
Warning against Sin's doom, Sin's cheat —
Thy Word, a lamp unto my feet.

Yet praise, O God, Thou God of grace,
That as I run the Christian race,
Thou wilt all enemies defeat —
Thy Word, a lamp unto my feet.

So shall I follow on and on,
Until the promised Land be won;
Where dwelling in the light indeed
My earthly lamp no more I need.

—Alexander B. Grosart[14]

WHENE'ER IN ERROR'S PATHS WE ROVE

Whene'er in error's paths we rove,
The living God through sin forsake,
Our conscience by Thy Word reprove,
Convince and bring the wanderers back,
Deep wounded by the Spirit's sword,
And then by Gilead's balm restored.

—Charles Wesley[15]

THE BIBLE

Lamp of our feet, whereby we trace
Our path, when wont to stray!
Stream from the fount of heavenly grace,
Brook by the traveller's way!

Bread of our souls, whereon we feed,
True manna from on high!
Our guide and chart, wherein we read
Of realms beyond the sky.

Pillar of fire through watches dark,
Or radiant cloud by day!
When waves would whelm our tossing bark,
Our anchor and our stay!

Pole-star on life's tempestuous deep!
Beacon, when doubts surround!
Compass, by which our course we keep,
Our deep sea-land to sound!

Riches in poverty! our aid
In every needful hour!
Unshaken rock,— the pilgrim's shade,
The soldier's fortress tower!

Our shield and buckler in the fight!
Victory's triumphant palm!

Give Me That Book!

Comfort in grief! in weakness, might!
In sickness, Gilead's balm!

Childhood's preceptor! manhood's trust!
Old age's firm ally!
Our hope when we go down to dust,
Of immortality!

Pure oracles of truth divine,
Unlike each fabled dream
Given forth from Delphos' mystic shrine,
Or groves of Academe!

Word of the ever-living God!
Will of his glorious Son!
Without thee how could earth be trod,
Or heaven itself be won?

Yet to unfold thy hidden worth,
Thy mysteries to reveal,
That Spirit which first gave thee forth
Thy volume must unseal!

And we, if we aright would learn
The wisdom it imparts,
Must to its heavenly teaching turn
With simple, childlike hearts!

—**Bernard Barton**[16]

THY WORD IS LIKE A GARDEN, LORD

Thy Word is like a garden, Lord,
With flowers bright and fair,
And every one who seeks may pluck
A lovely nosegay there.

Thy Word is like a deep, deep mine,
And jewels rich and rare
Are hidden in its mighty depths
For every searcher there.

Thy Word is like the starry host;
A thousand rays of light
Are seen to guide the traveller,
And make his pathway bright.

Thy Word is like a glorious choir,
And loud its anthems ring;
Though many tongues and parts unite,
It is one song they sing.

Thy Word is like an armoury,
Where soldiers may repair,
And find for life's long battle-day
All needful weapons there.

Oh, may I love Thy precious Word,
May I explore its mine!
May I its fragrant flowers glean,
May light upon me shine!

Oh! may I find my armour there,
Thy Word my trusty sword;
I'll learn to fight with every foe
The battle of the Lord.

—Edwin Hodder[17]

THERE IS A LAMP

There is a lamp whose steady light
Guides the poor traveller in the night;
'Tis God's own word; Its beaming ray
Can turn a midnight into day.

There is a storehouse of rich fare,
Supplied with plenty and to spare:
'Tis God's own word! It spreads a feast
For every hungering, thirsting guest.

There is a chart whose tracings show
The onward course when tempests blow:
'Tis God's own word! There, there is found
Direction for the homeward bound.

There is a tree whose leaves impart
Health to the burdened, contrite heart:
'Tis God's own word! It cures of sin,
And makes the guilty conscience clean.

Give me this lamp to read my road;
This storehouse for my daily food;
Give me this chart for life's rough sea;
These healing leaves, this heavenly tree.

—H.J. Betts[18]

BLESSED BIBLE!

Blessed Bible! how I love it!
How it doth my bosom cheer!
What hath earth like this to covet?
Oh, what stores of wealth are here!
Man was lost and doomed to sorrow;
Not one ray of light or bliss
Could he from earth's treasures borrow,
'Till his way was cheered by this.

Yes, I'll to my bosom press thee,
Precious Word, I'll hide thee here;
Sure my very heart will bless thee,
For thou ever sayest "good cheer:"
Speak, my heart, and tell thy ponderings,
Tell how far thy rovings led,
When this book brought back thy wanderings,
Speaking life as from the dead.

Yes, sweet Bible! I will hide thee
Deep, yes, deeper in this heart;
Thou, through all my life will guide me,
And in death we will not part.
Part in death? No! never! never!
Through death's vale I'll lean on thee;
Then, in worlds above, for ever,
Sweeter, still thy truths shall be!

—Phoebe Palmer[19]

GOD'S WONDERFUL WORD

Here is the spring where waters flow,
To quench our heart of sin;
Here is the tree where truth doth grow,
To lead our hearts therein.

Here is the Judge that stints the strife,
Where men's devices fail,
Here is the bread that feeds the life
That death cannot assail.

The tidings of salvation dear,
Come to our ears from hence;
The fortress of our faith is here,
And shield of our defence.

Then be not like the hog, that hath
A pearl at his desire;
But takes more pleasure in the trough,
And wallowing in the mire.

Read not this Book in any case,
But with a single eye;
Read not, but first desire God's grace
To understand thereby.

Pray still in faith with this respect—
To fructify therein;
That knowledge may bring this effect
To mortify thy sin.

Then happy thou, in all thy life,
What so to thee befalls;
Yea, doubly happy shalt thou be,
When God by death thee calls.

—**Author Unknown**[20]

HEAVENLY TEACHING

Father of mercies, in Thy Word
What endless glory shines!
For ever be Thy name adored
For these celestial lines.

Here may the wretched sons of want
Exhaustless riches find;
Riches, above what earth can grant,
And lasting as the mind.

Here the fair tree of knowledge grows,
And yields a free repast;
Sublimer sweets than nature knows,
Invite the longing taste.

Here the Redeemer's welcome voice
Spreads heavenly peace around;
And life, and everlasting joys,
Attend the blissful sound.

Here may the blind and hungry come,
And light and food receive:
Here shall the lowliest guest have room,
And taste and see and live.

Here springs of consolation rise
To cheer the fainting mind,
And thirsting souls receive supplies,
And sweet refreshments find.

Oh may these heavenly pages be
My ever dear delight;
And still new beauties may I see,
And still increasing light.

Divine Instructor, gracious Lord,
Be Thou for ever near:
Teach me to love Thy sacred Word,
And view my Saviour there.

—**Anne Steele**[21]

"FOR EVER, O LORD, THY WORD IS SETTLED IN HEAVEN"
(Psalm 119:89)

Lord, Thy Word abideth,
And our footsteps guideth;
Who its truth believeth
Light and joy receiveth.

When our foes are near us,
Then Thy Word doth cheer us,
Word of consolation,
Message of salvation.

When the storms are o'er us,
And dark clouds before us,
Then its light directeth,
And our way protecteth.

Who can tell the pleasure,
Who recount the treasure,
By Thy Word imparted
To the simple-hearted?

Word of mercy, giving
Succour to the living;
Word of life, supplying
Comfort to the dying!

Oh, that we discerning
Its most holy learning
Lord, may love and fear Thee,
Evermore, be near Thee!

—H.W. Baker[22]

O WORD OF GOD, INCARNATE

O Word of God Incarnate,
O Wisdom from on high,
O Truth unchanged, unchanging,
O Light of our dark sky;
We praise Thee for the radiance
That from the hallowed page,
A lantern to our footsteps,
Shines on from age to age.

The Church from her dear Master
Received the gift divine,
And still that light she lifteth
O'er all the earth to shine.
It is the golden casket
Where gems of truth are stored;
It is the heav'n-drawn picture
Of Christ the living Word.

It floateth like a banner
Before God's host unfurled;
It shineth like a beacon
Above the darkling world;
It is the chart and compass
That o'er life's surging sea,
'Mid mists and rocks and quicksands
Still guides, O Christ to Thee.

—**William W. How**[23]

THY WORD, O LORD

Thy Word, O Lord, like gentle dews,
Falls soft on hearts that pine;
Lord, to Thy garden ne'er refuse
This heavenly balm of Thine.
Water'd from Thee
Let every tree
Bud forth and blossom to Thy praise,
And bear much fruit in after days.

Thy Word is like a flaming sword,
A wedge that cleaveth stone;
Keen as a fire so burns Thy Word,
And pierceth flesh and bone.
Oh, send it forth
O'er all the earth,
To shatter all the might of sin,
The darken'd heart to cleanse and win.

Thy Word, a wondrous guiding star,
On pilgrim hearts doth rise,
Leads to their Lord who dwell afar,
And makes the simple wise.
Let not its light
E'er sink in night,
But still in every spirit shine,
That none may miss Thy light divine.

—Author Unknown[24]

THE SCRIPTURE CANNOT BE BROKEN
(John 5:35)

Upon the Word I rest,
Each pilgrim day;
This golden staff is best
For all the way.
What Jesus Christ hath spoken,
Cannot be broken!

Upon the Word I rest,
So strong, so sure,
So full of comfort blest,
So sweet, so pure!
The charter of salvation,
Faith's broad foundation.

Upon the Word I stand!
That cannot die!
Christ seals it in my hand,
He cannot lie!
The word that faileth never!
Abiding ever!

The Master hath said it! Rejoicing in this,
We ask not for sign or for token;
His Word is enough for our confident bliss, —
"The Scripture cannot be broken!"

—**Frances Ridley Havergal**[25]

THE SWORD

For the warfare gird it on;
Nor until the fight be won,
And the day's hot work is done,
Lay it by.

Sharp its edge; oh, use it well!
Strong against the strongest spell
Ever framed in earth or hell,
It will prove.

Give Me That Book!

Bright its blade; oh keep it bright,
For the battle, day and night!
Stainless as the flashing light
Let it shine.

With it hew thy onward way
Through hell's thickest way-array;
Nothing let thy soul dismay,
To the last.

Weapon of the true and just;
Trust it strongly, warrior, trust;
Keep it free from earthly rust;
Win it must.

Strike for God, and let each blow
Tell on Satan's overthrow,
Be the ruin of a foe:
Strike for God!

Not for angels was it made,
Man alone can wield that blade,
Soldiers of the great crusade, —
Host of God!

Sword of God, thy power we hail;
He who has thee cannot fail,
He who trusts thee must prevail:
Mighty sword!

Rich in victories untold,
Still the precious sword of old,
Steel and gems and glorious gold,
To the last.

Till the warfare shall be done,
Till the victory be won,
Till the triumph be begun,
Grasp we thee!

—**Horatius Bonar**[26]

THE BOOK OF GOD

Thy thoughts are here, my God,
Expressed in words divine,
The utterance of heavenly lips
In every sacred line.

Across the ages they
Have reached us from afar;
Than the bright gold more golden they,
Purer than purest star.

More durable they stand
Than the eternal hills;
Far sweeter and more musical
Than music of earth's rills.

Fairer in their fair hues
Than the fresh flowers of earth;
More fragrant than the fragrant climes
Where odours have their birth.

Each word of Thine a gem
From the celestial mines;
A sunbeam from that holy heaven
Where holy sunlight shines.

Thine, Thine, this book, though given
In man's poor human speech,
Telling of things unseen, unheard,
Beyond all human reach.

No strength it craves or needs
From this world's wisdom vain;
No filling up from human wells,
Or sublunary rain.

No light from suns of time,
Nor brilliance from its gold;

Give Me That Book!

It sparkles with its own glad light,
As in the ages old.

A thousand hammers keen,
With fiery force and strain,
Brought down on it in rage and hate,
Have struck this gem in vain.

Against this sea-swept rock
Ten thousand storms their will
Of foam and rage have wildly spent;
It lifts its calm face still.

It standeth and will stand,
Without or change or age,
The word of majesty and light,
The Church's heritage.

—**Horatius Bonar**[27]

GOD'S WORD TO HIS CHILDREN

The Word is milk to feed (1 Peter 2:2),
Th' imparted life (1 Peter 1:23);
This is the fare we need (Jeremiah 15:16),
In peace and strife (1 John 2:14).

The Word is food to mould (Acts 20:32),
The man within (Ephesians 3:16);
And makes him strong and bold (Joel 2:11),
The fight to win (Revelations 12:11).

The Word is honey sweet (Psalm 119:103),
Refined and pure (Psalm 18:30).
If fills with joy complete (1 Thessalonians 1:6),
Unspoil'd and sure (Psalm 93:5).

The Word's a living fount (Psalm 36:9),
'Tis pure and clear (Psalm 12:6);
It makes the soul to mount (Isaiah 40:31),
To Christ most dear (1 Peter 2:4-6).

The Word's a running stream (Isaiah 33:21),
'Tis broad and deep (Psalm 65:9);
His love in it doth gleam (Jeremiah 31:3),
The soul to keep (Jude 21).

The Word's a fire of love (Jeremiah 20:9),
To make aglow (Psalm 39:3)
The soul, to things above (Colossians 3:1),
While here below (Proverbs 15:24).

The Word's a lamp to light (Psalm 119:105),
Through life's dark way (Proverbs 6:23).
It guides us safe and right (Isaiah 58:11),
To realms of day (Psalm 43:3).

The Word's a safe guide book (Psalm 73:24)
To map the way (Psalm 119:9).

To this we need to look (James 1:25),
Lest we should stray (Psalm 119:11).

The Word's a mirror bright (James 1:25),
In which is seen (Job 42:5, 6)
Dark self — hideous sight (Romans 7:18);
The flesh — unclean (Isaiah 64:6).

The Word's a hammer hard (Jeremiah 23:29),
The heart it breaks (2 Kings 22:11–13).
Its force can none retard (John 5:25),
The soul it shakes (Jeremiah 23:9).

The Word's a balm to heal (Psalm 107:20),
The broken heart (Psalm 147:3);
New life, and strength, and zeal (John 6:63)
It doth impart (1 Kings 18:1).

The Word's a girdle sure (Ephesians 6:14)
To brace the loins (Luke 12:35);
It girds us to endure (Psalm 18:39),
What truth enjoins (1 Peter 1:13).

The Word's the Spirit's sword (Ephesians 6:17),
As sharp as steel (Hebrews 4:12),
To kill unholy words (1 Thessalonians 2:13);
Its power we feel (Acts 19:20).

The Word's the pilgrim's stay (Isaiah 50:10),
While here below (Isaiah 50:4, R.V.);
It helps us on our way (Psalm 119:54),
As home we go (2 Corinthians 5:8).

The Word's a casket rare (Psalm 139:17),
Its gems are great (2 Peter 1:4);
Its cost can none declare (Job 28:16),
On earth's estate (Psalm 119:72).

—F.E. Marsh[28]

O WORTHY GIFT

O worthy gift of heavenly love to man!
Blessed exposition of salvation's plan!
By truth confirmed through each important line
A revelation of the Will divine!
The rule to which our stubborn hearts should bend,
The rich man's monitor, the poor man's friend!
The good man's trust, the scoffers secret dread!
A song of peace to soothe death's fearful bed,
Of peace from God, long tempted, oft denied,
To man the contrite, humble child of pride!

—**H. Selwyn**[29]

THE BIBLE! THERE IT STANDS!

Where childhood needs a standard
Or youth a beacon light,
Where sorrow sighs for comfort
Or weakness longs for might,
Bring forth the Holy Bible,
The Bible! There it stands!
Resolving all life's problems
And meeting its demands.

Though sophistry conceal it,
The Bible! There it stands!
Though Pharisees profane it,
Its influence expands;
It fills the world with fragrance
Whose sweetness never cloys,
It lifts our eyes to heaven,
It heightens human joys.

Despised and torn in pieces,
By infidels decried —
The thunderbolts of hatred
The haughty cynic's pride —
All these have railed against it
In this and other lands,
Yet dynasties have fallen,
And still the Bible stands!

To paradise a highway,
The Bible! There it stands!
Its promises unfailing,
Nor grievous its commands;
It points man to the Saviour,
The lover of his soul;
Salvation is its watchword,
Eternity its goal!

—**James M. Gray**[30]

HOUSE OF TREASURES!

House of treasures! Here I find
Food and medicine for the mind,
Sword to wield
Against the foe,
Helm and shield
To ward his blow,
Garments for the heavenly born,
Gems, the spirit to adorn;
Songs of praise in sunny hours,
Dirges when the tempest lowers;
But I need not thus go on
Naming treasures one by one —
Why should I the rest recall?
Christ is here — and Christ is *all*.

—**A.A. Rees**[31]

THE HOLY BOOK

I open it, my fingers trace the lines
That Wesley's, Moody's, Spurgeon's eyes have scanned.
Beneath my fingertips a promise shines,
A diamond unearthed by my seeking hand,
A gem that countless saints have touched before
And left among this jewel casket's store.

I searched as one who searches long for gold,
And oh, what gleaming nuggets I unearthed.
All that my seeking heart and hands can hold
I gather, and I know their precious worth,
And strange, the vein has never failed, though man
Has mined its channel since the world began.

The Holy Book, that gives its wealth unpriced
To every seeker after God and Christ.

—**Grace Noll Crowell**[32]

AS THE RAIN COMETH DOWN
(Isaiah 55:10, 11)

Softly the rain is falling in the night,
Over the hills and valleys, promising
God will reclothe His world in robes of bright
And living verdure. Soon there will be Spring.
Along the barren bough new life will creep
And quicken in each tender blade and shoot:
The earth will waken from her long, long sleep,
There will be bud and blossom, leaf and fruit.

Into my heart His gentle promise falls
Like falling rain. All is not yet destroyed:
Though strife and sorrow rule, and sin appalls,
God's Word shall not return unto Him void —
It shall accomplish all His purpose planned.
Upon this blessed hope the heart can stand.

—Helen Frazee-Bower[33]

"STUDY TO SHOW THYSELF APPROVED"

God's Word, as a lamp to the feet, shines bright;
    'Tis a brilliant light to the way;
It will keep aright in the darkest night;
    Who walks by it never can stray.

"Study to show thyself approved unto God:
A workman that needeth not to be ashamed;
    Rightly dividing, rightly dividing,
    Rightly dividing the Word of truth."

God's Word is the food for a hungry soul;
    'Tis a morsel sweet to the taste;
Give the Word control, if thou would'st be whole,
    It builds up the dreariest waste.

God's Word is a song on our pilgrim way;
    'Tis an anthem sweet to the ear;
It will cheer each day, let there come what may;
    It dries up the bitterest tear.

—R. Clements[34]

THE BOOKS OF THE BIBLE

Sixty-six singers, singing sweet and true,
And setting all the world to singing too.

Sixty-six soldiers, vigorous and strong,
Valiantly attacking cruelty and wrong.

Sixty-six judges, learned in the law,
Uttering decisions free from fear or flaw.

Sixty-six artists — wondrously they paint
Kings and sages, common folk, angel, devil, saint.

Sixty-six explorers, keen to search and find
All the hidden secrets of life and death and mind.

Sixty-six masons, marvellously skilled;
One majestic temple they unite to build.

Sixty-six farmers, planting holy seed,
Happily upspringing in holy thought and deed.

Sixty-six teachers, keeping perfect school,
Where faith the law is, and love the rule.

Sixty-six doctors, knowing well to cure,
Masters of a medicine healing swift and sure.

Sixty-six sailors, bearing us away
To a better country, to a brighter day.
                                        —**Author Unknown**[35]

THE WORD OF GOD

This Book unfolds Jehovah's mind:
This Voice invites in accents kind.
This Fountain has its source on high:
This Friend will all our need supply.
This Mine affords us boundless wealth:
This Good Physician gives us health.
This Sun renews and warms the soul:
This Sword both wounds and makes us whole.
This Letter shows our sins forgiven:
This Guide conducts us safe to heaven.
This Charter has been sealed with blood:
This Volume is the Word of God.

—**Author Unknown**[36]

THE WRIT OF GOD

The Bible grows each day, each hour we pause
To feast upon its royal fare and drink
Its wine. It grows, and dearer, as we think
Its thoughts, deliberate upon a clause
Or verse, and find new truth in ancient laws.
It grows as memory and purpose link
The precious words to brain and tongue, and sink
Their beauty in the soul. Whoever draws
From this vast store of wisdom finds the store
Unlimited, exhaustless, infinite!
The heights and depths, the sum and all, who knows?
What countless gems, what wealth of shining ore,
Its truth, as yet untapped, shall yield! The Writ
of God, when lived and loved, forever grows.

—**Gwynn McLendon Day**[37]

THE WONDER BOOK

Oh, how I love this Word, this Wonder Book
That God has given me! So rich, so sweet,
So full of truth and light, of drink and meat,
And priceless treasures for the eyes which look
With faith and prayer upon its script! O brook
No task to crowd it out, but pause to greet
The Master here each day in soul retreat.
Poor and blind is he who never took
The time to seek its hidden wealth and joy.
What exultation from the fountain flows,
What cleansing comes, what strength and beauty lift
The heart and mind! No power can destroy
The faith of him who cherishes, who knows
This vital Volume, heaven's timeless Gift.

—Gwynn McLendon Day[38]

A WONDERFUL PEARL OF EXCEEDING PRICE

"O lady fair, these silks of mine are beautiful and rare —
The richest web of the Indian loom,
which beauty's queen might wear;
And my pearls are pure as thy own fair neck,
with whose radiant light they vie;
I have brought them with me a weary way —
will my gentle lady buy?"

And the lady smiled on the worn old man
through the dark and clustering curls
Which veiled her brow as she bent to view
his silks and glittering pearls;
And she placed their price in the old man's hand,
and lightly turned away,
But she paused at the wanderer's earnest call —
"My gentle lady, stay!"

"O lady fair, I have yet a gem which a purer lustre flings,
Than the diamond flash of the jewelled crown
on the lofty brow of kings —
A wonderful pearl of exceeding price,
whose virtues shall not decay,
Whose light shall be as a spell to thee
and a blessing on thy way!"

The lady glanced at the mirroring steel
where her form of grace was seen,
Where her eyes shone clear, and her dark locks waved
their clasping pearls between,
"Bring forth thy pearl of exceeding worth,
thou traveller gray and old —
And name the price of thy precious gem,
and my page shall count thy gold."

The cloud went off from the pilgrim's brow,
as a small and meagre book,

Uncased with gold or gem of cost,
from his folding robe he took!
"Here, lady fair, is the pearl of price,
may it prove as such to thee!
Nay — keep thy gold — I ask it not,
for the word of God is free!"

The hoary traveller went his way, but the gift he left behind
Hath had its pure and perfect work
on the high-born maiden's mind,
And she hath turned from the pride of sin
to the lowliness of truth,
And given her human heart to God
in its beautiful hour of youth!

And she hath left the gray old halls,
where an evil faith had power,
The courtly knights of her father's train,
and the maidens of her bower;
And she hath gone to the Vaudois
vales by lordly feet untrod,
Where the poor and needy of earth are rich
in the perfect love of God!

—John G. Whittier[39]

Index of Poems

Alphabetical Listing of the Symbols

Notes and Sources

Preface

1. See Appendix 1, "The Symbols in Prose"
2. A.C. Thiselton, *With the Prophets* (London: James Nisbet, 1882), p. 167
3. See, for example, F.E. Marsh, *Emblems of the Holy Spirit* (Grand Rapids: Kregel, 1957), & Charles Stanford, *Symbols of Christ* (London: Religious Tract Society, n.d.)
4. S.T. Coleridge (as quoted by D.L. Moody) in the Preface to *One Thousand and One Thoughts from My Library* (Grand Rapids: Baker, 1979), p. 7
5. Quoted by J.L. Nye as the Frontispiece, *Anecdotes Illustrating Bible Texts* (London: The Sunday School Union, n.d.)

Study 1: GOD'S WORD IS SUPERLATIVE

1. Adapted from Eleanor L. Doan, Compiler, *The Speaker's Sourcebook* (Grand Rapids: Zondervan, 1960), pp. 29–30
2. F.E. Marsh, *Fully Furnished* (London: Pickering & Inglis, n.d.), p. 184
3. Norman B. Harrison, *His Things of Power* (The Bible Institute Colportage Ass'n, 1935), p. 11
4. Lloyd M. Perry & Robert D. Culver, *How To Search the Scriptures* (Grand Rapids: Baker, 1967), p. 22
5. A.T. Pierson, *The Key Words of the Bible* (London: Hodder & Stoughton, 1898), p. x
6. A.T. Pierson, *Knowing the Scriptures* (Los Angeles: Biola Book Room, 1910), p. 312
7. Lloyd M. Perry & Robert D. Culver, *op. cit.*, pp. 22–23
8. W.H. Griffith Thomas, *Life Abiding and Abounding* (Chicago: The Bible Institute Colportage Ass'n, n.d.), p. 31
9. Allon Poole, *The Bible Wonder Book* (London: Pickering & Inglis, n.d.), p. 34
10. W.A. Rice, *The Precious Jewel of the Word* (London: Marshall, Morgan & Scott, n.d.), p. 93
11. Robert Burdette (quoted by W.A. Rice), *Ibid.*, pp. 94–95

12. Miles Smith, *The Translators to the Readers: An Introduction to the King James Version of the Bible* (Portland: Multnomah School of the Bible, 1963), pp. 7–8, as rendered into modern English by E.W. Goodrick
13. Eleanor L. Doan, *op. cit.*, p. 36
14. *Ibid.*, p. 32
15. *Ibid.*, p. 33
16. *Ibid.*
17. Will H. Houghton, *Let's Go Back to the Bible* (New York: Revell, 1939), pp. 45–46
18. D.J. Burrell, *Why I Believe the Bible* (New York: Revell, 1917), p. 195
19. Allon Poole, *op. cit.*, p. 91
20. *Ibid.*, p. 55
21. *Ibid.*, p. 94
22. D.J. Burrell, *op. cit.*, p. 199
23. W.H. Houghton, *op. cit.*, p. 65

Study 2: GOD'S WORD IS ILLUMINATIVE

1. Adapted from R.A. Bertram, *A Homiletic Encyclopaedia* (London: No Publisher, n.d.), p. 87
2. William W. How in *Golden Bells* (London: C.S.S.M., 1925), Hymn 588, verse 1
3. A.T. Pierson, *The Bible and Spiritual Criticism* (London: Nisbet, 1906), p. 276
4. Sarah Stock, *Windows* (London: Sunday School Union, n.d.), pp. 40–41
5. Robert E. Lee (as quoted by W.B. Knight), *Three Thousand Illustrations* (Grand Rapids: Eerdmans, 1957), p. 43
6. William Adamson, *The Religious Anecdotes of Scotland* (Glasgow: Morison, 1885), p. 204
7. Matthew Henry (source unknown)
8. As quoted by Aquilla Webb, *One Thousand Evangelistic Illustrations* (New York: Harper & Brothers, 1921), p. 317
9. Monier Williams (as quoted by A.E. Richardson), *This Is the Way* (London: Marshall, n.d.), p. 85
10. As quoted by W.B. Knight, *op. cit.*, p. 40

11. Archibald Naismith, *1,200 Notes, Quotes & Anecdotes* (London: Pickering & Inglis, 1962), p. 120

12. As quoted by Walter Baxendale, *Dictionary of Illustrations for Pulpit and Platform* (Chicago: Moody, 1949), p. 37

13. Mildred Gable and Francesca French, *Towards Spiritual Maturity* (London: Hodder & Stoughton, 1950), p. 135

14. Samuel Hayes in H.C. Adams, Editor, *Sacred Poetical Quotations* (London: Groombridge, 1882), p. 64

15. Reginald Heber in *Redemption Songs* (London: Pickering & Inglis, n.d.), Hymn 626, verse 3

16. Horatius Bonar in *The Keswick Hymn Book* (London: Marshall, Morgan & Scott, n.d.), Hymn 292, verse 5

17. Henry M. King in *Sacred Songs & Solos* (London: Marshall, Morgan & Scott, n.d.), Hymn 262, verse 2

18. As quoted by Clarence E. Macartney, *Macartney's Illustrations* (New York: Abingdon, 1946), p. 30

19. As quoted by W.B. Knight, *Knight's Master Book of New Illustrations* (Grand Rapids: Eerdmans, 1956), p. 36

Study 3: GOD'S WORD IS REGENERATIVE

1. Archibald Naismith, *1,200 Notes, Quotes & Anecdotes* (London: Pickering & Inglis, 1962), p. 177

2. G.J. Polkinghorne in G.C.D. Howley, *et al*, Editor, *A New Testament Commentary* (Grand Rapids: Zondervan, 1969), p. 588

3. Daniel W. Whittle in Ira D. Sankey, Compiler, *Sacred Songs & Solos* (London: Morgan & Scott, n.d.), Hymn 857, verse 3

4. Wilbur M. Smith in Carl F.H. Henry, Editor, *The Biblical Expositor* (Philadelphia: A.J. Holman, 1960), vol. 1, p. 8

5. E.L. Langston in Walter B. Knight, *3,000 Illustrations for Christian Service* (Grand Rapids: Eerdmans, 1957), p. 32

6. George F. Pentecost, *In the Volume of the Book* (London: Morgan & Scott, 1882), p. 41

7. Allon Poole, *The Bible Wonder Book* (London: Pickering & Inglis, n.d.), p. 80

8. Mary Warburton Booth, *They That Sow* (London: Pickering & Inglis, n.d.), p. 171

9. Fay Inchfawn, *Songs of the Ups and Downs* (London: Ward, Lock & Co., n.d.), p. 128

10. Archibald Naismith, *op. cit.*, p. 143

Study 4: GOD'S WORD IS PRODUCTIVE

1. A.J. Gordon (as quoted by E.B. Gordon), *Adoniram Judson Gordon* (New York: Revell, 1896), p. 288

2. J.R. Miller, *Devotional Hours with the Bible* (London: Hodder & Stoughton, 1920), vol. 4, p. 288

3. W. Kay in F.C. Cook, Editor, *The Holy Bible with Commentary* (London: John Murray, 1880), vol. 5, p. 275

4. W.G.T. Shedd, *Sermons to the Spiritual Man* (Edinburgh: T.&T. Clark, 1884), p. 410

5. Ibid., p. 421

Study 5: GOD'S WORD IS NUTRITIVE

1. Donald G. Barnhouse, *Let Me Illustrate* (New York: Revell, 1967), pp. 29, 30

2. Howard M. Kelly (as quoted by Walter B. Knight), *Knight's Master Book of New Illustrations* (Grand Rapids: Eerdmans, 1958), p. 28

3. W.H. Griffith Thomas, *Life Abiding and Abounding* (Chicago: The Bible Institute Col. Ass'n, 1935), p. 29

4. Robert G. Lee, *Pickings* (Grand Rapids: Zondervan, 1938), pp. 119–120

5. J.S. Keiffer in F. Grether, *Our Daily Bread* (Ohio: Publishing House of the Reformed Church in the U.S., 1898), p. 17

6. Jabez Burns, *500 Sketches and Skeletons of Sermons* (Grand Rapids: Kregel, 1968), p. 595

7. H.P. Barker (as quoted by A. Naismith), *1,200 Notes, Quotes & Anecdotes* (London: Pickering & Inglis, 1962), p. 15

8. J.E. McKee (source unknown).

9. R.A. Torrey (as quoted by G.B.F. Hallock), *Five Thousand Best Modern Illustrations* (New York: Doran, 1927), pp. 72–73

10. Mary A. Lathbury in *Golden Bells* (London: CSSM, 1925), Hymn 572, verse 1

11. C.H. Spurgeon in G.B.F. Hallock, *Five Thousand Best Modern Illustrations* (New York, 1927), p. 631

12. G.F. Allee, *Evangelistic Illustrations for Pulpit and Platform* (Chicago: Moody, 1961), p. 33

13. A.E. Richardson, *This Is the Way* (London: Marshall Brothers, n.d.), p. 89

14. James M. Gray, "How To Eat the Word" (Chicago: Good News, n.d.), p. 2

15. Source unknown

16. As quoted by Walter B. Knight, *3,000 Illustrations for Christian Service* (Grand Rapids: Eerdmans, 1957), p. 39

17. A.J. Gordon, *Yet Speaking* (London: Baptist Tract & Book Society, n.d.), p. 78

18. Jabez Burns, *500 Sketches and Skeletons of Sermons* (Kregel, 1968), p. 595

Study 6: GOD'S WORD IS REFLECTIVE

1. Walter Baxendale, *Dictionary of Illustrations for Pulpit and Platform* (Chicago: Moody, 1949), p. 52

2. W.H. Griffith Thomas, *Life Abiding and Abounding* (Chicago: The Bible Institute Col. Ass'n, 1935), pp. 28–29

3. Amos R. Wells in Al Bryant, *Sourcebook of Poetry* (Grand Rapids: Zondervan, 1968), p. 37, verse 4

4. Mildred Cable & Francesca French, *Towards Spiritual Maturity* (London: Hodder & Stoughton, 1950), p. 135

5. John Hus (source unknown)

6. Archibald Naismith, *1,200 Notes, Quotes & Anecdotes* (London: Pickering & Inglis, 1962), p. 16

7. A.J. Gordon in E. B. Gordon, *Adoniram Judson Gordon* (New York: Revell, 1896), pp. 300–301

8. Harry Ironside, *Illustrations of Bible Truth* (Chicago: Moody, 1945), pp. 91–92

9. Walter B. Knight, *3,000 Illustrations for Christian Service* (Grand Rapids: Eerdmans, 1957), p. 39

10. H.P. Barker, *Windows in Words* (London: Pickering & Inglis, 1954), p. 17

11. J.D. Gilmore as quoted in *Footsteps of Truth* (London: John F. Shaw, 1901), vol. 19, p. 204

12. John Macbeath, *Lamps and Lamplighters* (London: John F. Shaw, 1901), vol. 19, p. 204

13. Augustine as quoted by Harrington C. Lees, *The Joy of Bible Study* (London: Longmans, Green & Co., 1910), p. 27

14. Incident reported in *The Calgary Herald* (Calgary: Southam, Inc., 1972), edition of July 12. Application is the author's.

15. John Macbeath, *op. cit.*, pp. 109–110

16. Amos R. Wells, *Think on These Things* (Boston: W.A. Wilde, 1928), p. 95

17. John Ruskin (source unknown)

18. Paul Radar, *Life's Greatest Adventure* (London: Victory Press, 1938), p. 89

19. John Macbeath, *op. cit.*, p. 110

20. Martin Luther as quoted in *Footsteps of the Flock* (London: John F. Shaw, 1899), vol. 17, p. 306

21. Alcuin as quoted by McLure, *The Supreme Book of Mankind*. Full bibliographical data not available.

22. Clarence E. Macartney, *Macartney's Illustrations* (New York: Abingdon, 1945), p. 325

23. Bob Jones, Jr., *Comments on Here and Hereafter* (New York: Loizeaux, 1946), pp. 108–109

24. Walter B. Knight, *op. cit.*, p. 67

25. Donald G. Barnhouse as quoted by Walter B. Knight, *Knight's Treasury of Illustrations* (Grand Rapids: Eerdmans, 1957), p. 67

26. John Macbeath, *op. cit.*, pp. 110–111

Study 7: GOD'S WORD IS PURGATIVE

1. Amy L. Person, *Illustrations from Literature* (Grand Rapids: Baker, 1966), p. 91

2. Adapted by the author from a story in G.B.F. Hallock, *Five Thousand Modern Illustrations* (New York: G.H. Doran, 1927), p. 345

3. W.H. Griffith Thomas, *Abiding and Abounding* (Chicago: The Bible Institute Colportage Ass'n, 1935), p. 28

4. Ibid., pp. 16–17

Study 8: GOD'S WORD IS PROTECTIVE

1. See article, "Perseus," *World Book* (Chicago: Field Enterprises Educational Corp., 1976), vol. 15, p. 261
2. Homer as quoted in *The Divine Panoply* (London: The Religious Tract Society, 1846), p. 100
3. Author's notes. Original source unknown.
4. Alexander Maclaren, *Expositions of Holy Scripture* (London: Hodder & Stoughton, 1908), p. 190
5. Charles Hodge, *Systematic Theology* (London: James Clarke, 1960), vol. 3, p. 437
6. Frances (source unknown)
7. Source unknown
8. *The Divine Panoply*, p. 91
9. Adapted from Hugh Macmillan, *The Spring of the Day* (London: Pitman, 1907), p. 166
10. John S. Howson, *The Metaphors of St. Paul* (London: Strahan, 1869), pp. 28–29
11. Martin Luther, *The Table Talk of Martin Luther* (Philadelphia: The Lutheran Publication Society, n.d.), p. 22
12. P.N. Corry, *The Whole Armour of God* (London: The Victory Press, 1931), p. 40
13. Martin Luther as adapted from Clarence Macartney, *Macartney's Illustrations* (New York: Abingdon, 1945), p. 35
14. David Livingstone as quoted by Alexander Naismith, *1,200 Notes, Quotes & Anecdotes* (London: Pickering & Inglis, 1962), p. 35
15. Edwin Hodder in *Golden Bells* (London: CSSM, 1925), Hymn 581, verse 3
16. Richard Crashaw in Frank S. Mead, Editor, *Encyclopedia of Religious Quotations* (London: Peter Davies, 1965), p. 26. (The Title of the poem is "Prayer Prefixed to a Little Prayer Book.")

Study 9: GOD'S WORD IS DEFENSIVE

1. As quoted by Walter Baxendale, *Dictionary of Illustrations for Pulpit and Platform* (Chicago: Moody Press, 1949), p. 65
2. Charles H. Spurgeon (source unknown)

3. Richard Moulton as quoted by K.A. Amsler, "Rules for Bible Study" (Chicago: Good News, n.d.), pp. 3–4

4. Wilfred Grenfell as quoted by Walter B. Knight, *Knight's Up-to-the-Minute Illustrations* (Chicago: Moody Press, 1974), p. 19

5. Nansen (source unknown)

6. Edwin Hodder as in *Golden Bells* (London: CSSM, n.d.), Hymn 581, verse 3

7. M.B. Williams, *Among Many Witnesses* (New York: Revell, 1891), pp. 220–221

8. E. Paxton Hood (source unknown)

9. For information on King Arthur's Sword see *World Book* (Chicago: Field Enterprises, 1976), vol. 1, p. 335

10. George F. Pentecost, *"In the Volume of the Book"* (London: Morgan & Scott, 1882), p. 52

11. Billy Graham. (There are various accounts of this experience.) See J.C. Pollock, *Billy Graham* (New York: McGraw Hill, 1966), pp. 51–53

12. Quoted by D.L. Pierson in *Arthur T. Pierson* (London: James Nisbet, 1912), p. 77

13. As in G.B.F. Hallock, *2,500 Best Modern Illustrations* (New York: Harper, 1935), p. 271

14. Walter B. Knight, *Knight's Master Book of Illustrations* (Chicago: Eerdmans, 1958), p. 43

15. Ralph C. Norton as quoted by Walter B. Knight, *3,000 Illustrations for Christian Service* (Chicago: Eerdmans, 1957), p. 41

16. Allon Poole, *The Bible Wonder Book* (London: Pickering & Inglis, n.d.), p. 91

17. James Montgomery, *The Poetical Works of James Montgomery* (London: Gall & Inglis, n.d.), p. 409

18. Quoted by James A. Stahr, Editor, *Interest* (Wheaton, Illinois: Letters of Interest Associates), Issue of July–August, 1972

19. G. Woods (source unknown)

20. As told by P.N. Corry, *The Whole Armour of God* (London: Victory Press, 1931), pp. 64–65

21. Henry Melville (source unknown)

22. Alexander Maclaren, *Expositions of Holy Scripture* (London: Hodder & Stoughton, 1909), p. 380

23. T.H. McGuffie (source unknown)
24. Adapted by the author from a story of unknown origin.
25. Author and source unknown
26. J.H. Jowett, *The Whole Armour of God* (London: Hodder & Stoughton, 1916), p. 119
27. Martin Luther, *The Table Talk of Martin Luther* (Baker, 1979), p. 191
28. Caesar Malan as quoted by Walter B. Knight, *Knight's Master Book of New Illustrations* (Grand Rapids: Eerdmans, 1958), p. 34
29. John Ridley, *The Unsheathed Sword* (Melbourne: Bacon, n.d.), p. 6
30. *Ibid.*, p. 7
31. A.J. Gordon in E.B. Gordon, *Adoniram Judson Gordon* (New York: Revell, 1896), p. 282
32. Aquilla Webb, *1,001 Illustrations for Pulpit and Platform* (New York: Harper, 1926), p. 55
33. Henry Thorne
34. For—origin of Excalibur, see Note 9
35. James Burns, *Illustrations from Art* (London: Clarke, n.d.), pp. 85–86
36. Alfred Tennyson in James D. Morrison, Editor, *Masterpieces of Religious Verse* (Baker, 1977), p. 376

Study 10: GOD'S WORD IS CURATIVE

1. W.M. Tidwell, *Pointed Illustrations* (Kansas City: Beacon Hill, 1949), pp. 11–12
2. Richard W. DeHaan, *Our Daily Bread* (Grand Rapids: The Radio Bible Class), issue not known.
3. Walter B. Knight, *Knight's Master Book of New Illustrations* (Grand Rapids: Eerdmans, 1958), pp. 34–35
4. T.H. Darlow, *The Greatest Book in the World* (London: Hodder & Stoughton, 1927), pp. 177–178
5. Walter Shepherd, *Sent by the Sovereign* (Nutley, New Jersey: Presbyterian & Reformed, 1958), p. 92
6. Thomas Ken in Al Bryant, Editor, *Sourcebook of Poetry* (Grand Rapids: Zondervan, 1968), p. 214
7. Walter B. Knight, *Knight's Treasury of Illustrations* (Grand Rapids: Eerdmans, 1963), p. 19

8. Amos R. Wells, *A Cyclopedia of Twentieth Century Illustrations* (New York: Revell, 1918), p. 29
9. Walter B. Knight, *Knight's Treasury*, p. 16
10. G. Franklin Allee, *Evangelistic Illustrations for Pulpit and Platform* (Chicago: Moody Press, 1961), p. 159

Study 11: GOD'S WORD IS STIMULATIVE

1. E.A. Stuart as quoted by Thomas Payne, *Apostolic Christianity* (London: Christian Herald, n.d.). p. 57
2. J.H. Lord as quoted by O.J. Smith, *The Revival We Need* (London: Marshall, Morgan & Scott, 1933), p. 49
3. Source unknown
4. Mrs. Fletcher as quoted by Thomas Payne, *Revivals: How Promoted* (London: Morgan & Scott, n.d.), pp. 26–27
5. T. DeWitt Talmage in May Talmage, *Wisdom and Wit of T. DeWitt Talmage* (New York: G.H. Doran, 1922), p. 28
6. James Gilmour in Richard Lovett, Editor, *James Gilmour of Mongolia* (London: Religious Tract Society, 1895), p. 39

Study 12: GOD'S WORD IS PENETRATIVE

1. G.B.F. Hallock, *2,500 Best Modern Illustrations* (New York: Harper & row, 1935), p. 281
2. C.H. Spurgeon as quoted by Thomas Payne, *Apostolic Christianity* (London: Christian Herald Office, n.d.), pp. 48–49
3. Charles Edwards, *A Box of Nails* (London: H.R. Allenson, 1897), pp. 2–3
4. William Carey as quoted by W.O. Carver, *The Course of Christian Missions* (New York: Revell, 1939), p. 139
5. William Luff in C. Edwards, *A Box of Nails*, p. viii
6. Ron Jordahl, Librarian at Prairie Bible Institute, in a personal note to the author.
7. Paxton Hood as quoted by C.H. Spurgeon, *The Art of Illustration* (Pasadena, Texas: Pilgrim, 1971), p. 52
8. Quoted by J.C. Hutchinson, *Fugitive Poetry* (London: Frederick Warne, 1878), p. 144
9. C.H. Spurgeon, *The Art of Illustration*, p. 46

Study 13: GOD'S WORD IS DESTRUCTIVE

1. Samuel Wilberforce in Joseph Excell, Editor, *The Biblical Illustrator* (Grand Rapids: Baker, 1959), vol. 24, p. 39
2. As quoted by J.H. Bomberger, *Three Thousand Practical Illustrations* (Ohio: Central Publishing House, n.d.), p. 8
3. Alexander Stewart, *Jeremiah* (Edinburgh: W.F. Henderson, 1936), pp. 187–188
4. Hugh Macmillan, *The Corn of Heaven* (London: Macmillan, 1901), p. 138
5. Adapted from H.P. Barker, *Windows in Words* (London: Pickering & Inglis, 1954), p. 27
6. Sidney Collet, *The Scripture of Truth* (London: Partridge, 1905), p. 71
7. Jabez Burns, *500 Sketches and Skeletons of Sermons* (Grand Rapids: Kregel, 1968), p. 599
8. Macmillan, *op. cit.*, p. 142
9. H.P. Buddicum as quoted by Joseph Excell, *op. cit.*, p. 39
10. Jabez Burns, *op. cit.*
11. J.B. Courtney as quoted by Joseph Excell, *op. cit.*, p. 41
12. W.F. Foshag, "Exploring the World of Gems," in *The National Geographic Magazine* (Washington, D.C., National Geographic Society, 1950), vol. 98, p. 782
13. Jabez Burns, *op. cit.*
14. See H.P. Barker, *op. cit.*

Study 14: GOD'S WORD IS COMPULSIVE

1. Ralph G. Turnbull, *A Minister's Obstacles* (Grand Rapids: Baker, 1972), p. 12

Study 15: GOD'S WORD IS CONSULTATIVE

1. Keith L. Brooks, *Gleanings from the Word* (Wheaton: Van Kampen Press, 1951), p. 19
2. Author unknown [see similar list in Eleanor L. Doan, *The Speaker's Sourcebook* (Grand Rapids: Zondervan, 1960)], pp. 31–32
3. Edgar A. Guest as quoted in J.D. Morrison, *Masterpieces of Religious Verse* (Grand Rapids: Baker, 1977), p. 91

4. As given by Walter B. Knight, *Knight's Master Book of New Illustrations* (Grand Rapids: Eerdmans, 1958), p. 268

5. Adapted and abridged from Harry Ironside, *Illustrations of Bible Truth* (Chicago: Moody Press, 1945), pp. 35–37

6. Adapted from Walter B. Knight, *Knight's Treasury of Illustrations* (Grand Rapids: Eerdmans, 1963), p. 150

7. Attributed to "Morris" in A.C. Dixon, *Lights and Shadows in American Life* (New York: Revell, 1898), p. 130

Study 17: GOD'S WORD IS FESTIVE

1. *Newsweek* (Dayton, Ohio: Newsweek, 1972), vol. 79, no. 18, pp. 87–88

2. D.J. Burrell, *Why I Believe the Bible* (New York: Revell, 1917), p. 55

3. John G. Whittier in James D. Morrison, Editor, *Masterpieces of Religious Verse* (Grand Rapids: Baker, 1978), p. 341

4. Sir Walter Scott in James D. Morrison, Editor, *ibid.*, p. 384

5. W.P. Whyte, *Thinking Through the Scriptures* (Los Angeles: Stationers Corporation, 1935), page not known.

6. John Dryden as quoted by H.G. Adams, *Sacred Poetical Quotations* (London: Groombridge, 1892), p. 61

7. T. DeWitt Talmage in May Talmage, *Fifty Short Sermons* (New York: G.H. Doran, 1923), p. 59

8. Author unknown. This stanza of the poem is taken from E.L. Doan, *The Speaker's Sourcebook* (Grand Rapids: Zondervan, 1960), pp. 34–35

9. Erasmus as quoted by W.A. Rice, *The Precious Jewel of the Word* (London: Marshall, Morgan & Scott, n.d.), p. 36

10. W.A. Rice, *op. cit.*, p. 87

11. Robert Ingersoll as quoted by W.B. Knight, *Knight's Master Book of Illustrations* (Grand Rapids: Eerdmans, 1956), p. 29

12. Charles Wesley as quoted by E.F. & L. Harvey, *The Christian's Daily Challenge* (MOVE Press, Blackburn, Lancs., UK, 1973), p. 45

Study 18: GOD'S WORD IS COMPETITIVE

1. *New American Standard Bible.* Reference ed. Chicago: Moody Press, 1975.

2. Beck, William F. *The New Testament, in the Language of Today.* Saint Louis, Mo.: Concordia Pub. House, 1963.

3. Verkuyl, Gerrit. *The Holy Bible, the Berkeley Version in Modern English Containing the Old and New Testaments.* Grand Rapids: Zondervan Pub. House, 1959.
4. Matthew Simpson (source unknown)
5. Ingersoll as quoted in W.B. Knight, *Knight's Master Book of New Illustrations* (Grand Rapids: Eerdmans, 1956), p. 29
6. Isaac Taylor (source unknown)
7. Samuel M. Zwemer as quoted by W.B. Knight, *op. cit.*, p. 31
8. John Clifford in James D. Morrison, Editor, *Masterpiece of Religious Verse* (Grand Rapids: Baker, 1978), p. 493
9. *Telenotes* (Edmonton, Alberta: Alberta Government Telephones, date not known)
10. A.W. Tozer (source unknown)
11. Dick Hillis, *Sayings of Mao and of Jesus* (Glendale, CA: Regal, 1972), p. 3
12. *Ibid.*, p. 82
13. C.H. Spurgeon as quoted by W.B. Knight, *Knight's Treasury of Illustrations* (Grand Rapids: Eerdmans, 1963), p. 13

Study 19: GOD'S WORD IS TRANSFORMATIVE

1. Bishop Bedell as in *Anecdotes Illustrative of Old Testament Texts* (London: Hodder & Stoughton, n.d.), p. 128
2. George Whitefield in E.F. & L. Harvey, *The Christian's Daily Challenge* (MOVE Press, Blackburn, Lancs., UK, 1973), p. 226
3. Henry Ward Beecher (source unknown)
4. Joy Ridderhof in a message given at Prairie Bible Institute, Three Hills, Alberta, Canada.

Study 20: GOD'S WORD IS DISCRIMINATIVE

1. J.H. Thayer, *A Greek-English Lexicon of the New Testament* (Edinburgh: T. & T. Clark, 1901), p. 362
2. W.B. Knight, *Knight's Treasury of Illustrations* (Grand Rapids: Eerdmans, 1963), p. 12
3. In *The Gospel Herald* as quoted by W.B. Knight, *3,000 Illustrations for Christian Service* (Grand Rapids: Eerdmans, 1957), p. 33
4. *Ibid.*

5. As quoted by W.B. Knight, *Knight's Master Book of New Illustrations* (Grand Rapids: Eerdmans, 1958), p. 26

6. *Ibid.*, p. 39

7. A. Naismith, *1,200 Notes, Quotes & Anecdotes* (London: Pickering & Inglis, 1962), pp. 13–14

8. W.B. Knight, *op. cit.*, pp. 64–65

9. F.W. Boreham (source unknown)

10. John Burton as quoted by Al Bryant, *Sourcebook of Poetry* (Grand Rapids: Zondervan, 1968), p. 25

11. W.B. Knight, *op. cit.*, p. 40

12. G.F. Allee, *Evangelistic Illustrations for Pulpit and Platform* (Chicago: Moody Press, 1961), p. 35

13. *Ibid.*, p. 34

Study 21: GOD'S WORD IS CONSTRUCTIVE

1. G.B.F. Hallock, *Five Thousand Best Modern Illustrations* (New York: Doran, 1927), p. 74

2. T. DeWitt Talmage (source unknown)

3. Hugh T. Kerr, *Children's Everyland Story-Sermons* (London: Oliphants, 1955), pp. 63–64

4. William Souper in *The Report of the Mundesley Bible Conference, 1914* (London: Morgan & Scott, 1914), pp. 147–148

5. H.P. Barker, *Windows in Words* (London: Pickering & Inglis, 1954), p. 18

6. M.R. DeHaan & H.G. Bosch, Editors, *Our Daily Bread* (Grand Rapids: Zondervan, 1959), Reading for May 21.

7. David J. Burrell, *Why I Believe the Bible* (New York: Revell, 1917), pp. 157–158

8. J. Reid Howatt (source unknown)

9. C.H. Spurgeon (source unknown)

10. A.W. Pink, *Spiritual Growth* (Grand Rapids: Baker, 1971), p. 127

11. Martin Luther in J.H. Merle D'Aubigne, *The Life and Times of Martin Luther* (Chicago: Moody Press, 1950), p. 433

Study 22: GOD'S WORD IS FORMATIVE

1. Adapted by the author from a story of unknown origin.

2. Gwynn M. Day, *The Wonder of the Word* (Chicago: Moody Press, n.d.), p. 199

3. *Ibid.*, p. 8

4. James Burns, *Illustrations from Art* (London: Clarke, n.d.), p. 29

5. Mary Lathbury in *Golden Bells* (London: CSSM, 1925), Hymn 572, verse 3

6. A.B. Simpson. Source unknown; see G.B.F. Hallock, *2,500 Best Modern Illustrations* (New York: Harper & Row,1935), p. 28, for a similar use of this picture.

7. Annie Johnson Flint. (I have not been able to track down the source of this poem in volumes of the author's poetry.)

8. Maude Frazer Jackson in James D. Morrison, Editor, *Masterpieces of Religious Verse* (Grand Rapids: Baker, 1978), p. 383

9. Source unknown

10. This is one version of a story found in various volumes of illustrations. See H.P. Barker, *Windows in Words* (London: Pickering & Inglis, 1954), p. 126

11. Adapted by the author from a story of unknown origin

12. As in George F. Pentecost, *"In the Volume of the Book"* (London: Morgan & Scott, n.d.), p. 36

13. This account is given in various forms. This version is taken from Walter B. Knight, *Knight's Master Book of New Illustrations* (Grand Rapids, Eerdmans, 1958), p. 299

14. George F. Pentecost, *op. cit.*, pp. 113–114

Study 23: GOD'S WORD IS REMUNERATIVE

1. Archibald Naismith, *1,200 Notes, Quotes & Anecdotes* (London: Pickering & Inglis, 1962), p. 17

2. Charles Simeon, *Expository Outlines on the Whole Bible* (Grand Rapids: Zondervan, n.d.), vol. 14, p. 226

3. William W. How as in *Golden Bells* (London: CSSM, n.d.), Hymn 588, v.1

4. Edwin Hodder, *ibid.*, Hymn 581, v. 2

5. Anne Steele as in *Sacred Songs & Solos* (London: Morgan & Scott, n.d.), Hymn 258, v. 2

6. Isaac Watts as in C.H. Spurgeon, Compiler, *Our Own Hymn Book* (London: Passmore & Alabaster, 1892), Hymn 478, v. 3

7. Julia Sterling (source unknown)

8. John Burton as in *Golden Bells* (London: CSSM, 1925), Hymn 580, v. 1

9. Thomas Guthrie in R.A. Bertram, *A Homiletic Encyclopedia* (No publisher & no date), p. 84

10. W.B. Knight, *3,000 Illustrations* (Grand Rapids: Eerdmans, 1957), pp. 62–63

11. Archibald Naismith, *op. cit.*, pp. 16–17

12. John Bate, *A Cyclopaedia of Illustrations* (London: Jarrold, 1875), p. 72

13. Aquilla Webb, *1,000 Evangelistic Illustrations* (New York: Harper, 1921), p. 41

14. Author unknown. As in W.B. Knight, *Knight's Master Book of New Illustrations* (Grand Rapids: Eerdmans, 1956), p. 87

15. Louis A. Banks, *Windows for Sermons* (New York: Funk & Wagnails, 1909), pp. 305–306

16. J.E. Wolfe, *Gold from Ophir* (Chicago: Evan. Pub. Co., 1889), p. vii

17. J. Todd as quoted by John Bate, *op. cit.*, p. 75

18. Source unknown

19. Sir Walter Scott as in R.A. Bertram, *op. cit.*, p. 84

20. J.J.S. Perowne, *Homiletical and Pastoral Lectures* (London: Hodder & Stoughton, 1879), p. 327

21. George F. Pentecost, "In the Volume of the Book" (London: Morgan & Scott, 1882), p. 97

22. Archibald Naismith, *op. cit.*, p. 17

23. Maria V.G. Havergal, *Memorials of Frances Ridley Havergal* (London: Nisbet, 1880), p. 209

24. D.L. Moody (source unknown)

25. A.T. Pierson, *Knowing the Scriptures* (Los Angeles: Biola Book Room, 1910), pp. 12–13

26. R.E. Neighbour, *Games of Gold* (Ohio: McMillen-Neighbour, n.d.), Frontispiece

27. Source unknown

28. Chrysostom (source unknown)

29. Matthew Simpson, *Lectures on Preaching* (New York: Phillips & Hunt, 1879), p. 104

30. J.H. Vincent in G.F. Pentecost, "In the Volume of the Book" (London: Morgan & Scott, n.d.), p.x
31. J. Edwards (source unknown)
32. John Ruskin (source unknown)
33. Amos R. Wells, *Think on These Things* (Boston: W.A. Wilde, 1928), p. 117
34. Edwin Hodder, *op. cit.*, verse 3
35. Eleanor L. Doan, *The Speaker's Sourcebook* (Grand Rapids: Zondervan, 1960), pp. 38–39
36. See "The Value of the Bible" by John G. Whittier in Elon Foster, Editor, *Cyclopaedia of Poetry* (New York: Thomas Y. Crowell, 1872), p. 65
37. H.W. Baker in *The Keswick Hymn-Book* (London: Marshall, Morgan & Scott, n.d.), Hymn 527, verse 4

Study 24: GOD'S WORD IS COMPENSATIVE
1. Author unknown. Quoted by E.F. & L. Harvey, *Daily Challenge* (Samlesbury, Preston, Lancs., England: MOVE Press, 1961), p. 85
2. M.J. Smith in *Golden Bells* (London: CSSM, 1925), Hymn 575, verses 1–2
3. W.M. Whittemore in *The Sunday School Hymnary* (London: Publisher not known, n.d.), Hymn 303, verse 2
4. Charles H. Spurgeon in Hy. Pickering, Editor, *One Thousand Tales Worth Telling* (London: Pickering & Inglis, n.d.), p. 69
5. *Golden Bells*, Hymn 583, verse 1
6. Goethe as quoted by W.M. MacGregor, *Christian Freedom* (London: Hodder & Stoughton, 1914), pp. 83–84
7. D.L. Moody
8. Henry G. Weston as quoted by Walter B. Knight, *Knight's Treasury of Illustrations* (Grand Rapids, Eerdmans, 1963), p. 12
9. Author unknown
10. Author unknown
11. G.B.F. Hallock, *Five Thousand Best Modern Illustrations* (New York: G.H. Doran, 1927), p. 65
12. Author unknown
13. Allan A. MacRae in brochure of the Biblical School of Theology

14. As quoted by H.P. Barker, *Windows in Words* (London: Pickering & Inglis, 1954), p. 38

15. Walter B. Knight, *Knight's Treasury of Illustrations* (Grand Rapids: Eerdmans, 1963), p. 9

16. Charles Gulston, *No Greater Heritage* (London: The Paternoster Press, 1960), p. 249

Appendix 2: THE SYMBOLS IN POETRY

1. Bishop Richard Mant in Elon Foster, Editor, *Cyclopaedia of Poetry* (New York: Thomas Y. Crowell, 1872), First Series, poem 234

2. George Herbert, *The Poetical Works of George Herbert* (London: Bickers & Bush, 1863), p. 53

3. Christopher Harvey in *The Poetical Works of George Herbert*, pp. 239–241. Although often ascribed to George Herbert, this poem was written by Christopher Harvey in imitation of Herbert's style. See p. 224

4. Peter Heylyn. This poem is found in various sources. See Archibald Naismith, *A Treasury of Notes, Quotes & Anecdotes* (Grand Rapids: Baker, 1976), p. 24

5. Gerhardt Ter Steegen in Frances Bevan, Editor, *Hymns of Ter Steegen* (New York: Loizeaux, 1894), First series, p. 24

6. Isaac Watts in *Selection* (London: Haddon, 1858), pp. 473–374

7. *Ibid.*, pp. 213–214

8. *Ibid.*, p. 216

9. William Cowper in C.H. Spurgeon, *Our Own Hymn Book* (London: Passmore & Alabaster, 1892), Hymn 479

10. John Newton in Cowper & Newton, *Olney Hymns* (Edinburgh: Taylor, n.d.), Hymn 287

11. Reginald Heber, *The Poetical Works of Reginald Heber* (London: John Murray, 1875), p. 60

12. Cawood in *The Psalms of David* (Toronto: C. Blackett Robinson, n.d.), no. 109

13. Alexander B. Grosart, *Songs of the Day and Night* (Printed for private circulation, n.d.), p. 134

14. *Ibid.*, p. 135

15. Charles Wesley in *The Methodist Hymnbook* (Toronto: The Methodist Church, n.d.), Hymn 639, verse 3

16. Bernard Barton in *A Library of Religious Poetry* (New York: Funk & Wagnalls, 1889), p. 593

17. Edwin Hodder in *Golden Bells* (London: CSSM, 1925), Hymn 581

18. H.J. Betts in *Golden Bells*, Hymn 586

19. Phoebe Palmer in Elon Foster, Editor, *Cyclopaedia of Poetry* (New York: Thomas Y. Crowell, 1872), no. 234

20. Author unknown. As in *Fully Furnished* (Grand Rapids: Kregel, 1969) by F.E. Marsh, p. 172

21. Anne Steele in C.H. Spurgeon, Editor, *Our Own Hymn Book* (London: Passmore & Alabaster, 1892), Hymn 482

22. H.W. Baker in *The Keswick Hymn-Book* (London: Marshall, Morgan & Scott, n.d.), Hymn 527

23. William W. How in Al Bryant, Compiler, *Sourcebook of Poetry* (Grand Rapids: Zondervan, 1968), p. 40

24. Author unknown. In Catherine Winkworth, Translator, *Lyra Germanica* (London: James Nisbet, 1884), vol. 2, p. 396

25. Frances Ridley Havergal, *The Poetical Works of Frances Ridley Havergal* (London: James Nisbet, 1884), vol. 2, p. 396

26. Horatius Bonar, *Hymns of Faith and Hope* (London: James Nisbet, 1876), p. 233

27. *Ibid.*, p. 301

28. F.E. Marsh, *Five Hundred Bible Readings* (London: Pickering & Inglis, n.d.), pp. xv–xvi

29. H. Selwyn in Cornelius Zylstra, Editor, *Source Book of Poetry* (Grand Rapids: Baker, 1960), no. 36

30. James M. Gray in Eleanor Doan, Compiler, *Sourcebook for Speakers* (Grand Rapids: Zondervan, 1968), p. 43

31. A.A. Rees in C. Russell Hurditch, Editor, *Footsteps of Truth* (London: J.F. Shaw, 1884), p. 279

32. Grace Noll Crowell in E.F. & L. Harvey, *The Christian's Daily Challenge* (Samlesbury, Preston, Lancs., England: MOVE, 1961), p. 229

33. Helen Frazee-Bower, *He Came with Music* (Chicago: Moody Press, 1965), p. 23

34. J.R. Clements in C. Russell Hurditch, Editor, *Footsteps of Truth* (London: J.F. Shaw, 1902), vol. 20, p. 236

35. Author unknown. As in Hugh T. Kerr, *Children's Gospel Story Sermons* (London: Oliphants, 1962), p. 81

36. Author unknown. As in David Kirk, *The Wonderful Word of God* (New York: Loizeaux, 1947), p. 62

37. Gwynn McLendon Day, *The Wonder of the Word* (Chicago: Moody Press, n.d.), p. 222

38. *Ibid.*, p. 254

39. John G. Whittier in Elon Foster, Editor, *Cyclopaedia of Poetry* (New York: Thomas Y. Crowell, 1872), p. 65

Bibliography

Adams, H.G., ed., *Sacred Poetical Quotations*. London: Groombridge, 1882

Adamson, William. *The Religious Anecdotes of Scotland*. Glasgow: Morison, 1885

Allee, G. Franklin. *Evangelistic Illustrations for Pulpit and Platform*. Chicago: Moody Press, 1961

Amsler, K.A. "Rules for Bible Study." Chicago: Good News, n.d.

Banks, Louis A. *Windows for Sermons*. New York: Funk & Wagnalls, 1909

Barker, H.P. *Windows in Words*. London: Pickering & Inglis, 1954

Barnhouse, Donald G. *Let Me Illustrate*. New York: Revell, 1967

Barton, Bernard. *A Library of Religious Poetry*. New York: Funk & Wagnalls, 1889

Bate, John. *A Cyclopaedia of Illustrations*. London: Jarrold, 1875

Baxendale, Walter. *Dictionary of Illustrations for Pulpit and Platform*. Chicago: Moody, 1949

Bedell, Bishop. *Anecdotes Illustrative of Old Testament Texts*. London: Hodder & Soughton, n.d.

Bertram, R.A. *A Homiletic Encyclopaedia*. London: No publisher, n.d.

Bomberger, J.H. *Three Thousand Practical Illustrations*. Ohio: Central Publishing House, n.d.

Bonar, Horatius. *Hymns of Faith and Hope*. London: James Nisbet, 1876

Booth, Mary Warburton. "They That Sow." London: Pickering & Inglis, n.d.

Brooks, Keith L. *Gleanings from the Word*. Wheaton: Van Kampen Press, 1951

Bryant, Al, ed., *Sourcebook of Poetry*. Grand Rapids: Zondervan, 1968

Burns, Jabez. *500 Sketches and Skeletons of Sermons*. Grand Rapids: Kregel, 1968

Burns, James. *Illustrations from Art*. London: Clarke, n.d.

Burrell, David J. *Why I Believe the Bible*. New York: Revell, 1917

Cable, Mildred, and Francesca French. *Towards Spiritual Maturity*. London: Hodder & Stoughton, 1950

Carver, W.O. *The Course of Christian Missions*. New York: Revell, 1939

Collet, Sidney. *The Scripture of Truth*. London: Partridge, 1905

Cook, F.D., ed., *The Holy Bible with Commentary*. London: John Murray, 1880

Corry, P.N. *The Whole Armour of God*. London: The Victory Press, 1931

Cowper, William, and John Newton. *Olney Hymns*. Edinburgh: Taylor, n.d.

Darlow, T.H. *The Greatest Book in the World*. London: Hodder & Stoughton, 1927

D'Aubigne, J.H. Merle. *The Life and Times of Martin Luther*. Chicago: Moody Press, 1950

Day, Gwynn McLendon. *The Wonder of the Word*. Chicago: Moody Press, n.d.

DeHaan, M.R., and H.G. Bosch, eds., *Our Daily Bread*. Grand Rapids: Zondervan, 1959

Dixon, A.C. *Lights and Shadows in American Life*. New York: Revell, 1898.

Doan, Eleanor, Compiler, *Sourcebook for Speakers*. Grand Rapids: Zondervan, 1968

___. *The Speaker's Sourcebook*. Grand Rapids: Zondervan, 1960

Edwards, Charles. *A Box of Nails*. London: H.R. Allenson, 1897

Excell, Joseph, ed., *The Biblical Illustrator*. Grand Rapids: Baker, 1959

Footsteps of Truth. London: John F. Shaw, 1901

Foster, Elon, ed., *Cyclopaedia of Poetry*. New York: Thomas Y. Crowell, 1872

Frazee-Bower, Helen. *He Came with Music*. Chicago: Moody Press, 1963

Golden Bells. London: CSSS, 1925

Gordon, A.J. *Yet Speaking*. London: Baptist Tract & Book Society, n.d.

Gordon, Ernest B. *Adoniram Judson Gordon*. New York: Revell, 1896

Gray, James M. "How To Eat the Word." Chicago: Good News, n.d.

Grether, F. *Our Daily Bread*. Ohio: Publishing House of the Reformed Church in the U.S., 1898

Grosart, Alexander B. *Songs of the Day and Night*. Printed for private circulation, n.d.

Gulston, Charles. *No Greater Heritage*. London: The Paternoster Press, 1960

Hallock, G.B.F. *Five Thousand Best Modern Illustrations*. New York: Doran, 1927

____ . *2,500 Best Modern Illustrations*. New York: Harper, 1935

Harrison, Norman B. *His Things of Power*. The Bible Institute Colportage Association, 1935

Harvey, E.F. & L. *The Christian's Daily Challenge*. Samlesbury, Preston, Lancs., England: MOVE, 1961

Havergal, Frances Ridley. *The Poetical Works of Frances Ridley Havergal* London: James Nisbet, 1884

Havergal, Maria V.G. *Memorials of Frances Ridley Havergal*. London: Nisbet, 1880

Heber, Reginald. *The Poetical Works of Reginald Heber*. London: John Murray, 1875

Henry, Carl F.H., ed., *The Biblical Expositor*. Philadelphia: A.J. Holman, 1960

Herbert, George. *The Poetical Works of George Herbert*. London: Bickers and Bush, 1863

Hillis, Dick. *Sayings of Mao and of Jesus*. Glendale, CA: Regal, 1972

Hodge, Charles. *Systematic Theology*. London: James Clarke, 1960

Houghton, Will H. *Let's Go Back to the Bible*. New York: Revell, 1939

Howley, G.C.D., et al., ed., *A New Testament Commentary*. Grand Rapids: Zondervan, 1969

Howson, John S. *The Metaphors of St. Paul*. London: Strahan, 1869

Hurditch, C. Russell, ed., *Footsteps of Truth*. London: J.F. Shaw, 1884

Hutchinson, J.C. *Fugitive Poetry*. London: Frederick Warne, 1878

Hymns of Ter Steegen. Frances Bevan, Editor. New York: Loizeaux, 1894

Inchfawn, Fay. *Songs of the Ups and Downs*. London: Ward, Lock & Co., n.d.

Ironside, Harry. *Illustrations of Bible Truth*. Chicago: Moody, 1945

Jones, Bob Jr. *Comments on Here and Hereafter*. New York: Loizeaux, 1946

Jowett, J.H. *The Whole Armour of God*. London: Hodder & Stoughton, 1916

Kerr, Hugh T. *Children's Everyland Story-Sermons*. London: Oliphants, 1962

Kirk, David. *The Wonderful Word of God*. New York: Loizeaux, 1947

Knight, W.B. *Knight's Master Book of New Illustrations*. Grand Rapids: Eerdmans, 1956

____. *Knight's Treasury of Illustrations*. Grand Rapids: Eerdmans, 1963

____. *Knight's Up-to-the-Minute Illustrations*. Chicago: Moody Press, 1974

____. *3,000 Illustrations*. Grand Rapids: Eerdmans, 1957

Lees, Harrington C. *The Joy of Bible Study*. London: Longmans, Green & Co., 1910

Lovett, Richard, ed., *James Gilmour of Mongolia*. London: Religious Tract Society, 1895

Luther, Martin. *Footsteps of the Flock*. London: John F. Shaw, 1899

____. *The Table Talk of Martin Luther*. Grand Rapids: Baker, 1979

Macartney, Clarence E. *Macartney's Illustrations*. New York: Abingdon, 1946

Macbeath, John. *Lamps and Lamplighters*. London: The Carey Press, n.d.

MacGregor, W.M. *Christian Freedom*. London: Hodder & Stoughton, 1914

Maclaren, Alexander. *Expositions of Holy Scripture*. London: Hodder and Stoughton, 1908

Macmillan, Hugh. *The Corn of Heaven*. London: Macmillan, 1901

___. *The Spring of the Day*. London: Pitman, 1907

Marsh, F.E. *Emblems of the Holy Spirit*. Grand Rapids: Kregel, 1957

___. *Five Hundred Bible Readings*. London: Pickering & Inglis, n.d.

___. *Fully Furnished*. London: Pickering & Inglis, n.d.

Mead, Frank S., ed., *Encyclopedia of Religious Quotations*. London: Peter Davies, 1965

Miller, J.R. *Devotional Hours with the Bible*. London: Hodder & Stoughton, 1920

Montgomery, James. *The Poetical Works of James Montgomery*. London: Gall & Inglis, n.c.

Moody, D.L., ed., *One Thousand and One Thoughts from My Library*. Grand Rapids: Baker, 1979

Morrison, James D., ed., *Masterpieces of Religious Verse*. Grand Rapids: Baker, 1978

Naismith, Archibald. *A Treasury of Notes, Quotes & Anecdotes*. Grand Rapids: Baker, 1976

___. *1,200 Notes, Quotes & Anecdotes*. London: Pickering & Inglis, 1962

Neighbour, R.E. *Gems of Gold*. Ohio: McMillen-Neighbour, n.d.

Nye, J.L. in the Frontispiece of *Anecdotes Illustrating Bible Texts*. London: The Sunday School Union, n.d.

Payne, Thomas. *Apostolic Christianity*. London: Christian Herald Office, n.d.

___. *Revivals: How Promoted*. London: Morgan & Scott, n.d.

Pentecost, George F. "*In the Volume of the Book*." London: Morgan & Scott, 1882

Perowne, J.J.S. *Homiletical and Pastoral Lectures.* London: Hodder & Stoughton, 1879

Perry, Lloyd M. and Robert D. Culver. *How To Search the Scriptures.* Grand Rapids: Baker, 1967

Person, Amy L. *Illustrations from Literature.* Grand Rapids: Baker, 1966

Pickering, Hy., ed., *One Thousand Tales Worth Telling.* London: Pickering & Inglis, n.d.

Pierson, A.T. *Knowing the Scriptures.* Los Angeles: Biola Book Room, 1910

___. *The Bible and Spiritual Criticism.* London: Nisbet, 1906

___. *The Key Words of the Bible.* London: Hodder & Stoughton, 1898

Pierson, D.L. *Arthur T. Pierson.* London: James Nisbet, 1912

Pink, A.W. *Spiritual Growth.* Grand Rapids: Baker, 1971

Pollock, J.C. *Billy Graham.* New York: McGraw Hill, 1966

Poole, Allon. *The Bible Wonder Book.* London: Pickering & Inglis, n.d.

Radar, Paul. *Life's Greatest Adventure.* London: Victory Press, 1938

Rice, W.A. *The Precious Jewel of the Word.* London: Marshall, Morgan & Scott, n.d.

Redemption Songs. London: Pickering & Inglis, n.d.

Richardson, A.E. *This Is the Way.* London: Marshall Brothers, n.d.

Ridley, John. *The Unsheathed Sword.* Melbourne: Bacon, n.d.

Sankey, Ira D., compiler, *Sacred Songs & Solos.* London: Morgan & Scott, n.d.

Selection. London: Haddon, 1858

Shedd, W.G.T. *Sermons to the Spiritual Man.* Edinburgh: T. & T. Clark, 1884

Shepherd, Walter. *Sent by the Sovereign.* Nutley, New Jersey: Presbyterian & Reformed, 1958

Simeon, Charles. *Expository Outlines on the Whole Bible.* Grand Rapids: Zondervan, n.d.

Simpson, Matthew. *Lectures on Preaching*. New York: Phillips & Hunt, 1879

Smith, Miles. *The Translators to the Readers: An Introduction to the King James Version of the Bible*. Portland, Oregon: Multnomah School of the Bible, 1963. Rendered into modern English by E.W. Goodrick.

Smith, O.J. *The Revival We Need*. London: Marshall, Morgan & Scott, 1933

Souper, William. *The Report of the Mundesley Bible Conference*, 1914. London: Morgan & Scott, 1914

Spurgeon, C.H. *The Art of Illustration*. Pasadena, Texas: Pilgrim, 1971

___. Editor, *Our Own Hymn Book*. London: Passmore & Alabaster, 1892

Stahr, James A., ed. *Interest*. Wheaton, Illinois: Letters of Interest Associates. Issue of July–August, 1972

Stanford, Charles. *Symbols of Christ*. London: Religious Tract Society, n.d.

Stewart, Alexander. *Jeremiah*. Edinburgh: W.F. Henderson, 1936

Stock, Sarah. *Windows*. London: Sunday School Union, n.d.

Talmage, May. *Fifty Short Sermons*. New York: G.H. Doran, 1923

___. *Wisdom and Wit of T. DeWitt Talmage*. New York: G.H. Doran, 1922

Thayer, J.H. *A Greek-English Lexicon of the New Testament*. Edinburgh: T. & T. Clark, 1901

The Divine Panoply. London: The Religious Tract Society, 1846

The Keswick Hymn Book. London: Marshall, Morgan & Scott, n.d.

The Methodist Hymnbook. Toronto: The Methodist Church, n.d.

The Psalms of David. Toronto: C. Blackett Robinson, n.d.

The Sunday School Hymnary. London: Publisher not known, n.d.

Thiselton, A.C. *With the Prophets*. London: James Nisbet, 1882

Thomas, W.H. Griffith. *Life Abiding and Abounding*. Chicago: The Bible Institute Col. Ass'n, 1935

Tidwell, W.M. *Pointed Illustrations*. Kansas City: Beacon Hill, 1949

Give Me That Book!

Turnbull, Ralph G. *A Minister's Obstacles*. Grand Rapids: Baker, 1972

Webb, Aquilla. *One Thousand Evangelistic Illustrations*. New York: Harper & Brothers, 1921

____. *1,001 Illustrations for Pulpit and Platform*. New York: Harper, 1926

Wells, Amos R. *A Cyclopedia of Twentieth Century Illustrations*. New York: Revell, 1918

____. *Think on These Things*. Boston: W.A. Wilde, 1928

Whyte, W.P. *Thinking Through the Scriptures*. Los Angeles: Stationers Corporation, 1935

Williams, M.B. *Among Many Witnesses*. New York: Revell, 1891

Winkworth, Catherine, Translator, *Lyra Germanica*. London: George Routledge, n.d.

Wolfe, J.E. *Gold from Ophir*. Chicago: Evan. Pub. Co., 1889

Zylstra, Cornelius, ed., *Source Book of Poetry*. Grand Rapids: Baker, 1960

OTHER TITLES BY TED S. RENDALL PUBLISHED BY VICTORY BAPTIST PRESS

Discipleship in Depth

Fire in the Church

In God's School

Jeremiah: Prophet of Crisis

Living the Abundant Life

Nehemiah: Laws of Leadership